Indochina Monographs

The U.S. Adviser

by

General Cao Van Vien/Lt. Gen. Ngo Quang Truong
Lt. Gen. Dong Van Khuyen/Maj. Gen. Nguyen Duy Hinh
Brig. Gen. Tran Dinh Tho/Col. Hoang Ngoc Lung
and Lt. Col. Chu Xuan Vien

U.S. ARMY CENTER OF MILITARY HISTORY

WASHINGTON, D.C.

Library of Congress Cataloging in Publication Data
Main entry under title:

The U. S. adviser.

   (Indochina monographs)
   Supt. of Docs. no.: D 114.18:Ad9
   1. Vietnamese Conflict, 1961-1975--United States.
2. U.S. Military Assistance Command, Vietnam.
I. Vien, Cao Van. II. Series.
DS558.2.U17   959.704'33'73   80-607108

This book is not copyrighted and may be reproduced in whole or in part without consulting the publisher

First printing 1980

Indochina Monographs

This is one of a series published by the U.S. Army Center of Military History. They were written by officers who held responsible positions in the Cambodian, Laotian, and South Vietnamese armed forces during the war in Indochina. The General Research Corporation provided writing facilities and other necessary support under an Army contract with the Center of Military History. The monographs were not edited or altered and reflect the views of their authors--not necessarily those of the U.S. Army or the Department of Defense. The authors were not attempting to write definitive accounts but to set down how they saw the war in Southeast Asia.

Colonel William E. Le Gro, U.S. Army, retired, has written a forthcoming work allied with this series, Vietnam: From Cease-Fire to Capitulation. Another book, The Final Collapse by General Cao Van Vien, the last chairman of the South Vietnamese Joint General Staff, will be formally published and sold by the Superintendent of Documents.

Taken together these works should provide useful source materials for serious historians pending publication of the more definitive series, the U.S. Army in Vietnam.

JAMES L. COLLINS, JR.
Brigadier General, USA
Chief of Military History

Preface

The United States advisory mission in South Vietnam encompassed many fields of endeavor and affected almost every level of the Republic of Vietnam Armed Forces. It was a demanding exercise of professional duties and a unique human experience for the American adviser who had not only to struggle with problems of environment and culture differences and face the complexities and hazards of the war, but also devote his time and energy to supplement our Vietnamese experience with US Army professionalism. The total effort by US advisers contributed directly and immeasurably to the development and modernization of the Vietnamese Armed Forces.

To the Vietnamese officers and men who benefited from his expertise and experience, the US adviser was both a mentor and a samaritan. Regardless of his level of assignment or branch of service, he could be subsumed by a common trait: a sincere desire to help and devotion to those he advised. Whatever his approach to advisory duties, he always performed with dedication and competence. For nearly two decades, these qualities were the hallmark of the US adviser in South Vietnam.

To analyze and evaluate the United States advisory experience in its entirety is not an easy task. It cannot be accomplished thoroughly and effectively by a single author since there were several types of advisers representing different areas of specialty but all dedicated to a common goal. Therefore, each member of the Control Group for the Indochina Refugee Authored Monograph Program has made a significant contribution as we presented the Vietnamese point of view.

As the last Chairman of the Joint General Staff, RVNAF, a position I held for a decade, I have contributed the chapter concerning the relationship between *The JGS and MACV*. As I see it, the advisory effort at that level was largely a matter of personal relationship which set the tone and example for the entire system. I am sure that the tributes I pay to the successive MACV commanders, living or deceased, are but a small part of their towering contributions and achievements.

Lieutenant General Ngo Quang Truong, former commander of the 1st Infantry Division and IV Corps and the last commander of I Corps, has provided our evaluation of *The Tactical Adviser*, a subject for which I am sure no one else is better qualified. A professional soldier who held command positions at every tactical echelon during his distinguished career, General Truong presents a candid appraisal of the US tactical adviser, his role, and his contributions at every level, drawing from his invaluable combat experience. *The Intelligence Adviser* has been prepared by Colonel Hoang Ngoc Lung, former chief J-2, JGS and our foremost expert in RVNAF intelligence. In his assessment of the US intelligence adviser, Colonel Lung is backed by years of cooperation with US Army intelligence agencies. Lieutenant General Dong Van Khuyen, commander of the Central Logistics Command, RVNAF, and the last Chief of Staff, JGS, has produced *The Logistic and Technical Adviser*. His truthful account of the US logistical advisory effort reflects the long experience of a man involved with the system he helped develop from the start with the assistance of US advisers. *The Pacification Adviser* has been written by Major General Nguyen Duy Hinh, the last commander of the ARVN 3d Infantry Division, who draws from his experience as Chief of Staff of III Corps and I Corps, Deputy Commander for Territorial Security, IV Corps and as Chief of Staff of the RF and PF Command during the middle 1960's. Brigadier General Tran Dinh Tho, has developed our contribution on *The Training Adviser*, drawing on his experience as a division and corps G-3, and seven years as the J-3 of the Joint General Staff.

To provide cohesiveness and unity for the monograph, the authors and I have relied on the editorial services of Lieutenant Colonel Chu Xuan Vien, our last Army Attache serving at the Embassy of Vietnam in

Washington, D.C. Colonel Vien, a knowledgeable analyst with a keen sense of military history and an author in his own right, compiled the introductory and closing chapters. The observations and conclusions are an excellent compendium of suggestions and comments made by the individual authors who, like myself, all feel we owe him a special debt of gratitude.

Finally, we are all indebted to Ms. Pham Thi Bong, formerly a Captain in the Republic of Vietnam Armed Forces and also a former member of the Vietnamese Embassy staff who spent long hours typing, editing and in the administrative preparation of this manuscript in final form.

McLean, Virginia
31 May 1977

Cao Van Vien
General, ARVN

Contents

Chapter		Page
I.	INTRODUCTION	1
	A Brief Comparative Historical Account	1
	The U.S. Advisory System	9
	Vietnamese Requirements For Advisory Assistance and Support to the U.S. Advisory Effort	16
II.	THE JGS AND MACV	22
	A Matter of Personal Relationship	22
	Reorganization and Development of the RVNAF	24
	Highlights of a Fruitful Relationship	31
	Procedures for Cooperation	38
	An Evaluation	42
III.	ARVN BATTALION TO CORPS AND THE TACTICAL ADVISER	46
	The Tactical Advisory System	46
	The Tactical Adviser's Responsibilities	53
	The Adviser's Role in Operational Planning and Combat Intelligence	58
	U.S. Support and the Problem of Leverage	65
	Observations on Tours of Duty and Relationships	69
	An Evaluation	73
IV.	THE INTELLIGENCE ADVISER	77
	A Pioneering Effort	77
	Increasing Commitment	79
	The Period of Full-Fledged Cooperation	83
	Anatomy of a Relationship	89
V.	THE LOGISTIC AND TECHNICAL ADVISER	96
	Significant Milestones	96
	The Base Depot Upgrade Program	106
	Path-Finder I and Path-Finder II	107
	Observations of the U.S. Logistical Advisory Effort	110
	Some Lessons Learned	119

Chapter	Page
VI. THE PACIFICATION ADVISER	122
The U.S. Response to Insurgency	122
CORDS Organization and Operations	126
Relations and Contributions	137
Some Lessons Learned	153
VII. THE TRAINING ADVISER	157
A Monumental Achievement	157
Organization for Training and Training Support . . .	162
Training Advisory Activities	168
Observations and Comments	181
VIII. OBSERVATIONS AND CONCLUSIONS	186

Appendix

A.	PRINCIPLES AUTHORIZING TRIM ADVISERS WITH UNITS AND FORMATIONS OF THE VIETNAMESE NATIONAL ARMED FORCES	199
B.	THE ASSISTANCE OF AMERICAN ADVISERS	202
GLOSSARY		204

Charts

No.		Page
1.	Organization, U.S. Advisory System, 1970	11
2.	Organization, MACV Headquarters Staff Advisers, 1970 . .	12
3.	Organization, Military Assistance Advisory Group, Vietnam, 1956	26
4.	Organization, U.S. Military Assistance Command, Vietnam 1972	35
5.	Organization, Joint General Staff and Armed Forces Structure, 1972	36
6.	Organization, U.S. Army Advisory System, Corps Tactical Zone	48
7.	Organization, Regional Assistance Command, 1971-1972 . .	50
8.	Organization, Temporary Equipment Recovery Mission, 1956	97
9.	CORDS in MACV Command Channel	127
10.	Organization, Office of the Assistant Chief of Staff for CORDS, MACV	129
11.	Organization, CTZ/Region CORDS	130
12.	Advisory Relationships, Corps, Province and District Levels	132
13.	Advisory Relationships, ARVN Hierarchy	150
14.	Organization, MACV Training Directorate	166
15.	Organization, Central Training Command	167

Maps

No.		Page
1.	Location, Military Academies and Service Schools	163
2.	Location, National Territorial Force Training Centers . .	164

Illustrations

No.	Page
FRAC Ending A Fruitful Relationship with I Corps, 20 March, 1973	52
An Odd-Looking But Harmonious Couple: The ARVN Tactical Commander and His Adviser	54
ARVN Rangers Going Out on a Patrol with U.S. Adviser (Ba To, Quang Ngai, Dec. 1970)	55
CIDG Troopers and U.S. Special Forces Adviser Back From Patrol (Ban Me Thuot, March 1962)	56
ARVN 8th Marine Bn Staff Discussing Operational Plan with U.S. Adviser (Quang Tri, Sept. 1970)	59
ARVN Battalion Commander (9th Infantry Division) Reviewing Position with His Adviser During Combat Operation (Kien Phong, Dec. 1970)	60
U.S. Advisers Briefing ARVN Rangers Prior to Long Range Reconnaissance Mission (Near Cambodian Border, Nov. 1970)	67
On-The-Job Training Provided by U.S. Photography Technician (Oct. 1970)	102
Civilian Technicians and Specialists of the U.S. Army Materiel Command as Advisers to the Army Arsenal, 1972	105
MAT In Action: On A Firing Range with PF Troops (Long An, December 1970)	133
MAT Members Checking Targets After PF Troops Practice Firing the M-16 Rifle (Long An, Dec. 1970)	134
A First-Aid Class for PF Troopers by MAT Member (Dec. 1970)	135
MAT Member as Adviser to Vietnamese NP Field Force (Da Nang, 1970)	136
U.S. Adviser Instructing ARVN Troops on Helilift Procedures (March, 1962)	160
ARVN Paratroopers in Combat Assault Training, 1966	161
Assisting Students at the RVNAF Language School (Dec. 1970)	170
The National Military Academy at Dalat: A Significant Contribution of U.S. Advisory Effort	173
The Cadets of Dalat NMA: A Source of Pride for the RVNAF	174
Training ARVN Rangers How to Use Compass to Bring In a Helicopter for Landing (Oct. 1970)	179
Advisers Looking On as Ranger Student Successfully Guides Helicopter on Landing Pad (Oct. 1970)	180

CHAPTER I

Introduction

A Brief Comparative Historical Account

To understand and appreciate the full impact of the United States adviser on the RVN Armed Forces from the Vietnamese viewpoint, it is desirable first to review briefly the evolution of the advisory system to include how it was organized, supported and how it functioned at different echelons.

The United States began providing direct military advisory assistance to the Vietnamese National Army in early 1955. However, American commitment in Indochina had started five years earlier when, coming to the help of a hard-pressed war ally, the US supplied war materiel to the French Expeditionary Corps which was fighting a dubious war against the Communists-led Viet Minh, then the champion of a strong cause for national independence.

When the US Military Assistance Advisory Group (MAAG), Indochina was established in late 1950 under Brigadier General Francis G. Brink to administer this aid, the new state of Vietnam had been born only a year earlier as a result of compromises between ex-Emperor Bao Dai, Chief of State, and the French who sought to set up a regime capable of competing with the Viet Minh. The US had promptly recognized Bao Dai and signed with France and the "Associated States" of Indochina (Vietnam, Cambodia, Laos) in December 1950 what came to be known as the Pentalateral Agreements. These agreements formed the basis of US economic and military aid for Vietnam, the first step toward a growing commitment which terminated only a quarter of a century later.

As an Associated State of the French Union, Vietnam was granted some degree of autonomy, but not total independence, which came only in the aftermath of the French defeat at Dien Bien Phu in 1954. It was during this period that the National Army of Vietnam came into being, its creation sanctioned by the French need to Vietnamize the war. The Vietnamese Army, which initially consisted of auxiliary elements recruited, trained, and led by French cadre, was gradually upgraded into infantry battalions, then mobile groups by 1953, all under the command of Vietnamese officers. During 1952, command and control of the new national army was established, first with the General Staff, then four military region headquarters, but these bodies were still heavily staffed by French officers. During all this time, the United States Military Assistance Advisory Group (MAAG) remained far removed from the scene. Its main function was to make sure that US equipment was delivered and properly maintained through liaison with the French High Command. Most Vietnamese tactical commanders in the field were even unaware of its existence until 1953 when they received the first visits by MAAG officers.

The nature of US commitment in Vietnam radically changed after the 1954 Geneva Accords to become a true military assistance and advisory role with the advent of South Vietnam, now a separate nation south of the 17th parallel. This came about as a result of an agreement reached between General J. Lawton Collins, President Eisenhower's special envoy and General Paul Ely, the French High Commissioner and Commander-in-Chief of the French Expeditionary Corps in Indochina. Under the terms of the agreement, the Vietnamese Armed Forces were to receive organization and training assistance from the MAAG as of 1 January 1955 and to become fully autonomous six months later. By this time, the General Staff had become all-Vietnamese under Major General Le Van Ty and after the regrouping of the 3d Military Region units from North Vietnam, the entire Vietnamese Armed Forces strength stood at 215,997, to include 179,197 regular troops who made up about 168 infantry battalions. The day the Collins-Ely agreement went into effect was also the day that three infantry divisions, the 11th, 21st and 31st, were activated for the first time.

Such was the general status of the Vietnamese Army when the MAAG began its organization and training efforts. In cooperation with the French,

Lieutenant General John W. O'Daniel, who replaced Major General Thomas J. H. Trapnell as Chief MAAG in April 1954, organized the Training Relations and Instruction Mission (TRIM) on 1 February 1955. TRIM was essentially an American concept but for the purpose of political convenience, its staff also included French officers who performed mostly in a consultant's role. The first TRIM advisory training teams, largely composed of US Army officers, began their field assignments in April 1955. They were attached to infantry divisions, the airborne brigade, service schools and training centers. One month later the first US advisers were placed at military region headquarters.

As defined in a memorandum published by the Vietnamese General Staff on 10 April 1955, the mission of TRIM advisers was "to assist and advise, on strictly technical aspects, Vietnamese military commanders to whom they were assigned, in order to rapidly and effectively rebuild the Vietnamese Armed Forces on a new basis."[1] The insistence on "strictly technical aspects" set the tone and direction for the US Army advisory effort which was to remain technically-oriented throughout its existence. The "new basis" for reorganization needed no clarification: it was understood to be the doctrine of the US Army.

These combined arrangements for training and reorganizing the Vietnamese Army continued for more than a year. When the French High Command in Indochina was deactivated on 28 April 1956, TRIM personnel were immediately reassigned to the MAAG's Combat Arms Training and Organization (CATO) Division. It was only then that the Vietnamese Armed Forces became fully autonomous after taking over all military responsibilities from the departing French. But French officers continued advising and training the Vietnamese Navy and Air Force for another year, until asked by the Government of Vietnam to terminate their mission in May 1957.

---

[1] Memorandum No 1891/TTM/MG, dated 10 April 1955, and signed by Major General Le Van Ty, Chief of the General Staff.

During this period, the major difficulties of MAAG stemmed from the ceiling imposed on US military personnel by the Geneva Accords. Faced with an increasing commitment to training activities and growing logistical problems, the MAAG was authorized only 342 spaces, of which about two-thirds were devoted to training. The Vietnamese General Staff was also hard pressed by the same problem of a ceiling which was imposed, not by the Geneva Accords, but by the MAAG at the 150,000 level.

With the support of direct US economic and military assistance, South Vietnam confidently began its task of nation-building. On 26 October 1955, Prime Minister Ngo Dinh Diem proclaimed the Republic of Vietnam and installed himself as President and Supreme Commander of the Armed Forces. The National Armed Forces of Vietnam became the Republic of Vietnam Armed Forces (RVNAF) and the National Army took on its acronym ARVN so familiar to US Army advisers. At about the same time, MAAG, Indochina was redesignated MAAG, Vietnam, marking the separation of duties for Vietnam, Laos and Cambodia.

The final pullout of the French Expeditionary Corps from South Vietnam resulted in logistical problems which plagued both the RVNAF General Staff and the MAAG. Not being adequately organized and trained for the handling of logistic support, the RVNAF found themselves unprepared for it. On his part, the new Chief MAAG-V, Lieutenant General Samuel T. Williams, who succeeded General O'Daniel in November 1955, had to face problems caused by the difficulty in locating, recovering and shipping out excess MDAP equipment left behind unaccounted for by French forces. The RVNAF did not even know exactly how much equipment there was in the inventory. These requirements led to the creation of the Temporary Equipment Recovery Mission (TERM) in June 1956 to clean up the logistical mess and to assist the RVNAF in establishing a workable logistical support system. TERM personnel were later integrated into MAAG-V, which brought total US advisory strength to 692 by 1960.

In the meantime, the Vietnamese Army undertook a long and arduous process of reorganization under the auspices of MAAG advisers. During the first stage, it was agreed that ten infantry divisions (6 light and 4 field) would constitute the ARVN backbone. This was accomplished by the end of 1955. The search for an optimum-type division for the ARVN, however, continued to preoccupy the MAAG for the next three years. After discarding hundreds of tentative TOEs, it was decided in 1958 that seven regular infantry divisions of 10,500 men each were required by RVN to defend itself against overt aggression from the North. To solve the problem of auxiliary forces which were not eligible for US military assistance, the GVN instituted the Civil Guard and People's Militia (or Self-Defense Corps) under the control of the Ministry of the Interior.

By the time the ARVN reorganization was completed, the Republic of Vietnam had consolidated its political and economic base. The resettlement of nearly one million refugees fleeing the North had been accomplished, dissidents defeated and central authority firmly established. Against the chaotic background of its formative years, the emergence of a strong and stable South Vietnam was indeed a miraculous achievement that surprised friends and foes alike, particularly North Vietnam. Determined to gain control of the South after missing the chance of a legal take-over through elections in 1956, the North Vietnamese Lao Dong (Communist) Party proceeded to wage a "war of liberation" by reintroducing selected personnel who had previously lived in the South and directing local Viet Minh agents into action. The insurgents became known as the Viet Cong (literally, Vietnamese Communists) who fought under the political aegis of the National Liberation Front, created by Hanoi in December 1960.

Beginning in 1957, the Viet Cong expanded and intensified guerrilla warfare actions, to include terror, sabotage, kidnapping and assassination, severely threatening the GVN control in the countryside. Faced with this mounting crisis, the RVN outlawed Communist activities and requested additional US military assistance. Recognizing the unconventional nature of the war, the GVN successively created a 5,000-man Ranger Command and the Special Forces in 1960. The US, on its part, began re-evaluating its advisory effort which resulted in a comprehensive Counterinsurgency Plan allowing an increase in the RVNAF strength from 150,000 to 170,000 men, MAP support for a 68,000-man Civil Guard and a 40,000-man People's Militia, and providing more US advisers. As a result, for the first time, US advisory teams were assigned to ARVN battalions on a selective basis and US Special Forces teams initiated the training of ARVN Ranger companies.

The new Kennedy administration not only approved the Counterinsurgency Plan in early 1961 but also organized a special staff, called Task Force, Vietnam, to look after the Vietnam problem and recommend appropriate actions. In Saigon, the US Ambassador, the Chief, MAAG, and heads of US agencies also made up a similar task force to direct the US assistance and advisory effort. President Kennedy's concern over Vietnam was further reflected by his sending two survey missions to Saigon during 1961, one headed by Dr. Eugene Staley and the other by General Maxwell D. Taylor and Dr. Walt W. Rostow. Both missions seemed to confirm that counterinsurgency should be a concerted military-economic effort and that assistance should be substantially increased in terms of advisers, combat support, and expansion of the Vietnamese armed forces. Most particularly, the Taylor-Rostow mission recommended US support for the GVN strategic hamlet program which was a pacification strategy based upon fortifying vulnerable, isolated hamlets. By the end of 1961, the US advisory effort had expanded to most ARVN battalions and to provinces as well. In the central highlands, US Special Forces teams were organizing, arming, and training Montagnards to fight as units which became known as Civilian Irregular Defense Groups (CIDG). In addition, to direct the increased military commitment effectively, it was decided to establish the US Military Assistance Command, Vietnam (MACV) and General Paul D. Harkins was selected as commander. The Military Assistance Advisory Group was still retained, however, under Major General Charles J. Timmes who continued directing the military assistance program and the advisory and training effort for the RVNAF.

A month after General Harkins activated Headquarters, MACV in early February, 1962, the GVN launched the strategic hamlet program with the objective of pacifying the countryside. Although termed a success by the GVN, the program was not popular with the rural population because it required many to leave their own farms in insecure areas and move to fortified areas, and it did not receive substantial support from the United States.

The introduction of US tactical aircraft and helicopters brought total American advisory and support personnel to approximately 11,000 by the end of 1962, including 26 Special Forces teams. ARVN units were initiated to airmobile operations transported in US Army helicopters which were operationally controlled by US advisers.

In spite of this progress, the military coup that overthrew the Diem governnment on 1 November 1963 ushered in an era of political turmoil and instability which proved nearly fatal to South Vietnam. The enemy took advantage of this opportunity to speed up a military victory. He began infiltrating regular units from the North and systematically wrecked the largely neglected strategic hamlet program. By the end of 1964, the situation had so deteriorated that President Johnson had to make the fateful decision in early 1965 to bomb North Vietnam and engage in the ground war in the South. The US advisory system had by now extended to the district level. To streamline command and control, MAAG was dissolved in May 1964 and the military assistance and advisory effort placed under direct control of MACV. A month later, General William C. Westmoreland took over as commander, USMACV.

The buildup of US forces which started in mid-1965 and the intensification of the war during the next few years towered above the advisory effort and turned US advisers into liaison officers whose primary role was to maintain coordination between ARVN and US units and to obtain US combat support for the ARVN. To help the ARVN carry out effectively its assigned role of pacification support, Mobile Training Teams (MTT) were organized to train and motivate ARVN maneuver battalions for their new task. The US renewed interest in pacification also led to the establishment in 1967 of the Civil Operations and Rural Development Support (CORDS) system which paralleled and advised the GVN system of Pacification and Development Councils. The MACV commander was given overall military-civilian control for the conduct of the war and was assisted by a Deputy CORDS, an official of ambassadorial rank. At the field level, the US Field Force commander as senior adviser to the ARVN corps commander was also assisted by a Deputy CORDS. During 1967 a total of 4,000 military personnel and 800 civilians were involved in the CORDS organization. Subsequent increases in US advisory strength was devoted to training and advising the Regional and Popular Forces (formerly Civil Guard and People's Militia, respectively).

By 1968, MACV had about 2,500 fewer advisers assigned than authorized and these shortages fell mostly in the CORDS and RF-PF advisory areas. To assist in offsetting this, MACV used five-man Mobile Advisory Teams (MAT) that rotated among RF-PF units to train and advise them. This expansion of the RF-PF advisory effort was done incrementally, however, with in-country resources and reaching toward a planned goal of 354 such teams by the end of 1968. When Vietnamization was officially proclaimed in mid-1969, total US Army advisory strength stood at about 13,500, half of which was assigned to CORDS organizations. In Saigon, General Creighton W. Abrams had succeeded General Westmoreland as Commander, USMACV since July 1968.

The advent of Vietnamization radically changed the direction of the US advisory effort. The goal now was to expand and improve the RVNAF combat effectiveness to such an extent that they were capable of taking over combat responsibilities from US forces which were gradually being withdrawn by increments. As a result of successive force structure increases, total RVNAF strength was brought up to 717,214 for 1968, then jumped quickly to the 1.1 million mark within the space of the next four years. ARVN force structure, meanwhile, accounted for only a modest increase, from 321,056 in 1968 to 448,953 by the time of the cease-fire. During this period, US advisory strength was gradually reduced in keeping with the phasing out of the US presence in South Vietnam.

Efforts at improving the RVNAF combat effectiveness and enabling them to replace US forces in all aspects of combat and service support had been undertaken at an accelerated pace under several programs since 1969. Most noteworthy among them were the combined operations programs initiated by US Field Forces such as the Dong Tien and Pair-Off campaigns, and the extensive on-the-job training programs conducted by the US 1st Logistical Command for the benefit of ARVN logistical and technical service units. It was during this period that the RVNAF really came of age, operationally as well as logistically. The development and maturity of the ARVN were particularly proved during the two major cross-border campaigns, in 1970 and 1971, conducted without the participation of US advisers.[2] The ARVN also took over the operation of major US logistical facilities without serious problems. As a result of the standdown and redeployment of US forces, Regional Assistance Commands (RAC) were activated to replace US Field Forces in the four corps areas during 1971 and 1972, signifying the end of the US combat role in South Vietnam.

The US advisory effort terminated on the cease-fire day, 28 January 1973. To manage the continuing Security Assistance Program for the RVN, the US Defense Attache Office (USDAO) was established with a very limited number of military personnel. But its relationship with the RVNAF was essentially one of co-workers, not a relationship between advisers and advisees as it had been. All CORDS functions were taken over by USAID and its residual personnel absorbed into four US Consulates General, one for each military region. At the province level, US civilian personnel were grouped into 20 area offices, responsible for civil operations. But even these offices were subsequently dissolved and finally the US presence in each province was reduced to a small liaison team.

The U.S. Advisory System

Despite the evolution of the system, the objectives contemplated by the US advisory effort in South Vietnam remained essentially consistent throughout its existence. These objectives were to organize, train, and equip the Vietnamese armed forces and develop their combat effectiveness to such an extent as to enable them to maintain internal security and to defend the nation against outside aggression. The presence of such a military force was vital for the GVN in its task of nation-building and national defense in the face of a hostile North Vietnam

---

[2] American advisers accompanied ARVN units in the initial phases of the Cambodian operation but were gradually withdrawn until by 1 July, all ARVN units operating in Cambodia were without advisers.

whose avowed goal was to dominate the South.

The United States advisory system was firmly established only after the creation of the Military Assistance Command, Vietnam and its subsequent reorganization in 1964 when it took over all military assistance and advisory functions from the MAAG which was dissolved. *(Chart 1)* MACV's mission in South Vietnam derived basically from the American advocacy of the self-determination principle which would allow countries to determine their own future without outside interference. Up to 1969, however, in keeping with the US policy of confrontation towards the hard-line Communist countries MACV was assigned the mission of assisting the GVN and its armed forces to defeat the VC/NVA forces and to attain an independent, secure, non-Communist society in South Vietnam. With the advent of Vietnamization and a switch of US policy to negotiation, MACV's mission was reworded as "To assist the GVN to defeat externally directed and supported Communist subversion and aggression in order to attain an environment which would allow the people of the RVN to determine their future without outside interference."[3]

The scope of MACV's mission thus defined transcended the military advisory and training functions previously assigned to MAAG-V during nearly a decade of its existence. It clearly encompassed the civil operations in support of the GVN pacification and development program. The difference in mission between MACV and MAAG-V also stemmed from the fact that MACV also functioned as a US theater-type troop command. As a result, only part of MACV Headquarters staff personnel actually served in a true advisory capacity. In 1970, for example, only 397 out of 1668 authorized spaces in MACV's 15 staff agencies were designed officially as "advisers" to the GVN and the JGS/RVNAF. *(Chart 2)* The MACV command group consisted of only three advisers: the commander, MACV, the deputy commander and the deputy CORDS.

---

[3] MACV Directive No. 10-11, dated 4 May 1971.

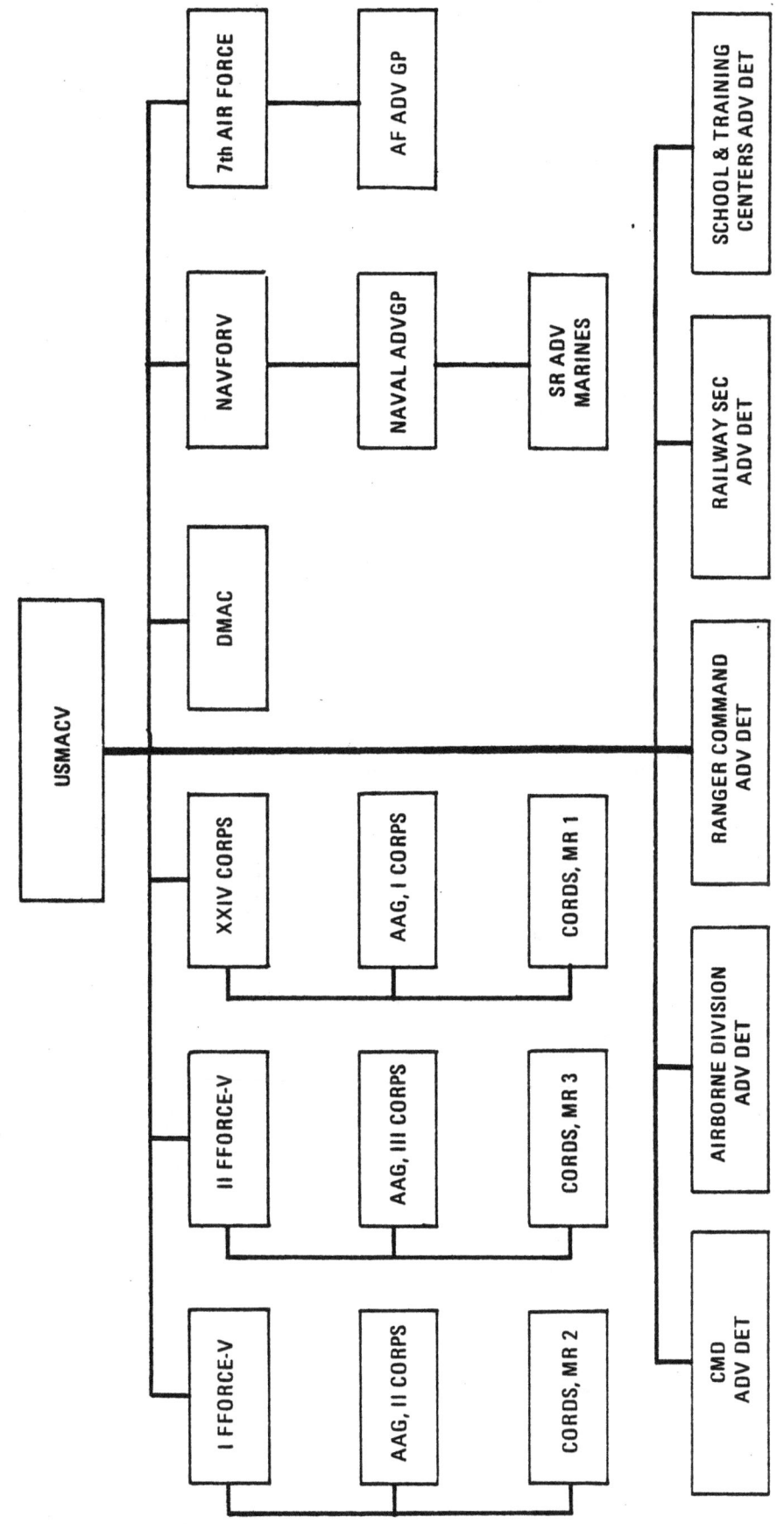

Chart 1 — Organization, U.S. Advisory System, 1970

Chart 2 — Organization, MACV Headquarters Staff Advisers, 1970

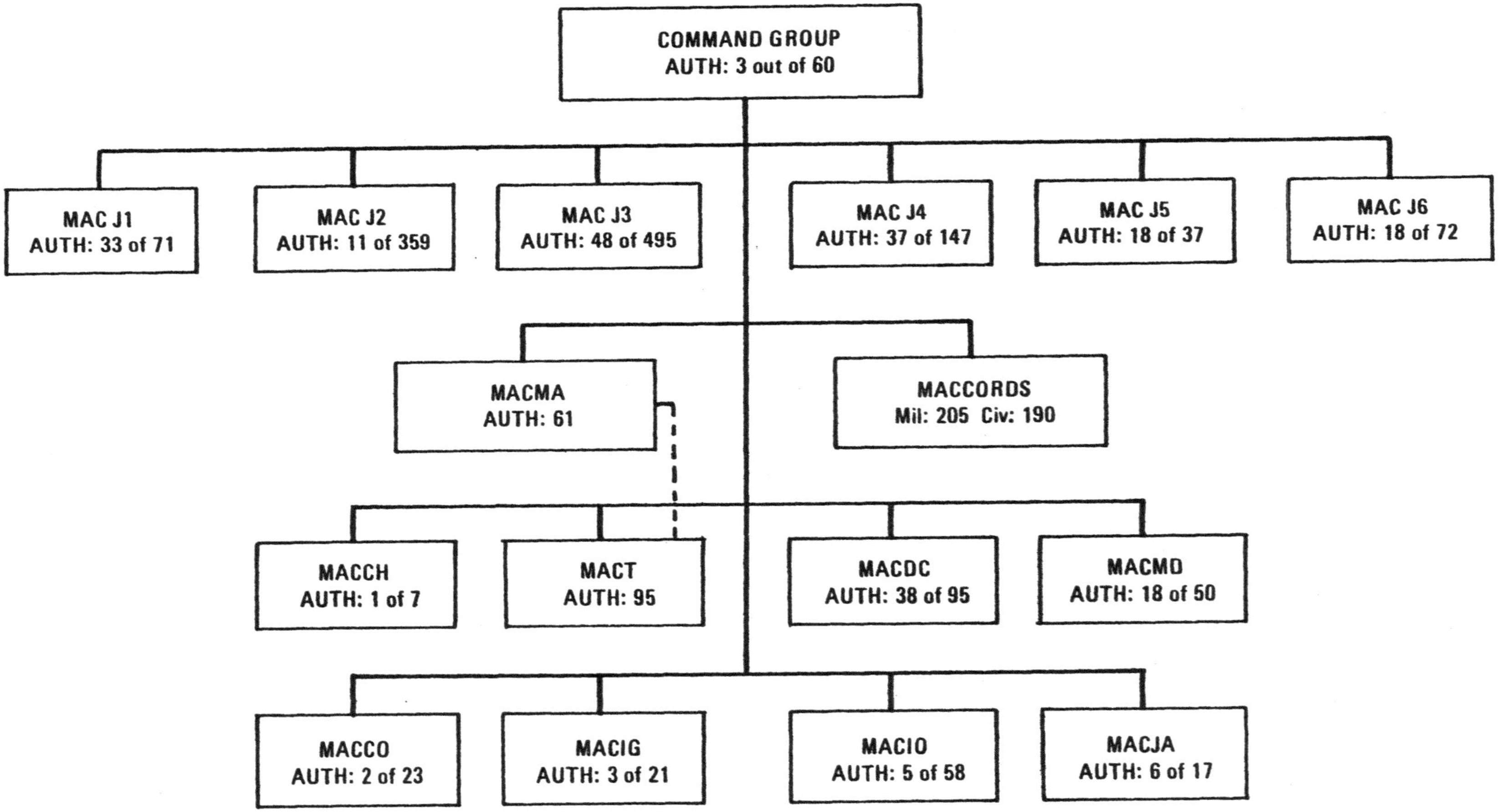

- COMMAND GROUP
  AUTH: 3 out of 60
  - MAC J1
    AUTH: 33 of 71
  - MAC J2
    AUTH: 11 of 359
  - MAC J3
    AUTH: 48 of 495
  - MAC J4
    AUTH: 37 of 147
  - MAC J5
    AUTH: 18 of 37
  - MAC J6
    AUTH: 18 of 72
  - MACMA
    AUTH: 61
  - MACCORDS
    Mil: 205 Civ: 190
  - MACCH
    AUTH: 1 of 7
  - MACT
    AUTH: 95
  - MACMD
    AUTH: 18 of 50
  - MACCO
    AUTH: 2 of 23
  - MACIG
    AUTH: 3 of 21
  - MACDC
    AUTH: 38 of 95
  - MACIO
    AUTH: 5 of 58
  - MACJA
    AUTH: 6 of 17

Only three MACV staff agencies were exclusively involved in advisory and support efforts: the office of the Assistant Chief of Staff for Military Assistance (MACMA), established in 1967 to serve as a focal point for all advisory matters for the Army, Navy, and Air Force advisory groups; the Training Directorate (MACT) which evolved from the original CATO Division, MAAG-V, and served as principal US adviser to the Central Training Command/JGS; and CORDS.

The Assistant Chief of Staff for CORDS was the principal staff assistant to the MACV commander on US civil/military support for the GVN pacification and development program. Within CORDS, there were staffs for each component of the program. Those concerned with civil-oriented programs, such as Refugee Resettlement, Chieu Hoi (the effort to encourage enemy defections and to exploit and care for those who did) Public Safety and Community Development, were staffed mainly by USAID and State Department civilians and their directors served as advisers to counterpart GVN agencies. The mission of advising the RF/PF was assigned to the Territorial Security Directorate, which was staffed mostly by military personnel. In addition, there were Department of Defense civilians working with RD cadre and in the Phoenix program.[4]

MACV general and special staff agencies were all involved in the advisory effort to a certain extent. The Assistant Chief of Staff for Personnel (MACJ1) was the principal adviser to the Minister of War Veterans, GVN, the Director General of Mobilization, Ministry of Defense, and to the J-1, JGS on personnel matters. The Assistant Chief of Staff for Intelligence (MACJ2) was the principal adviser to his counterpart, the J-2, JGS on RVNAF intelligence programs, training, and actions relating to the improvement and modernization of RVNAF intelligence elements. The Assistant Chief of Staff for Operations (MACJ3) was the principal adviser to the JGS on all matters pertaining to operations and current plans. He exercised supervision and control over the

---

[4]Rural Development (RD) cadre were teams of specialists and technicians deployed to villages to assist the people in improving local conditions, primarily in agricultural and management fields. The Phoenix program was designed to root out the VC infrastructure.

Railway Security Advisory Detachment and airborne advisers to the ARVN Airborne Division, and provided primary liaison and assistance to the RVNAF General Political Warfare Department. The Assistant Chief of Staff for Logistics (MACJ4) was the principal adviser to RVNAF on materiel systems development, logistics operation, organization, and plans, and directed the advisory effort of the RVNAF Central Logistics Command, the Technical Service Advisory Divisions, and the Area Logistics Command, the Technical Service Advisory Divisions, and the Area Logistics Commands (ALC) advisory teams. The Assistant Chief of Staff for Plans (MACJ5) provided advisory assistance, conducted combined contingency planning with the JGS, and exercised joint staff supervision for the Free World Military Assistance Organization (FWMAO). The Assistant Chief of Staff for Communications-Electronics (MACJ6) was the senior adviser to the GVN and RVNAF on matters pertaining to the improvement and modernization of communications-electronics and provided direct advisory assistance to ARVN C-E staffs and signal units directly under the operational control of the JGS and ARVN Signal Department. The Comptroller (MACCO) served as an adviser to the RVN on the development and execution of the defense budget and as the senior adviser to the GVN Ministry of Defense on accounting and finance matters. Other special staff agencies such as Provost Marshall, Inspector General, Chaplain, etc. all performed advisory functions in addition to their normal staff duties of a United States military headquarters.

At the corps level, the US field force commander served as senior adviser to the ARVN corps commander. In this capacity, he was assisted by two deputies: a deputy for CORDS and a deputy senior adviser who was actually the chief of the US Army Advisory Group attached to the ARVN Corps headquarters. The Deputy CORDS was the principal adviser to the ARVN corps commander for his responsibilities as chairman of the Corps Pacification and Development Council. His advisory duties were related to territorial security, i.e., improving the effectiveness of the RF/PF, National Field Force Police, and armed RD cadre and PSDF.[5]

---

[5] Armed RD Cadre accompanied the RD teams to protect them in the insecure hamlets in which they worked. The People's Self Defense Forces (PSDF) were the local, lightly armed militia organized solely to protect their own hamlets from VC incursions.

He was also the direct supervisor of the senior advisers assigned to the provinces. The Deputy Senior Adviser directed and supervised the US Army Advisory Group (USAAG) at corps headquarters whose mission was to provide advice and assistance to the ARVN corps commander and his staff in command, administration, training, combat operations, intelligence, security, logistics, political warfare, and civil affairs. He determined requirements for and coordinated US tactical air, airlift support, helicopter, and artillery support for the ARVN corps, and also coordinated with US and FWMAF on joint plans, operations, and training. In addition, he was responsible for establishing, maintaining, operating, and providing advisory functions for a combined Corps Tactical Operations Center/Direct Air Support Center (TOC/DASC) in conjunction with RVNAF elements.

In 1971-1972, to consolidate the corps advisory system during the reduction of US personnel, US Field Forces were replaced by Regional Assistance Commands (RAC). The Delta Military Assistance Command (DMAC) had been established first in late 1969 as the brigade of the US 9th Infantry Division withdrew from IV Corps area. It was redesignated DRAC in 1971. Then in early 1972, the First Regional Assistance Command (FRAC), the Third Regional Assistance Command (TRAC) and the Second Regional Assistance Command (SRAC) were successively established.

The mission of Regional Assistance Commands was to: (1) Provide assistance to the GVN in developing and maintaining an effective military capability by advising and supporting RVNAF military and paramilitary commanders and staffs at all levels in military operations, training, intelligence, personnel management, and combat support and combat service support activities; (2) Provide advice, assistance, and support to RVNAF at corps, division/special zone, sector, and subsector level in planning and executing coordinated pacification and development programs, to include civic actions by US units, and; (3) Develop, in coordination with the ARVN corps commander, recommendations for RVNAF and paramilitary force materiel, personnel, and organizational requirements in the military region. As the corps senior adviser, the RAC commander exercised operational control over the corps US Army Advisory Group and the CORDS organization for the military region.

The division advisory team's mission was to advise and assist the ARVN division commander and his staff in command, administration, training, tactical operations, intelligence, security, logistics, and certain elements of political warfare. The team assisted the ARVN division commander in obtaining and coordinating US combat support. It obtained necessary MAP materiels and equipment for ARVN and kept higher headquarters informed on the combat effectiveness of the division; it also assisted in the operation of the division Tactical Operations Center. The division senior adviser exercised control over regiment and battalion advisory teams, each composed of from three to five US Army personnel.

At the province level, the senior adviser (PSA) was either military or civilian depending on the security situation. Of the 44 province advisers, in 1970, there were 25 military and 19 civilians. If the PSA was military, his deputy was a civilian and vice versa. The PSA's counterpart was the province chief, usually a military officer who commanded the RF/PF as well as GVN administrative personnel. The PSA maintained direct control over each of the district senior advisers (DSA) and with his staff, provided support services and guidance to district and mobile advisory teams.

In 1970, there were 236 districts authorized a DSA and staff. Most of the DSAs were military. The advisory staff at district level usually had eight members but the size varied according to the district particular needs and situation. For example, the DSA for Binh Chanh District (Gia Dinh Province) had a 14-member team to advise and assist the district chief on military and civil aspects of the pacification and development program. In addition to the advisory relationship with the district chief, the DSA had operational control of the mobile advisory teams (MAT) working in the villages and hamlets of that district.

*Vietnamese Requirements For Advisory Assistance
and Support to the U.S. Advisory Effort*

The US advisory effort in South Vietnam was a gradual buildup that responded to the needs of the RVNAF and the military situation. Strange as it may seem, the RVNAF requirements for US advisory assistance were never determined by the Vietnamese themselves. From the beginning to the end of the US advisory effort, the RVNAF never requested a specific quota of advisers nor were they ever able to determine completely what types of advisers were required for their own needs.

The process of determining the requirements for advisory assistance, therefore, was largely based on estimates and progress and it was always a function performed by the US senior military headquarters in South Vietnam. Up to 1960, MAAG-V was bound by a strength ceiling imposed by the Geneva Accords which seriously limited the extent and range of its advisory effort. As of 1961, and in particular with the establishment of MACV, the US advisory effort seemed no longer restrained by the Geneva provisions after North Vietnam publicly vowed to conquer the South. During the Diem administration, however, despite the 1961 Treaty of Amity and Economic Relations with the US, the GVN tended to view the growing US advisory effort with a suspicious eye, particularly as it related to the assignment of advisers to provinces and to the activities of the United States Special Forces. This suspicion seemed to derive from the fact that as an autocratic ruler, President Diem was reluctant to let any outsider be privy to the way he ruled the country from his palace.

The successive military governments after Mr. Diem took a more realistic view of the US advisory assistance effort which the military especially regarded as indispensable after the 1964 near-disaster. The expansion of the US advisory system during the following years came as a natural response to the growing Communist threat. Still, neither the GVN nor the JGS ever recommended how many or what types of advisers would be required to help South Vietnam achieve the desired objectives.

There were several reasons for this. First, the decisions to deploy more or fewer United States personnel were always made by US leaders after general consultation with the GVN which was never in a position to disagree. Second, neither the GVN nor the JGS was familiar with the different categories of US Army occupational specialties, much less with the US government civil service system. Third, the JGS never knew for certain how much financial and material aid the RVNAF would receive from the Military Assistance Program each year in order to plan accurately for force structure increases or other improvement programs, hence the requirements for additional advisory assistance. It seemed as if the JGS was always resigned to the position of a blind-folded recipient of military aid and advisory assistance, leaving all the details of programming and funding to the donor.

The requirements for US Army officers assigned to advisory duties in Vietnam seemed to be based on three major criteria: language ability, branch of service, and training. Some degree of fluency in Vietnamese, for example, was required of officers assigned to the RF/PF, particularly those advising the PF training centers and the district chiefs. Experience, however, showed that this linguistic requirement was seldom restrictive and that these advisers rarely achieved a desirable fluency for effective professional communication. US Army officers selected for staff or technical service advisory duties were usually matched branch for branch, but here again, this requirement was sometimes not strictly observed, chiefly when the advisory position was classified as branch-immaterial. The training criterion applied mostly to key advisory positions or specialized areas of duty. Depending on the level, graduates of the National or Army War Colleges, Command and General Staff College, branch Career or Advanced courses were required. Specialized areas of duty usually related to such courses as Counterinsurgency and Special Warfare, Psychological Operations, Special Forces, Civil Affairs, etc. The majority of advisory positions, however, required graduates of the Military Assistance Institute or Military Assistance Training Advisory Course. But regardless of position or specialization, the one-year tour seemed not conducive to more extensive preparation of US officers for advisory duties other than perfunctory requirements and a brief orientation course prior to field deployment.

The RVNAF support for the US advisory effort dated back to the early days of TRIM. However, this support was adequate and significant only during the existence of MAAG-V. The advent of MACV and the subsequent growth of the United States advisory effort gradually transcended the RVNAF capabilities to provide support. As a result, Vietnamese support to the advisory effort was only modest, in view of its limited assets.

When the first US advisers were assigned to field duties back in 1955, they were almost exclusively supported by the ARVN units to which they were attached. In fact, a basic directive issued by the Vietnamese General Staff in 1955 and reiterated three years later concerning support for US advisers emphasized that it was the responsibility of Vietnamese Armed Forces officers to ensure that US advisers were provided with: (1) Security; (2) Satisfaction in their operational requirements, and (3) Billets, office space, vehicles, drivers, mess personnel, interpreters, communications and emergency medical service.

During the first few years when advisory personnel were limited and mostly concentrated in the Saigon area, service and logistical support was provided for them by the 1st ARVN Headquarters and Service Battalion. Its responsibilities included the administration of Vietnamese base facilities made available to MAAG-V such as General Staff's old headquarters at 606, Tran Hung Dao Boulevard which was used for several years as the MAAG-V Headquarters, the operation of MAAG-V motor pool, including the control of Vietnamese drivers, and the provision of security personnel for MAAG-V Headquarters and personnel billets. In billeting support, the RVNAF provided a multi-story, downtown building which had been constructed and turned over by French Forces. This building was used as BOQs for US officers for many years and was named after the first MAAG chief, Brigadier General Francis G. Brink. Subsequently, as US forces increased many times and because of RVNAF limited assets, all billeting quarters and office requirements for US personnel in the Saigon area were provided by MACV.

In the field, US advisory teams permanently attached to ARVN units and schools were accommodated in Vietnamese facilities, to include office space, billets and mess service. These facilities were usually located in the same building complex occupied by the ARVN unit. In a few places where ARVN facilities were very limited, living quarters and a mess for US advisers were located in a separate area in town, however, offices were always co-located within the ARVN unit compound. A

substantial construction fund was set aside by the Construction
Directorate, RVNAF for the purpose of improving facilities reserved for
US advisers. Standards for this improvement work were normally higher
than those for ARVN facilities.

Vehicles and communications facilities were usually provided by
the ARVN unit out of its organic equipment. Drivers, interpreters, mess
and utility personnel were all ARVN servicemen from the unit's organic
personnel. Members of the advisory team were treated at the unit's
medical facility in case of minor illness and injury. In all aspects
of support, the United States advisory team was considered as an element
of the unit and the ARVN unit commander was held responsible for the
team's security and well being. The most significant difficulty for
most ARVN units with a US advisory team during the early years was
that neither vehicles, particularly 1/4 ton trucks, nor personnel
involved in the support of these US advisers were authorized within the
unit TOE.

By 1961, the advisory system had expanded to such an extent that it
was beyond the capability of RVNAF and the ARVN unit to provide adequate
support. As a result, vehicles, communication equipment and personnel
required for the support of US advisers were programmed and gradually
provided by MAAG-V. After MACV was established in 1962, all support
requirements for field advisory teams were processed through US support
channels. Vehicles and radio equipment that were earmarked for US
advisers were programmed for separately, but upon arrival in Vietnam
they were placed under RVNAF control. However, their distribution was
subject to orders issued by MACV J-4. Once these vehicles and radio
equipment had been issued, they were accounted for and maintained by
the ARVN unit to which the US advisory team was assigned.

For office and living quarters, US adviser's requirements were
handled by MACV either through new construction or leasing. Priority
in construction was given to office buildings located within ARVN compounds if land and space was available. The use of land outside ARVN
jurisdiction had to be approved by an Interministerial Commission on
Real Estate. Maintenance work on newly constructed buildings was the

responsibility of US support units. As to interpreters and drivers, requirements that seemed to multiply every year, an arrangement was made whereby if locally US recruited and paid civilians were not adequate, they were augmented with ARVN servicemen as appropriate.

By 1965, in view of the US force buildup, the support for United States advisers was provided entirely by MACV. It no longer was the responsibility of the RVNAF as had been initially determined. Conversely in 1972, to prepare for the pullout in the event of a cease-fire agreement, all facilities and equipment used by US advisers for their day-to-day operations were title-transfered to the RVNAF and became Vietnamese properties. US advisers signed for their temporary use and finally returned them to the RVNAF when they departed South Vietnam in compliance with the Paris Agreement of 28 January 1973.

Such was, in very broad terms, the evolution of the US advisory effort in South Vietnam from the day the Vietnamese armed forces became fully autonomous until the event of an illusory cease-fire forced its termination. The following chapters seek to analyze and evaluate the system from the Vietnamese point of view in terms of its achievements in every area of endeavor, its relations with the counterpart military organization at all levels and in terms of the constraints imposed upon it by national policies and cultural differences.

CHAPTER II

The JGS and MACV

A Matter of Personal Relationship

When I assumed the command responsibilities as Chief of the Joint General Staff (JGS) in October 1965, I did not really expect to serve in that capacity for nearly a decade. So eventful was my tenure of office that I hardly noticed the passing of time until the very last days of the Republic. During this period, I had the privilege of being a counterpart to three successive MACV commanders, General William C. Westmoreland, General Creighton W. Abrams, and General Frederick C. Weyand, all distinguished professional soldiers whom I admire and respect not only as military leaders but also as friends and advisers.

The decade of my command saw the Republic of Vietnam Armed Forces truly come of age in every respect. Within the space of eight years, they had more than doubled in force structure to become a strong, modern three-service military organization with 1.1 million men under arms by the time of the cease-fire. In early 1965, they were on the verge of losing the military war. In 1968, they stood up valiantly against a most vicious enemy offensive and turned it into a military victory. Twice in 1970 and 1971, they crossed the national borders and struck devastatingly against the enemy's inviolable sanctuaries and infiltration corridor. In 1972, they stalled and finally broke up a most ferocious and determined invasion by NVA regular divisions on three different fronts. All these exploits, although achieved with substantial support from American firepower, testified to the success of the U.S. military assistance and advisory program.

The relationship between the JGS and MACV had been purely advisory in nature until United States forces started to participate in the ground war. The buildup of U. S. combat forces beginning in mid-1965 added a new dimension to this relationship by making it one of coordination and cooperation for the conduct of the war since MACV had become a theater-type command. General Westmoreland was genuinely concerned, as all military strategists should, about the feasibility of a United Nations-type unified command and he sketched the idea to my immediate predecessor, Lieutenant General Tran Van Minh, and Lieutenant General Nguyen Van Thieu, then Minister of Defense, who was soon to become Chairman of the National Leadership Committee. As military men themselves, both understood his concern but were disturbed at the idea of sacrificing the national cause for the sake of the military war in the event an American general became supreme commander. After all, this was a Vietnamese conflict and national sensitivities aside, there was also the question of how world opinion would react if it was fought under the American banner. The matter was not discussed further and when I was appointed Chief of the JGS, the coexistence of two separate commands looked like the most natural way to manage the war effectively. Never again did General Westmoreland bring up the subject, as least as far as I was concerned.

I enjoyed the same kind of working relationship with the next MACV commander, General Creighton W. Abrams whose responsibility was to improve the RVNAF, oversee the gradual U.S. troop pullout and ensure that the RVNAF had the capabilities to assume the combat burden. His leadership and devotedness helped the RVNAF rapidly develop in strength and fighting ability. It was largely General Abram's idea of putting them to test. I most welcomed his suggestion of a spoiling attack against the enemy's supply bases and infiltration routes which resulted in the Cambodian Incursion of 1970 and LAM SON 719 in lower Laos in 1971. It was he again who, in the confusion of the first few hours after the NVA crossed the DMZ in early April 1972, personally informed me of the critical situation and the debacle of the 3d ARVN Infantry Division. Had it not been for his insight and solicitude, the JGS would have found itself in an embarrassing position after I Corps had apparently lost effective control. The next and last MACV commander, General Fred C. Weyand, who had served as II Field Force Commander, had only a brief tour, but was instrumental in bringing the RVNAF up to the required strength and combat capabilities. His finishing touch, the Enhance Plus program, which gave additional mobility and firepower to the RVNAF, brought the Vietnamization process to a successful conclusion.

Looking back over the years of U.S. advisory assistance and cooperation, I think that success owed a great deal to the personal relationship cultivated between the adviser and his counterpart. At the JGS and MACV level, this relationship was of utmost importance since it reflected on the entire system and could make or break the common war effort. But since its beginning, the U.S. advisory system had been built on solid ground as evidenced by the productive decade that preceded my tour of duty as Chief of the JGS. My predecessor, the venerated and paternal Marshal Le Van Ty, who presided over that earlier decade, was truly the pioneer who laid a solid foundation for the development of a fruitful U.S.-RVNAF relationship. What I later enjoyed was only the legacy of his exemplary leadership. During his time, he faced much less complex but more fundamental problems. What he had accomplished with the advisory assistance of various MAAG chiefs was to remain forever the basic framework on which the RVNAF were later developed.

Reorganization and Development of the RVNAF

It was in late 1954 that the Vietnamese General Staff became all-Vietnamese for the first time, without French officers and NCO cadre.[1] Major General Le Van Ty, then commander of the 1st Military Region, was appointed Chief of the General Staff, a position he held until his death in 1964. It was also then that Vietnamese began to be used as the official language in the armed forces in the place of French.

---

[1] The first Vietnamese officers appointed to key staff positions were: Colonel Tran Van Don, Chief of Staff; Lt. Colonel Tran Thien Khiem, Deputy Chief of Staff; Major Tu Cau, G-1; Major Trang Van Chinh, G-2; Lt. Colonel Nguyen Van Manh, G-3; Major Cao Van Vien, G-4; Major Tran Tu Oai, G-5 (Psywar); Lt. Colonel Tran Ngoc Tam, Training Bureau.

From the beginning, the General Staff of the Vietnamese National Armed Forces was predominantly army despite the existence of service components. The Deputies Chief of the General Staff for the Navy and Air Force were also the commanders of their respective components. When assuming its advisory and training role, the MAAG directed its primary effort toward the Vietnamese Army which was in fact the most important and by far the largest service. Within the MAAG organization, the Combat Arms Training and Organization (CATO) Division was the principal agency responsible for the reorganization and training of the Vietnamese Army. *(Chart 3)* This nucleus of training advisers was to develop in time into the Training Directorate under MACV.

The most pressing task faced by the Vietnamese General Staff after its creation in late 1954 was to take over responsibilities from the departing French forces by establishing a cohesive territorial system of command and organizing a regular combat force composed of nine infantry divisions and an airborne brigade in order to face the eventuality of renewed aggression by North Vietnam.

On 1 January 1955, the first three infantry divisions, the 11th, 21st, and 31st were activated. But this organizational momentum was soon impeded by the problem of a strength ceiling imposed by the MAAG. The Vietnamese forces' total strength by that date stood at 210,000 to include 172,000 of the regular forces and 37,800 assorted auxiliary troops (regional forces, French Union forces, Cao Dai and Hoa Hao armed units absorbed into the Vietnamese Army).[2] While the General Staff advocated

---

[2] There were about 25,000 Vietnamese serving in French Union forces to include 1,200 paratroopers and 3,000 commandos. Upon their departure, the French insisted that they be all reintegrated into the Vietnamese National Army. Only 10,000 were accepted by the Vietnamese General Staff. The remainder was either disbanded or rejoined French Forces in Algeria. The Cao Dai was a religious sect in Tay Ninh Province that maintained a private quasi-military force. About 2,400 of these men were absorbed into the Army. The Hoa Hao was a religious sect located in the Mekong Delta Province of Long Xuyen and 2,400 men of its private army were also integrated into the ARVN. Another military organization was maintained by the Catholics of Bien Hoa Province - the Unité Mobile de Defence de la Chrétienté (UMDC) - and 840 of these men were absorbed in the Vietnamese Army.

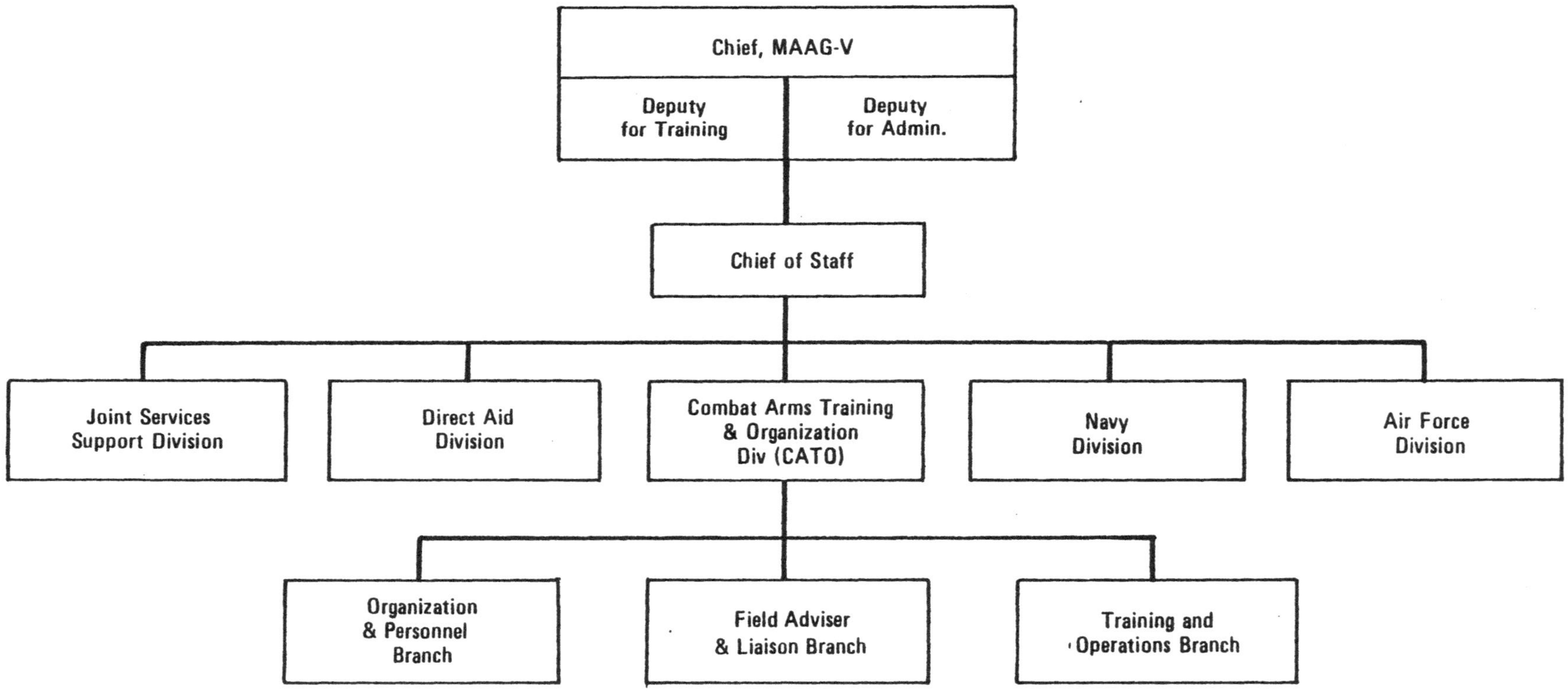

Chart 3 — Organization, Military Assistance Advisory Group, Vietnam, 1956

a 150,000-man regular force, the MAAG adamantly agreed to only 100,000 and further recommended that the strength reduction be made within six months.

In compliance with the MAAG's recommendations, the Vietnamese General Staff proceeded first to discharge the auxiliary forces, then the disabled, old, sick or wounded, mostly troops native of and regrouped from North Vietnam. This coercive measure generated a feeling of frustration among the troops which resulted in two riots by discharged servicemen, one in Nha Trang during February and the other in Hue in March, 1955, in protest against the discharge.

Hard-pressed by the mandatory strength ceiling and the problems created both by discharged servicemen and the need to maintain sufficient forces to combat the dissident sects, the government of Vietnam established the Civil Guard in April 1955 to absorb the veterans. By mid-June, when the MAAG approved the new 150,000-man force structure, the discharge orders were rescinded. The 150,000-man force structure was maintained, with slight fluctuations, as the basic strength of the Republic of Vietnam Armed Forces (RVNAF) for the next five years, then gradually increased to about 290,000 by the time the U.S. introduced combat forces for the ground war in South Vietnam in 1965.

With the new force structure plan approved, the MAAG and the General Staff agreed to build a national military force whose major combat components consisted of 10 infantry divisions (4 field and 6 light), 1 airborne brigade, 13 territorial regiments, 11 artillery battalions (including one 155-mm. artillery battalion), 4 armor regiments and 3 engineer combat groups. The navy and air force, meanwhile, had about 4,000 men each, poorly equipped and poorly trained. Following a MAAG suggestion, in October 1955, a standardized designation system was adopted for the infantry divisions. Thus the four 8,100-man field divisions were designated 1, 2, 3, 4 and the six 5,800-man light divisions were numbered from 11 to 16.

The period from 1956 to 1958 was devoted to extensive field tests initiated and conducted by the MAAG in search for an optimal type division for the Army of the Republic of Vietnam (ARVN). The restructuring effort was undertaken with the basic assumption of an overt invasion from the North and the organizational approach to it was purely conventional, undoubtedly under the influence of the Korean war experience. Tables of organization and equipment were prepared and tested. The guinea pig for these experimentations was the 4th Field Division (later redesignated 7th) at Bien Hoa.

By the end of 1959, the ARVN was reorganized into seven standard divisions of 10,450 men each and three army corps headquarters. In 1961, to cope with the mounting Communist insurgency, two new infantry divisions were activated, the 9th and 25th, and a fourth army corps headquarters was established. Still, each division had only one artillery battalion and company-size support units. The U.S. was then prepared to provide support for a regular army of 170,000 and an auxiliary force (Civil Guard) of 68,000.

Encouraged by the U.S. willingness to provide support as required, the JGS asked for a 15-division, 278,000-man regular army in mid-1961, a plan it had coveted to provide the ARVN with a strong combat backbone. The U.S. agreed to only 200,000 but began to send in more U.S. combat support assets to enhance the RVNAF capabilities in heliflift, air reconnaissance, and coastline and river patrolling. The strength of MAAG-V was also increased and it began attaching advisers to ARVN combat battalions. In view of consolidating the U.S. advisory and assistance effort in terms of command and control, the U.S. decided to establish the U.S. Military Assistance Command Vietnam (MACV) in February 1962, under Lieutenant General Paul D. Harkins. The MAAG continued to function as a separate headquarters responsible to MACV for advisory and operational support matters under Major General Charles J. Timmes who had succeeded Lieutenant General Lionel C. McGarr.

The years 1961 and 1962 were devoted to extensive training, field and command post exercises by infantry divisions, and emphasis was placed on improving the Civil Guard and People's Militia. The JGS itself underwent a radical change in organization when in mid-1962 it was decided to create an Army Command under Lieutenant General Tran Van Don, following an over-all defense structure reorganization which saw the establishment of four Corps Tactical Zones (CTZ), and Division Tactical

Areas (DTA). The JGS was to function as a genuine joint service general staff with personnel attached from the Air Force and Navy. At the same time a joint communications-electronics staff division, J-6, was created under the JGS for the first time.

The concept of a separate army component proved unsuccessful and the experimental Army Command was disbanded about six months later. It was concluded that the Army Command merely duplicated the functions being performed by the JGS which in fact remained essentially an army general staff with limited joint authority despite the inclusion of a handful of air force and naval staff officers.

After the November military *coup d' etat* of 1963 which overthrew President Ngo Dinh Diem, the JGS was transformed into an Armed Forces High Command under General Tran Thien Khiem and later, General Nguyen Kanh but its role and functions remained unchanged. This was a period of political uncertainty which saw several governments come and go in rapid succession. The new MACV commander, General William C. Westmoreland, must have had a hard time dealing with politically-ambitious ARVN generals who made up the Armed Forces Council and effectively controlled the RVNAF. After civilian rule was restored in early 1965, with the ousting of General Nguyen Khanh, the Armed Forces High Command was placed under the command of Lieutenant General Tran Van Minh. When the National Leadership Committee was formed in mid-1965 to rule the country under Lieutenant General Nguyen Van Thieu and Air "Vice Marshal" Nguyen Cao Ky, I was called upon to serve as Chief of the Joint General Staff, a position I held until the final days of South Vietnam. By this time, the RVNAF total strength had reached 435,000 to include 225,000 for the ARVN, a regular force still basically composed of nine infantry divisions.

The period from 1965 to 1969 saw a rapid expansion and modernization of the RVNAF. It was also a period of intensified fighting during which U.S. ground forces, introduced since mid-1965, took the lead in combat while the RVNAF assumed the more modest role of pacification support. Successive force structure increases brought total RVNAF strength to 633,645 in 1967, 685,739 in 1968, 875,790 in 1969, 953,673 in 1970, 992,837 in 1971, and finally to around 1.1 million men at the time of the cease-fire in January 1973. In the meantime, two new infantry divisions were created, the 10th (later redesignated 18th) in 1966, and the 3d, in early 1972. Having to cope with training and logistical support problems occasioned by the rapid force structure expansion, the JGS decided to create the Central Training Command and the Central Logistics Command in 1966 in an effort to consolidate and improve command and control regarding these major functions. To exercise supervision over the territorial (Regional and Popular) forces, which had become part of the RVNAF in 1964 and by 1966 made up about one half of total RVNAF strength, there was created the position of Deputy Chief of the JGS for Regional and Popular Forces.

With the institution of the Second Republic in 1967 under President Nguyen Van Thieu, who also effectively assumed his constitutional powers as Commander-in-Chief of the RVNAF, the role of the JGS greatly diminished in importance. Although by official decree it was the command body of the RVNAF, the JGS for all practical purposes was reduced to planning and supervising. The President reserved for himself the prerogative of appointing and promoting senior commanders, to include division commanders, technical service chiefs and province chiefs, and not infrequently he himself gave direct orders to field commanders. This state of things, unfortunately, continued until the collapse of the regime in April 1975.

In keeping with the turnabout of U.S. policy toward Vietnam, General Creighton W. Abrams succeeded General Westmoreland as Commander, USMACV in July 1968, with the mission of overseeing the accelerated program designed to improve the combat effectiveness of the RVNAF, thus preparing groundwork for the Vietnamization program which was formally announced in mid-1969. General Abrams also presided over the gradual redeployment of U.S. combat forces until he left Vietnam in April 1972 after accomplishing his difficult mission and reassuring the U.S. President that the RVNAF could "hack it" alone. He was replaced by General Fred C. Weyand who remained until MACV was disbanded after the cease-fire.

Highlights of a Fruitful Relationship

At the beginning of the U.S. advisory effort in South Vietnam which was initiated under TRIM, most U.S. field advisers were deployed to ARVN infantry division headquarters and major training centers. None of them had a rank higher than lieutenant colonel. An arrangement was made whereby if an American officer was appointed as senior adviser, he was assisted by a French deputy and vice-versa. At the General Staff and military region levels, the organization for advisory assistance at this state was skeletal and informal. All problems were solved through personal contracts or during meetings between the counterpart staffs.

The major obstacle then was the language barrier. Since most ARVN officers only spoke Vietnamese or French, there was the indispensable need for interpreters during every contact with U.S. advisers. In addition to language, there were also problems of dissimilar military background and training. Most ARVN officers then had only a scant knowledge of U.S. Army doctrine, organization, and operational technique. Added together, these problems complicated the task of reorganizing the ARVN and made it a time-consuming process. During discussions on new tables of organization and equipment, a minor difference in opinion was apt to take days to resolve. For example, while ARVN staff officers of the General Staff maintained that the only individual weapon a company commander ever needed was a cal .45 pistol, U.S. advisers contended that since a company commander was also required to fight like anybody else in the company, he had to be equipped with a cal .30 carbine. This type of problem gave rise to lengthy discussions which took twice as much time to get a point through because translation was required.

It was realized that for the advisory effort to be really beneficial, the problems of language and military knowledge, particularly about U.S. Army doctrine and organization, should be expediently resolved. Strange as it may have seemed, the subject of teaching Vietnamese or French to U.S. advisers was never brought up. A few advisers took private lessons on their own initiative but only for personal reasons and most never progressed beyond the greeting stage. Even later, over the war years, I know of no single instance in which a U.S. adviser effectively discussed

professional matters with his counterpart in Vietnamese. The learning
and development of a new language seemed to have no appeal for U.S.
advisers who must have found it not really worth the effort because of
the short tour of duty in Vietnam. So the effort was directed at giving
English lessons to Vietnamese servicemen. English courses conducted
after duty hours by U.S. advisers mushroomed in units and headquarters.
These were later complemented by regular courses given by the Vietnamese
American Association in Saigon.

In addition, a special command and staff course was conducted at
the 1st Training Center (later redesignated Quang Trung) in June 1955
for the benefit of ARVN officers who familiarized themselves with U.S.
Army doctrine and command and staff procedures for the first time. A
number of ARVN officers who spoke English well were also selected to
attend training courses at Fort Leavenworth, Fort Benning, and other U.S.
Army service schools beginning in August 1955, to be followed by specialized
offshore courses in the Philippines, Okinawa, and orientation tours in
Hawaii. All of these officers and specialists were earmarked for
assignments as instructors or staff officers upon graduation and return
to Vietnam.

When French advisers at the General Staff departed in early 1955
they were not immediately replaced by United States advisers. In the
interim an increased liaison was assumed by the Chief MAAG, Lieutenant
General Samuel T. Williams, himself, who usually met with the Chief of
the General Staff or his Chief of Staff for matters of mutual concern.
With the activation of TRIM and the assignment of field advisers, however,
there was a requirement for defining the specific mission, functions,
authority and responsibilities of TRIM advisers and the ARVN commanders'
duties and responsibilities toward U.S. advisers. This was the subject
of a memorandum published in April 1955 and signed by Major General Le Van Ty,
Chief of the General Staff. The memorandum laid the foundation and
set the tone for US-ARVN relations by defining, among other things:
(1) the general advisory mission which was to assist and advise ARVN
commanders on "strictly technical aspects"; (2) the advisers' responsibilities
which gave them no command nor supervisory authority, and (3) the ARVN

commanders' responsibilities which included providing security and support, inviting necessary counsel and exercising their own judgment in making use of the advice offered. The memorandum finally stressed a "courteous, inter-allied cooperative spirit" as the hallmark for a successful relationship.[3]

In some respects, this was indeed a solid milestone in US-ARVN relations, which was to develop into a most fruitful cooperation during the following years. It was also remarkable by the fact that this was the first official document ever published by the JGS concerning the role of U.S. advisers. Three years later, a second memorandum, similar in content and referring to the previous one as a reminder, emphasized the continued need for U.S. advisory assistance and admonished ARVN commanders to show "due consideration" to MAAG officials and all ARVN officers to be "civil and courteous" in their daily contact with American advisers.[4] Although it simply reiterated ARVN commanders' duties and responsibilities toward American advisers, the document was intended only for officers and stressed civility and courteousness as the basis for cooperation and association. This cooperation, in fact, worked so well during the following years that there was never a requirement to publish any other documents concerning this subject.

During this early period, U.S. officers served both as staff officers in their organization (TRIM, and later CATO, under MAAG) and as advisers for ARVN counterparts in the same branch of service. For example, the advisers attached to G-2, General Staff at that time came from the Combat Information Techniques Section, Training and Operations Branch.

---

[3] Memorandum No. 1891/TMT/MG, dated 10 April 1955, signed by Major General Le Van Ty, for general distribution.

[4] Memorandum No. 1442/TTM/TNCKH/KH/MK, dated 24 April 1958, signed by Lieutenant General Le Van Ty, for restricted distribution (officers only).

Field advisers, also under control of CATO, were assigned to infantry divisions, military schools and training centers while personnel from TERM served as advisers for ARVN logistical agencies. By the time the MAAG was reorganized with additional personnel in late 1960, absorbing TERM personnel in the process, the advisory system was well established throughout the RVNAF hierarchy even down to the battalion level on a selective basis. Cooperation between advisers and Vietnamese counterparts became closer and more effective since the initial barriers, language and unfamiliarity with the U.S. system, had been greatly reduced.

In February 1962, in keeping with the growing operational support role in South Vietnam, the United States activated the Military Assistance Command, Vietnam (MACV). However, the MAAG continued to function as a separate headquarters with its advisory role unchanged until it was dissolved and integrated into MACV in May 1964. Subsequently MACV underwent many organizational changes. *(Chart 4)* Its principal counterpart, the Joint General Staff, also went through some comprehensive reorganizations in keeping with the continually growing RVNAF force structure and functional changes in the overall defense structure. *(Chart 5)* Although the MACV commander dealt with three different levels of RVN defense organization (the President or Prime Minister, the Minister of Defense, and the Chairman, JGS) his principal counterpart was the Chairman of the JGS.

During the period from 1965 to 1972, MACV functioned not only as a sub-theater command which controlled U.S. combat forces in South Vietnam, but also in an advisory and assistance capacity with regard to the JGS. Thus, MACV staff division chiefs had the additional responsibility of serving as senior advisers to their JGS counterparts. In the MACV-JGS arrangement for coordination and cooperation, which practically amounted to a paralleled organization in terms of constituent components save for a few exceptions, all JGS general and special staff divisions, subordinate commands, arms and services benefited from the advisory effort. However, the number of U.S. advisers assigned to work with each JGS component or agency varied, depending on the relative importance or workload of

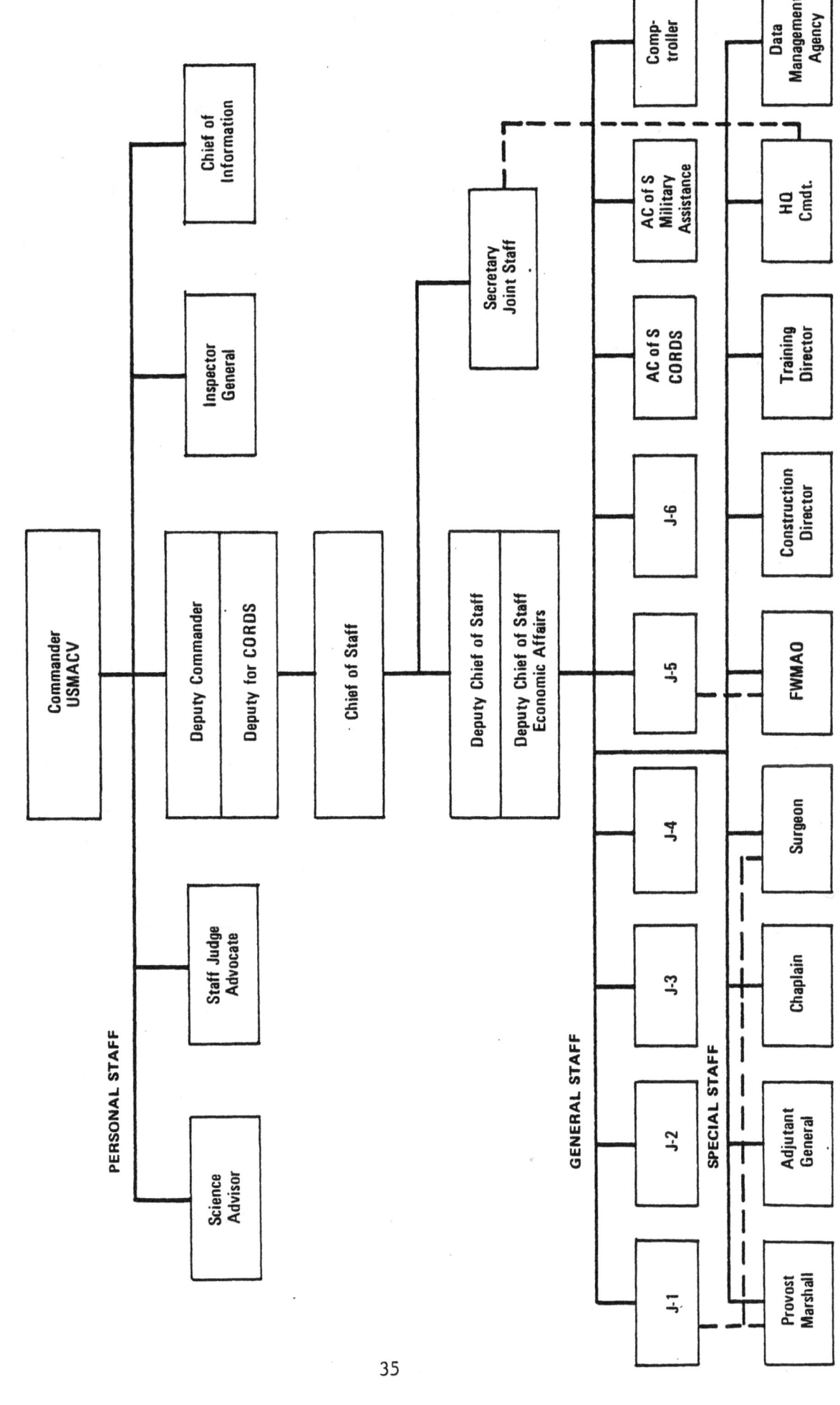

Chart 4 — Organization, US Military Assistance Command, Vietnam, 1972

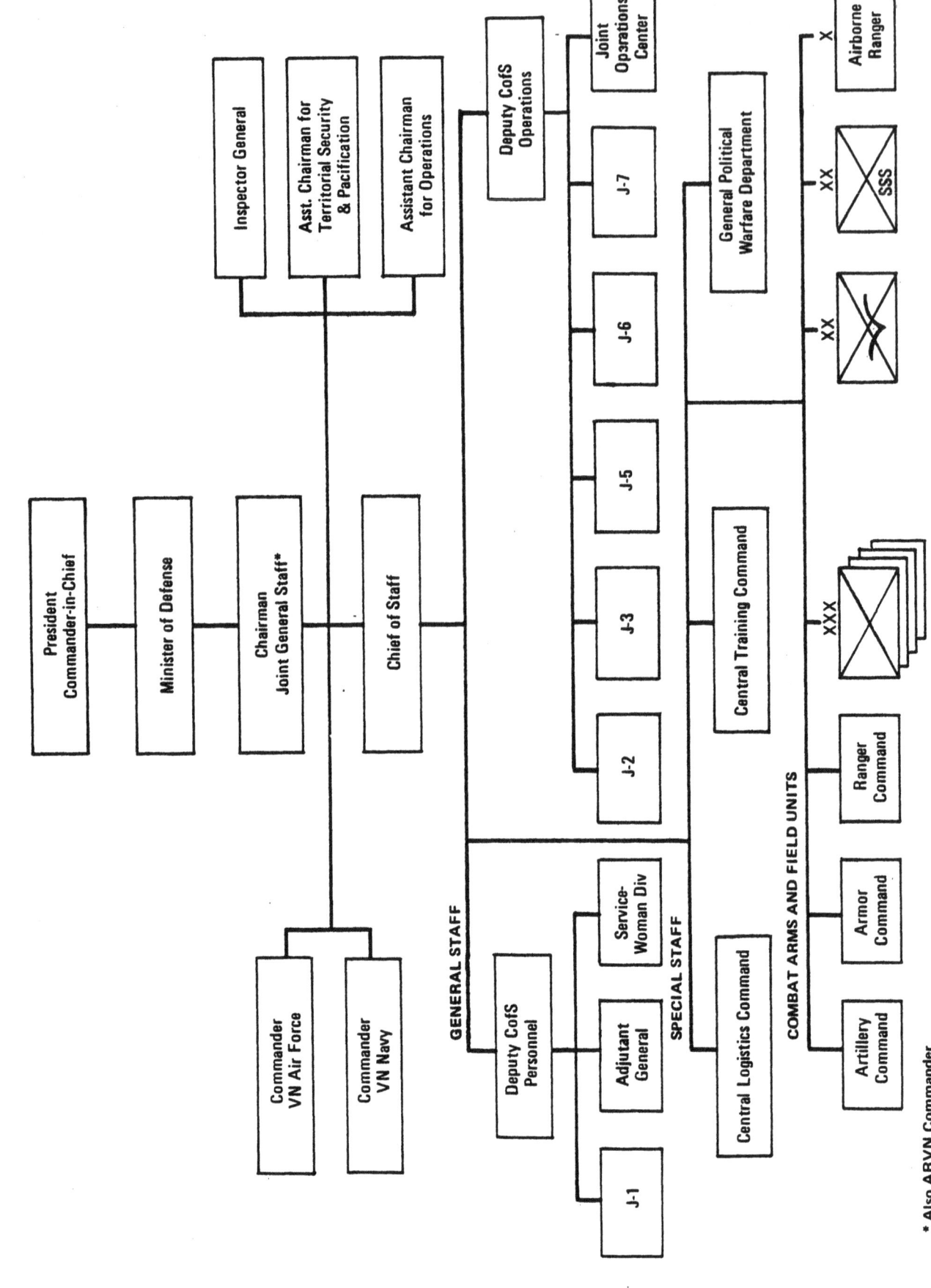

Chart 5 — Organization, Joint General Staff and Armed Forces Structure, 1972

that component or agency.

A few examples suffice to illustrate this working arrangement. The senior adviser to the Chief J-2 (Intelligence), JGS, was of course the MACV Assistant Chief of Staff J-2. But his permanent representatives at the Office of the J-2, JGS consisted of a liaison team composed of 4 officers (2 Army, 1 Air Force, 1 Navy) and 1 NCO. Also, at each of the four combined intelligence centers, there was a U.S. element working constantly in close coordination with the ARVN element sharing the same facilities and almost paralleling the ARVN organization.[5] The only difference was that the U.S. element had more personnel and a greater variety of specialists. The US-ARVN relationship at this working level was more of a co-worker than a regular advisor-counterpart arrangement, since the U.S. personnel assigned to these centers belonged to the 525th U.S. Military Intelligence Group, an operational unit under the command and control of MACV J-2.

At the J-3 division, JGS, there was also a liaison team of 4 officers and 1 NCO who worked directly with the Joint Operations Center. But the senior adviser to the Chief J-3, JGS was the MACV Assistant Chief of Staff J-3.

Prior to 1966, the J-4, JGS worked with both MACV J-4 and Headquarters U.S. Army, Vietnam, the former providing advisory assistance and the latter, materiel support. When the Vietnamese Central Logistics Command (CLC) was activated in 1966, all J-4 JGS functions were assumed by the Commander of CLC. The MACV J-4 then served as senior adviser and only point of contact for the Commander, CLC.

Some JGS staff divisions or agencies worked with more than one U.S. counterpart. For example, the J-7 division which was responsible for signal intelligence worked with both MACV J-2 and the U.S. Embassy. The same was true with some MACV staff divisions such as CORDS which provided

---

[5] The Combined Intelligence Center, Vietnam (CICV), the Combined Document Exploitation Center (CDEC), the Combined Military Interrogation Center (CMIC), and the Combined Materiel Exploitation Center (CMEC).

advice and assistance not only to J-3, JGS but also to the Central
Pacification and Development Council and various ministries of the GVN.
But those were exceptions rather than the rule.

Procedures for Cooperation

By the time the United States decided to commit combat troops to
help fight the war in South Vietnam, the initial language barrier and
Vietnamese unfamiliarity with American military doctrine and organization
were no longer stumbling blocks for the advisory effort. An Armed
Forces Language School had been added to the ARVN school system and it
was expanding. U.S. Army school curricular and instructional materials
were extensively used throughout the ARVN school and training center
system. Most ARVN officers were now able to communicate in English and
they were well familiar with U.S. military doctrine and organization.
The switch to the new system and language had been swift and thorough.

Still there were no detailed written procedures as to how US-ARVN
cooperation should be conducted. Most adviser-counterpart relations were
informal and unrestrained, shaped largely by improvisations and personalities. At the MACV-JGS level, for example, the procedures for cooperation
were determined by ad hoc verbal agreement between the Commander, USMACV
and me, his counterpart, the Chairman of the JGS. We agreed to meet
alone every Monday at 2:30 in the afternoon at the JGS for personal and
problem-solving discussions. During the week before the meeting I would
make notes as problems or issues arose that I wished to discuss with
General Westmoreland or General Abrams at our Monday meeting. Meanwhile,
my Chief of Staff would have the staff preparing fact sheets concerning
any matter they thought I should bring up with COMUSMACV. The chief
would bring these to me on Friday or Saturday and I would decide whether
or not to include them in our discussion. Sometimes I would direct
the staff officer to work out the matter with his counterpart first,
before I would broach it to COMUSMACV. I am sure that General Abrams
prepared for our meetings similarly, since he often passed to me fact
sheets prepared by his staff. We would settle some of the simpler
questions at our meetings, but often we would agree only to direct our

staffs to work together and present to us an agreed position at a later date. After each meeting I would inform my chief of staff of any answers or decisions reached and, of course, tell him what was necessary to get the staff working. In other words, the outcome of these meetings was a basis for the combined US-RVN military effort and all decisions jointly made by the two commanders were communicated to their chiefs of staff and related staff divisions for execution or further study. In addition to the regularly scheduled weekly meetings, it was also agreed that in case of an emergency, the two commanders would meet at any time, day or night. Less important problems in the meantime could be always solved by personal phone calls.

Many different types of issues and problems were raised, discussed and often solved during these weekly meetings, including a thorough review of the overall situation and appropriate follow-up actions. An extensive and complicated problem such as desertions in the RVNAF, as one example, was apt to require lengthy discussions before appropriate action was determined. The JGS was well aware of this debilitating problem and had initiated several measures of its own to alleviate it. But it was still a matter of deep concern for the MACV commander who submitted several recommendations for more effective control of personnel. His recommendations were discussed at length, possible solutions compared between the two staffs and agreements were reached on how best to solve the problem, either by initiating new actions or improving old ones. Most problems concerning personnel management were resolved in this way. However, COMUSMACV usually abstained from making specific recommendations concerning assignments, transfers and promotions of ARVN officers except for a few he had personally observed or his advisers in the field felt strongly should be promoted or assigned to key positions in view of their demonstrated merits. These recommendations were always reviewed carefully before any action was taken in order to avoid favoritism or to prevent insidious manipulations of U.S. advisers by ARVN officers.

With regard to reporting to me about Vietnamese officers that the American advisers considered ineffective, inept, or otherwise unsuited for command, Generals' Westmoreland and Abrams operated quite differently one from the other. It was General Westmoreland's practice to inform me, in detail, of any case where the U.S. adviser had determined that his counterpart should be relieved and he reached down as far as battalion commanders with this advice. Invariably I would have my chief of staff or J-1 investigate each case and, if the situation warranted, I would see that the appropriate changes were made. In the case of General Abrams, however, when he and I travelled together on field inspections he would often comment tersly on the state of the command and the ability of the commanders as he saw it. But he never suggested either the promotion or the relief of anyone.

In its limited role, the JGS usually provided combat support for ARVN corps through reinforcements from the general reserve force under its control, or by allotting the corps concerned additional tactical air missions. All operational support actions thus taken were immediately communicated to MACV; they did not always require joint discussions beforehand. B-52 missions flown in support of ARVN corps combat operations were allocated by COMUSMACV. But once they were allocated, the Chairman of JGS and the corps commanders were informed.

Plans which required extensive study were subject to a formal exchange of letters between the two headquarters. Studies were then made independently by each staff before being submitted for presentation and discussion at a joint meeting which would result in an agreed decision and general approach by the MACV Commander and the Chairman, JGS. Prior to the direct participation of U.S. combat forces in the war, the JGS developed an annual plan for the RVNAF conduct of the war in consultation with MACV. The resulting campaign plan, compiled under the supervision of J-3, JGS was then disseminated to ARVN Corps and other commands for implementation. This was the most important basic document published by the JGS which pertained to the strategic conduct of the war and was designed to defeat Communist aggression.

Beginning in 1965, with the active participation of U.S. and Free World Military Assistance Forces, this annual planning was undertaken jointly by the JGS and MACV and resulted in a Combined Campaign Plan.

Since the military effort in South Vietnam involved the coordination and cooperation of several national forces and agencies, the Combined Campaign Plan was developed by a joint MACV-JGS staff committee composed of representatives of the general staff divisions, usually J-2, J-3, J-4/CLC, and other U.S. and RVN agencies as required. The committee functioned under the joint chairmanship of the Assistant Chief of Staff for Operations, MACV and the Deputy Chief of Staff for Operations, JGS. Preparation and coordination usually took from two to three months to complete and the final draft was then submitted to the Commander, USMACV and the Chairman, JGS for approval. Finally, a simple ceremony was held at the JGS compound during which the Commander, USMACV, commanders of other FWMAF and myself as Chairman of the JGS formally approved the plans and signed the document.

In general, all JGS staff divisions followed a similar approach for effective coordination and cooperation with their MACV counterparts although there were some slight variations to suit the individual taste of personalities. There were no formally prepared standing operating procedures and none were required for these two highly professional headquarters. On the JGS side, there was never a need nor any compulsion for issuing instructions on how to take advantage of advisory assistance or how to obtain the most from an adviser.

It was common procedure for me, as the Chairman of the JGS, to devote two days each week for visits to field units, but these visits became sporadic after the cease-fire. Often I was accompanied by the Commander, USMACV. During these field trips we made a point of solving unit problems on the spot. Initially every month and later, every quarter, both commanders visited ARVN corps headquarters where they reviewed together the progress made by ARVN units in each corps area as projected in the Combined Campaign Plan.

To further enhance close coordination and cooperation General Westmoreland, when serving as COMUSMACV, assigned a general officer as his personal representative and liaison officer to the JGS. This general officer also served as senior adviser to the Assistant Chairman, JGS for Territorial Security and Pacification. Later, this position was reduced to a liaison function and assumed by a colonel.

The JGS and MACV never shared the same military compound or any common facilities. Initially the MAAG headquarters was located in Cho Lon; then in 1957 it moved to the compound vacated by the JGS on Tran Hung Dao Boulevard in Saigon. When MACV was activated in 1962, its headquarters was first located in a crammed apartment building on Pasteur Street. In 1966, it moved to a newly-built, modern headquarters complex near Tan Son Nhut, about one mile from the JGS headquarters. Although the two headquarters were physically separated, there was never any problem involved in liaison and communications which remained very close and effective throughout the war years.

An Evaluation

The Republic of Vietnam depended on U.S. military aid to fight the war against Communist aggression. Its military force, the RVNAF, was organized and operated in accordance with U.S. military doctrine and equipped with U.S. materiel. The presence of U.S. advisers at all echelons of the RVNAF hierarchy therefore was an obvious necessity. Consequently, a definite requirement always existed for close coordination, cooperation, and effective U.S. advice at the JGS and MACV echelons.

Throughout the war years, the U.S. Military Assistance Command, Vietnam effectively assisted the JGS in developing its plans and programs and provided the support required to implement them successfully. Its advice, assistance, and material support were most conspicuous in the areas of intelligence and logistics and made possible the expansion and modernization of ARVN intelligence and logistics agencies. These two accomplishments might be regarded as the most spectacular achievements.

In addition, MACV also helped the JGS with the means and resources to exercise better control over subordinate agencies and field units, particularly in times of operational emergencies. The most striking example of this help came in early 1972 when NVA forces crossed the DMZ and attacked Quang Tri. An event of such importance unfortunately remained unknown initially to the JGS because the I Corps commander at that time failed to report it. The JGS, as a result, was unable to take appropriate action until General Creighton W. Abrams, Commander USMACV, personally informed me of the offensive. It was also he who later correctly assessed and informed me that the commander of the 3d ARVN Infantry Division was no longer able to control his units and let Quang Tri fall into the hands of the enemy. These reports from MACV enabled the JGS to muster reinforcement troops, armor forces, tactical air, and request B-52 support missions for I Corps in a timely manner to effectively stop and eventually defeat the NVA advance.

At the field and unit level, there were of course some inevitable frictions and even head-on collisions between advisers and ARVN commanders. This was human and understandable, given the tremendous pressure placed on each adviser and commander by the tactical situation. But the problem was largely local and highly individual; it was limited to only a few cases of any importance. Two cases come to mind. The first concerned the commander of an ARVN division in 1967. This commander was an experienced, strong-willed officer who appeared aloof and reluctant to accept advice from his advisers. The Americans, frustrated in their attempts to influence the division commander, reported their difficulties through their channels and some pressure was exerted to secure his relief. Nevertheless, the Leadership Committee, which was the government at the time, was satisfied with the commander's performance and he remained in command for the normal tour. A succession of dissatisfied advisers passed through his headquarters during his tenure in command. Interestingly enough, this commander's attitude changed completely in later years and he was regarded by his American counterparts as being very cooperative and easy to deal with.

The other case involved a corps commander and his counterpart, the regional assistance command commander. It was during the 1972 Communist offensive when three major NVA thrusts threatened vital regions of the country. The American general, an aggressive man with a distinguished combat record, believed, essentially, that the corps commander was not performing an active enough role in the day-to-day command of the desperate battle then being waged in one sector of his area of responsibility. The American then took it upon himself to play the role of combat coordinator in the battle area and, meanwhile, reported his dissatisfaction with the corps commander to General Abrams. On his part, General Abrams never

discussed this matter with me and I do not know if he spoke to President
Thieu about it. I doubt it, however. In any event, the corps commander
remained in command for the normal tour. No such problem ever happened
at the MACV and JGS level; cooperation between advisers and counterparts
constantly remained close and sincere. The success of this productive
relationship derived from two cardinal factors: self-respect and mutual
respect. Despite differences in culture, language, traditions, customs
and personalities, the relationship remained unaffected because of the
common realization that without cooperation and unity, the combined military effort would stand no chance of success.

The advisory task was an effort involving human relations. To
ensure success, it had to be carried out with a full understanding of
human psychology, a deep devotion to duty, a knowledge of strengths and
weaknesses and in a tactful and courteous manner. The same rule applied
to the indigenous people who received advice and assistance. To achieve
this, MACV made commendable efforts in providing advisers with background knowledge on Vietnamese culture, traditions, and customs and
manners.

Throughout the years of JGS-MACV association, many Vietnamese officers
assigned to the JGS believed that their advisers were unduly restricted
and restrained by United States security regulations. As a result, and
despite the common effort, they never divulged the contents of highly
classified U.S. documents to their counterparts even though the information
could be of mutual concern. Perhaps because of these security constraints,
MACV never discussed nor ever informed the JGS of its annual military
assistance programming for the RVN. The JGS never knew how much force
structure increase, equipment or money were being programmed for a certain
year until after Washington had approved. Even then, whatever information
the JGS could obtain from MACV was usually sketchy and did not help very
much in making detailed plans for the judicious use of money and assets.

The common practice over the years was that all JGS recommendations
and requests regarding military aid were received with due respect but
never completely satisfied. MACV seldom provided an explanation concerning the logic or reasons which resulted in this curtailment of support.

This state of things changed only after the Paris Agreement was signed and MACV no longer existed.

In 1973 and 1974, the Ministry of National Defense, and to some extent, the JGS, became responsible for submitting to the USDAO—the American agency responsible for administering the military assistance program—a plan for maintaining, equipping, and fiscal management of the RVNAF. We had to do this without the benefit of advisers, but the USDAO did, of course, tell us how much money was available and whether what we asked for in the way of equipment was permitted under the Paris Agreement.

CHAPTER III

ARVN Battalion to Corps and the Tactical Adviser

The Tactical Advisory System

As a result of the expanded US advisory effort to help the RVNAF cope with aggravating insurgency problems, and with the approval of the Vietnamese Joint General Staff, the Military Assistance Advisory Group, Vietnam began to deploy advisers to selected ARVN battalions around the middle of 1961. The mission given to these tactical advisers was to help Vietnamese battalion commanders in operational, communications and logistic support matters with the understanding that they were not to engage in actual combat.

By the end of 1961, the US tactical advisory system was reflected in every ARVN combat arm and service battalion, sometimes down to company-level as in the case of armor units since they usually operated separately. The battalion was chosen as the lowest tactical level to receive advisers since infantry battalions made up the bulk of ARVN combat forces. The infantry battalion was also the lowest level unit to have a headquarters with planning and control capabilities and it was also the largest organization to be normally employed as a tactical unit. Therefore, the advisory effort, with its emphasis on operational and logistical matters was directed at the level which, it was believed, would most benefit from it.

A battalion advisory team consisted of three US Army personnel, a captain, a first lieutenant, and a sergeant. This was a logical arrangement to ensure that there would be at least two advisers to accompany the battalion in operations at all times if one should be sick, wounded or required rest and rehabilitation. Usually, one team member was detailed, in addition to his regular duties, to perform administrative matters for the team.

The advisory command system in the field paralleled the ARVN tactical chain of command in most cases. A senior adviser was assigned for each corps tactical zone (CTZ) and controlled division senior advisers. The division senior adviser was responsible for the regimental and battalion advisers. On the territorial side, the corps senior adviser also exercised control over province and district advisers. *(Chart 6)* The field advisory system had its own communications network which, like its Vietnamese counterpart, linked the various echelons together, from MACV headquarters to corps, divisions, regiments and battalions.

As of 1965, with the introduction of US ground combat forces in South Vietnam and following the establishment of US field commands in corps tactical zones, the US advisory system was modified appropriately in order to bring about better coordination and cooperation between ARVN and US forces in the military effort. When the US III Marine Amphibious Force closed in Da Nang, its commanding general was designated senior adviser to the I Corps commander, and the I Corps advisory group was placed under his operational control. The former senior adviser, a colonel, became his deputy. Similar arrangements took place in II and III Corps Tactical Zones when US Field Forces I and II were activated. Their commanding generals were designated senior advisers to II and III Corps respectively while the resident senior advisers now became deputies. This change in title in no way affected the conduct of advisory activities. US field force commanders, as a matter of fact, were more preoccupied with US units and their command and control problems than their advisory duties, which for all practical purposes, continued to be assumed by the former senior advisers - now deputies, as if nothing had been changed. It was in fact the deputy senior advisers who were in constant and direct contact with ARVN corps commanders.

In the Mekong Delta or IV Corps Tactical Zone, the advisory relationship with IV Corps underwent no change since there was no major US combat unit deployed to the area. In April 1969, however, the IV Corps advisory group was upgraded into the Delta Military Assistance Command (DMAC) to assume control responsibility over US Army units operating separately in the Mekong Delta, including one brigade of the US 9th Infantry Division.

Chart 6 — Organization, US Army Advisory System, Corps Tactical Zone

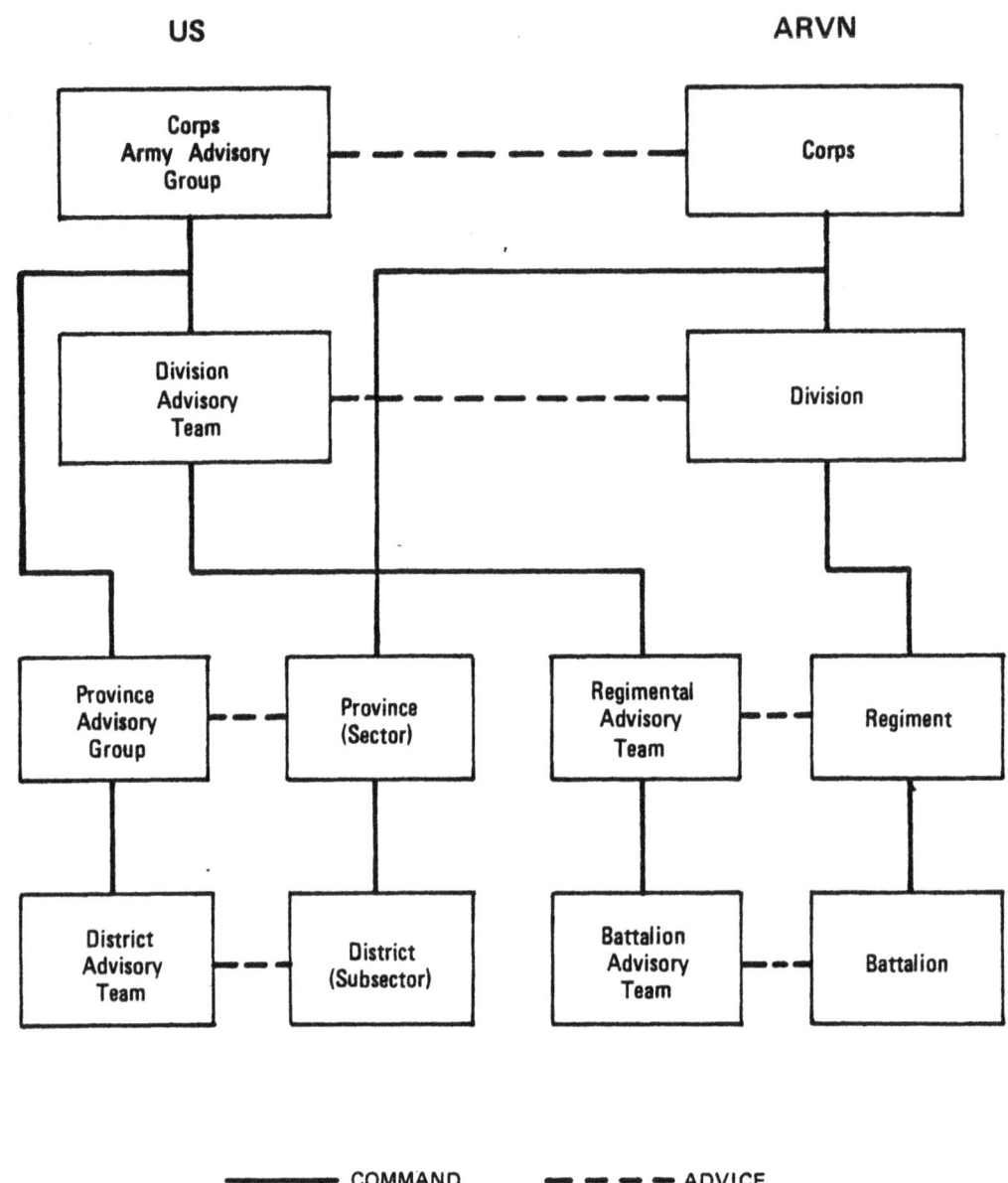

At the end of 1968, an evaluation was conducted of a new concept in organization for advisory assistance, called combat assistance teams (CAT). Its purpose was to determine the feasibility of replacing division advisory groups with smaller combat assistance teams. Immediate results of the experiment indicated that the CAT concept might help enhance leadership and initiative in ARVN units and also increase their independent capability to use US combat support assets. As a result, the commander, US MACV authorized corps senior advisers to reorganize tactical advisory elements in accordance with the CAT concept. However, subsequent evaluations of the concept failed to reveal any significant gains or a desired level of progress by ARVN units. It was apparent that a substantial permanent advisory effort was still needed, especially during major combat operations.

A re-evaluation of the CAT concept at regimental level, on the contrary, revealed the requirement for an even larger advisory staff because of two reasons. First, ARVN regimental staffs were relatively weak and second, ARVN regiments were being employed with greater frequency as major maneuver elements of divisions on large, extensive operations. Thus, the differences in missions, geographical areas of operation and available combat support assets precluded any attempt at standardizing the advisory effort, especially as it pertained to the division and special zone levels.

Finally, during the last two years of direct American involvement, 1971 and 1972, when most US ground combat units had redeployed from South Vietnam, Regional Assistance Commands (RAC) were established in the four corps areas, implying that the US combat role was terminated. *(Chart 7)* The Delta Regional Assistance Command (DRAC) was established first in MR 4 on 30 April 1971, being a redesignation of the Delta Military Assistance Command (DMAC). It was followed by the Second Regional Assistance Group (SRAG) which was activated as of May 1971 to replace Headquarters, I Field Force. SRAG was an exception in that its chief was a civilian, Mr. John Paul Vann, former deputy CORDS for DMAC, whose responsibility encompassed both military and civilian activities in MR 2. His deputy for military functions, Brigadier General Dewitt C. Armstrong III, was also commanding general of US Army forces in MR 2. After

Chart 7 — Organization, Regional Assistance Command, 1971–1972

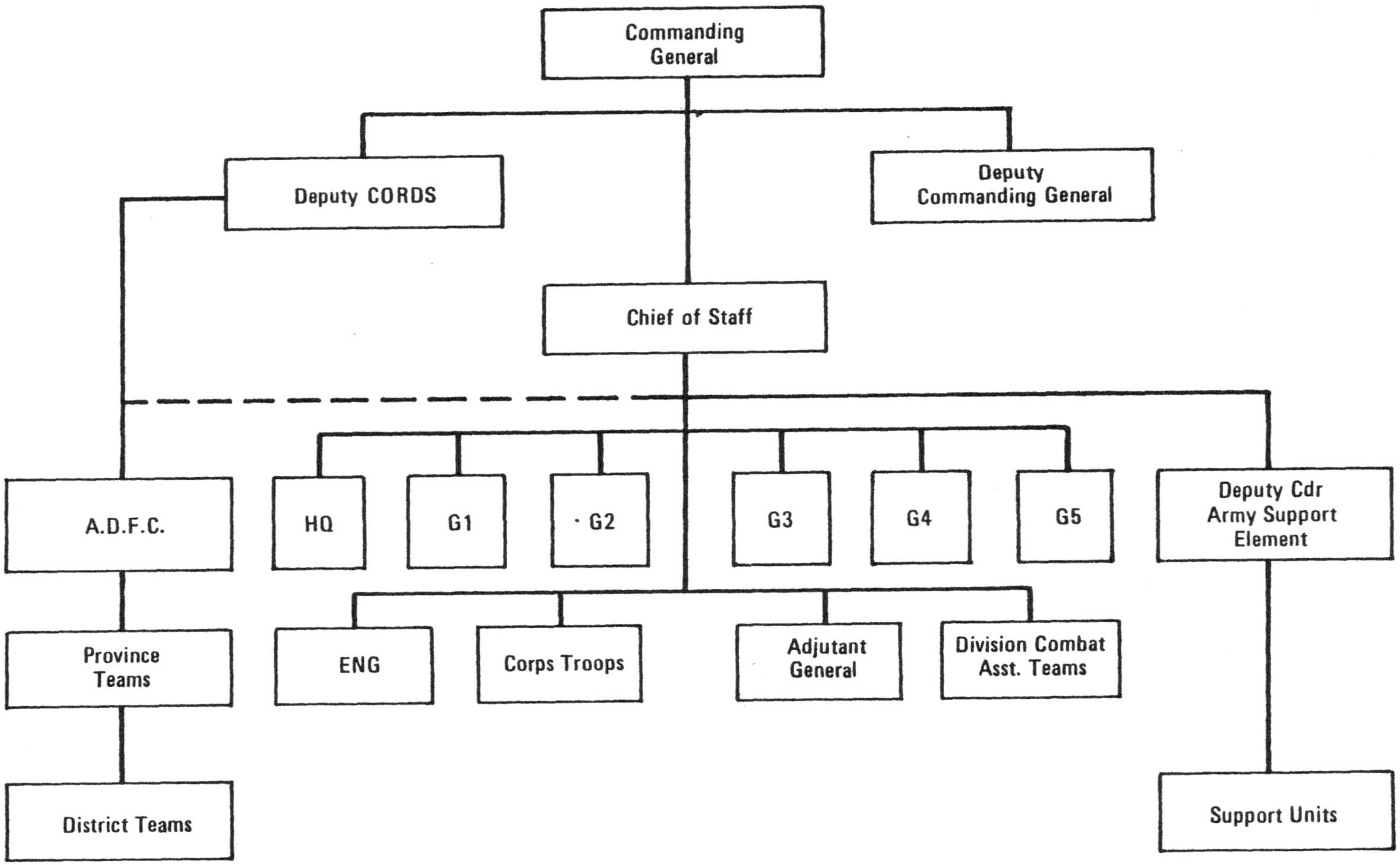

- Commanding General
  - Deputy Commanding General
  - Deputy CORDS
    - A.D.F.C.
      - Province Teams
        - District Teams
  - Chief of Staff
    - HQ
    - G1
    - G2
    - G3
    - G4
    - G5
    - ENG
    - Corps Troops
    - Adjutant General
    - Division Combat Asst. Teams
  - Deputy Cdr Army Support Element
    - Support Units

Mr. Vann's death in a helicopter accident, SRAG became a command as of 10 June 1972 like the others.[1] In MR 1, the US XXIV Corps was replaced by the First Regional Assistance Command (FRAC) on 19 March 1972. Then on 30 April 1972, II Field Force in MR-3 was the last US field command to convert to the new organization and was designated the Third Regional Assistance Command (TRAC).

Regional assistance commanders naturally served as senior advisers to ARVN corps commanders as their predecessors, the field force commanders, but maintained a more direct relationship with their counterparts. They also exercised operational control over designated US forces and were responsible for CORDS activities in support of pacification and development in their respective areas.

In addition to corps infantry and combat arms units, US advisers were also assigned to other combat forces such as the Airborne and Marine Divisions of the general reserve, Ranger and Special Forces units, and civilian irregular defense groups (CIDG). Advisory personnel assigned to Special Forces units and CIDGs, came from the US Army 5th Special Forces Group. Unlike the regular advisory system, the US Army Special Forces organization for advisory assistance was tailored to the specific missions assigned to each type of unit. Since these missions were predominantly border defense and unconventional warfare, US Special Forces advisory teams were sometimes deployed to platoon level, especially in Airborne Ranger companies and mobile strike task forces (Mike). In keeping with the Vietnamization program, the US 5th Special Forces Group stood down as of June 1970 and left South Vietnam on 1 March 1971 after converting CIDGs to ARVN Ranger units and regional force units.

With regard to territorial security and defense, the US advisory effort became particularly significant with the assignment of advisory teams to districts (subsectors) and the expansion of advisory personnel at province (sector) level in 1965. The buildup of US combat forces

---

[1] John Paul Vann chose to remain in Vietnam for many years as an adviser following a military assignment there. He was an aggressive professional who virtually assumed command of II Corps during the critical days before and during the battle of Kontum. The ARVN corps commander proved incapable of command during this crisis. His collapse was recognized by President Thieu, as well as by the JGS and Mr. Vann, and he was finally replaced.

FRAC Ending A Fruitful Relationship with I Corps,
20 March, 1973

and the emphasis placed on pacification made the role of these advisory teams especially important since it involved providing assistance to province and district chiefs in all matters related to the planning and execution of the pacification program, and the employment of territorial forces in support of the military plan.

The advisory effort in the provinces and districts was implemented in various ways, depending on requirements, the nature of the type of effort to be carried out and the specific areas of interest. In certain localities, the primary responsibility might focus on establishing or restoring local security; in others, the major task might be directed at improving the combat effectiveness and employment of RF and PF units. Still, in certain others, the principal emphasis might be placed on improving the political, social and economic institutions required by the central government. These differences in local situations naturally required different types of advisory personnel and a flexibility in organization which could readily meet the specific local requirements. In general, the US advisory effort in the field, be it in tactical or territorial organizations, was so deployed that it was reflected in almost every position or level of tactical endeavor.

The Tactical Adviser's Responsibilities

US Army advisers did not command, nor did they exercise operational control or responsibility for any part of the Army of the Republic of Vietnam (ARVN). Their mission and functions were to provide professional military advice and assistance in those specific areas of endeavor assigned by the Military Assistance Command, Vietnam, namely to advise and assist the counterpart ARVN commanders and their staffs in personnel management, training, combat operations, intelligence, security, logistics and psychological/civil affairs operations.

In each corps/military region, the US senior adviser supervised the activities of an Army Advisory Group (AAG) assigned to that particular corps/military region headquarters and exercised command of subordinate advisory teams (division, province). He was responsible for:

An Odd-Looking But Harmonious Couple:
The ARVN Tactical Commander and His Adviser

ARVN Rangers Going Out on a Patrol with U.S. Adviser
(Ba To, Quang Ngai, December 1970)

CIDG Troopers and U.S. Special Forces Adviser Back From Patrol (Ban Me Thuot, March 1962)

1. Providing liaison between the ARVN corps commander and United States and free world military assistance forces.

2. Establishing and operating US advisory tactical communications networks and providing assistance for the operation of ARVN networks.

3. Determining requirements for and coordinating US tactical air, airlift support, helicopter and artillery support.

4. Coordinating with US and FWMA forces on joint plans, operations, and training.

5. Establishing, maintaining, operating, and providing advisory functions for a combined corps tactical operations center/direct air support center (TOC/DASC) in conjunction with RVNAF elements.

6. Accompanying the ARVN corps commander and his staff, as appropriate, on field inspection trips and operations as required.[2]

Despite organizational changes of the advisory effort at the tactical levels, which were dictated by the local situation or progress made by ARVN units in terms of combat effectiveness, the adviser's role remained essentially unchanged. He continued to be an adviser, a coordinator of support for the benefit of ARVN units, and a liaison officer with US combat forces.

Restrained as it was by limitations in personnel, the US advisory effort was largely instrumental in the gradual improvement of ARVN units. Limitations in personnel did not discourage US advisers from doing all they could and striving constantly to make the units they sponsored better every day. In addition to providing the various assets that they could muster for the support of ARVN operational requirements, the adviser's professional knowledge and skills in planning, operations, tactics and technology contributed substantially to the performance of units in several instances. Their ARVN counterparts learned a great deal from them. In fact, the presence of advisers acted not only as a catalyst through which changes and improvements were attained, but also provided the incentive that stimulated and spurred actions on both the unit and its commander. The results obtained throughout the years

---

[2] USMACV Command History, p 69.

of US involvement showed that leadership and the management of units underwent a definite improvement and that combat effectiveness increased remarkably.

On the other hand, the adviser's overriding influence sometimes tended to stifle the ARVN commander's own initiative and diminish his authority and prestige. Usually the adviser confined himself to his advisory role; his relationship with the counterpart was essentially one built on and limited to mutual trust and respect. There were compelling instances, however, that required the adviser to trespass the line drawn and by so doing, he practically acted as a commander -- on the latter's behalf, naturally. This was what actually happened in a few ARVN units whose weak commanders wavered and were unable to make decisions under battlefield pressure. The prestige and power of the tactical adviser in such circumstances tended, in the long run, to tarnish the role of the ARVN commander in the eyes of his troops. Unit activities, for example, tended to follow exactly what the advisers had recommended; in other instances, the adviser was the one who solved the indecisive battle by bringing US tactical air and fire power to bear on the enemy; it was he who won the battle for the unit. Gradually, the ARVN commander's passivity made him excessively reliant and sometimes totally dependent on his adviser. The end result was that the commander's initiative, sense of responsibility and personal authority became seriously affected and in the long run, the adviser's presence had the undesirable effect of reducing his counterpart's chances for asserting and developing his command and leadership abilities.

The Adviser's Role in Operational Planning and Combat Intelligence

Poor planning was one of the most glaring deficiencies of ARVN units. This deficiency was most serious at regimental and battalion levels. There was not enough formal training in the ARVN to develop planning skills and the lack of capable personnel at these levels accounted for the absence of improvement in staff work. Whatever the reasons, the

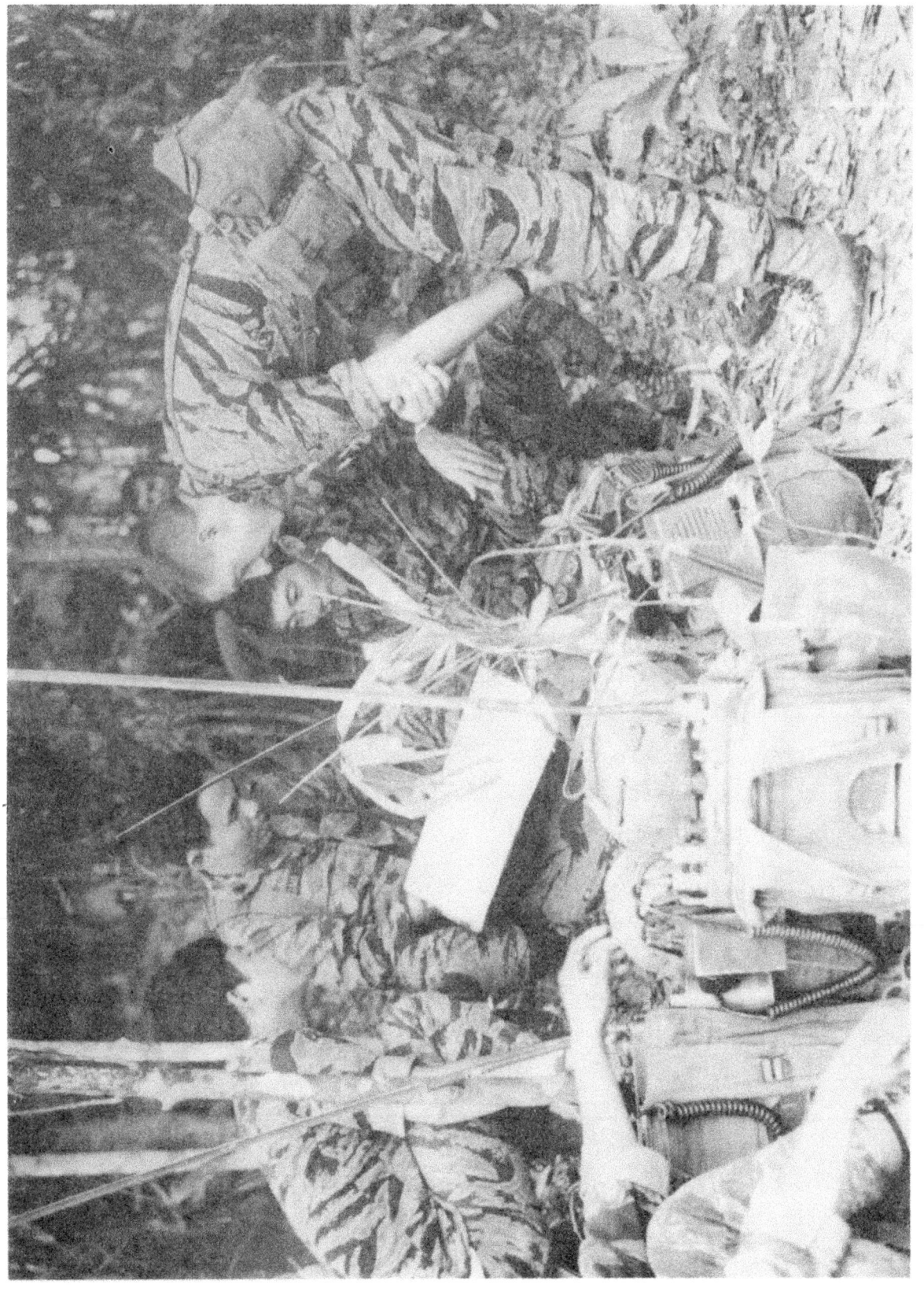

ARVN 8th Marine Bn Staff Discussing Operational Plan With U.S. Adviser (Quang Tri, Sept 1970)

ARVN Battalion Commander (9th Infantry Division) Reviewing Position With His Adviser During Combat Operation (Kien Phong, Dec 1970)

responsibility for this deficiency fell squarely on the unit commander, and if he were not demanding or aggressive, his staff would be less disposed to do acceptable staff work. Most ARVN tactical commanders at these echelons fought their battles without formal, detailed plans, but by personal improvisation. The commander was all and everything in the unit; his staff's contributions to the performance of the unit were minimal. It was the commander who decided everything, told them what to do, where and when to go, and how to conduct the operation from the beginning to the end. When he was absent, there was little his staff could do without his specific orders. Unfortunately, more often than not, if the commander was not there, his staff simply abstained from taking actions even if they knew what to do.

Because of these critical shortcomings, US advisers at nearly every level were compelled to participate in or even initiate planning for operations. Their contributions became even more important during the active participation of US forces, when almost all combat support assets were provided and controlled by US advisers. In these circumstances, there was little the ARVN unit commander could do except make decisions based on his adviser's recommendations, regardless of his own initiative. But regardless of how hard US advisers would like to push, they usually had to act in a most tactful manner in order to keep the relationship intact and maintain harmony.

There were instances in which US advisers presented their counterparts with a drafted plan with the hope that this plan would be translated into Vietnamese and implemented. Such an approach to the problem was tantamount to actually asking the ARVN commanders to take action and it usually worked. ARVN commanders felt bound, if not by the ready-made plan, at least by special consideration for their advisers.

There were also instances in which an adviser would just briefly make some remark or suggest an idea as to the course of action that the ARVN commander could take. The adviser thus tactfully encouraged his counterpart to elaborate on a suggested idea and develop his own plan based on it. In this way, the plan appeared to be a product that the ARVN commander had originated on his own initiative, something that bore his

personal mark rather than the adviser's. This approach indeed helped the
ARVN commander and his staff initiate their own effort and work toward
accomplishing it. But it was not always easy for the US adviser to achieve
this because he had to abstain from claiming any credit for the ideas that
he had suggested.

In other instances, US advisers simply put their assessment of the
tactical situation in writing, but refrained from any specific recommend-
ation with the deliberate purpose of leaving the matter up to their counterparts to see for themselves and develop their own planning and courses
of action. This method seemed to work best when an ARVN commander was
assisted by an able staff and when the adviser was reasonably certain that,
together, they could work out an adequate plan and carry it out to completion without assistance.

Generally speaking, US advisers contributed a great deal to the
operational planning conducted by ARVN units. By and large, they proved
remarkably adept and knowledgeable in this area of endeavor and their
advice was particularly effective when they had a thorough understanding
and appreciation of the situation.

During combined operations conducted by ARVN and US forces, US advisers
served as the point of contact for cooperation and coordination between
operational forces. They were also the liaison officers who put US
forces in touch with local governments in area security activities.
Usually, advisers coordinated with US unit staffs and provided essential
elements of information concerning the ARVN side to assist with the operational planning for US units. Sometimes they also provided specific
recommendations as to how the US unit could make the best contribution to
the combined operation.

The relationship between US advisers and US units depended partly
on the nature of the effort to be achieved, and partly on the individual
prestige enjoyed by each adviser. With regard to tactical advisers, especially at regimental and battalion levels, this relationship was not
always a happy one. For one thing, at the same unit level, the adviser
was usually outranked by the US commander. For another, some advisers
had not commanded troops in actual combat, even a unit at a lower level.

As a result, they became self-conscious of their standing and, therefore, were somewhat hampered in their coordination effort. US unit commanders sometimes tended to look down upon the US advisers whom they did not consider as co-equals. This was similar in some respect to the haughty attitude shown, for example, by an ARVN battalion commander toward a district chief, an attitude wholly unjustified and misleading for the simple reason that a district chief's responsibilities were much more complex and heavier by comparison. The district chief as well as the district adviser were required to have a solid professional capability in several respects and a tenacious determination to accomplish their difficult mission. By contrast, much of the tactical unit commander's advantage seemed to derive from a reliance on combat assets and ready-made standing operating procedures. It was really unfortunate that despite their heavy responsibilities, US advisers seemed to enjoy less prestige and less opportunities for personal advancement than US unit commanders. This lack of respect toward US advisers, added to certain prejudices against ARVN units in general on the part of some US unit commanders, often hindered effective coordination and cooperation efforts between ARVN and US forces.

With regard to coordination and cooperation with Free World Military Assistance units, especially with South Korean forces whose combat strength was the most sizeable after US forces, US advisers at ARVN divisions and down the tactical hierarchy usually played only a secondary role. Required planning, cooperation and coordination for combined operations in which forces of several nationalities participated were almost always worked out in complete detail at the corps level, except for routine activities concerning area security. In the II Corps area where two South Korean divisions were deployed, for example, plans for operational coordination were accomplished during monthly meetings attended by the field commanders of all three forces, the US I Field Force, II Corps and ROK forces in the II Corps area. In addition, a combined US-ARVN-ROK staff, made up of G-2 and G-3 representatives, was formed to discuss combined operational plans and report the results to their respective commanders for approval. This combined staff procedure prevented possible embarrassment to ARVN and ROK commanders. It was also determined throughout the war to be the best method of achieving effective cooperation.

Even though the complex nature of the war and terrain which favored the enemy tended to complicate friendly intelligence activities, the assistance provided by US advisers still brought about significant improvements and achievements in combat intelligence. This was possible because cooperation and coordination in intelligence activities were truly a combined effort based on mutual support and common objective.

At the tactical level, both the US and RVNAF combat intelligence systems had strengths and weaknesses. The US advisers enjoyed the backing of a system whose advantages were based on superior technology, abundant and sophisticated assets, a modern and extensive organization, rapid communications and well qualified experts. By contrast, the RVNAF system, while not as endowed as the US system, enjoyed a certain advantage in terms of intimate knowledge about the enemy, his psychology, his methods, and his culture and language. Thus, the two systems eventually complemented and reinforced each other to perfection, like a dovetailed joint.

At the corps level, G-2 advisers usually provided their counterparts with intelligence data collected through technical sources, aerial photography and reconnaissance and exploitation by US combat units. In return, the ARVN G-2 supplied his adviser with data collected through ARVN sources, primarily from prisoners of war and returnees, exploitation of documents and intelligence reports provided by ARVN agents. A similar procedure of coordination and exchange of intelligence data was also instituted at division and lower levels.

It was obvious that ARVN units relied heavily on US-supplied intelligence data in view of its reliability, validity and timeliness. Since their trust in these special reports was nearly absolute, the prestige of US advisers was particularly enhanced, not only because of their professional capability or knowledge of the enemy situation but because they were the providers of accurate information. The high validity that Vietnamese commanders usually attributed to US technical sources led to their inference that US advisers at higher levels should be completely knowledgeable about the enemy's policies and plans. Some ARVN tactical commanders believed, for example, that MACV and US Field Forces knew well in advance the enemy's plan for the 1968 Tet offensive but kept this information to themselves for political reasons and only divulged it to some degree to a few ARVN confidants.

In addition, with its methodical efficiency and abundant resources, the US intelligence advisory system helped its counterpart improve its own coordination and exchange of information in order to make intelligence more timely for the users. It also assisted its counterpart by providing guidance on certain scientific analysis techniques such as the pattern analysis method which was widely acclaimed by ARVN units.

The language barrier was probably the most obvious limiting factor affecting the US intelligence advisory effort. Language proficiency was not only required for daily contacts and coordination between advisers and counterparts but was also deemed indispensable for the accurate understanding and dissemination of intelligence data and to avoid misunderstanding or confusion when precise terminology, especially as used by the enemy, was concerned. To offset the language shortcoming, US advisers used indigenous interpreters who, at the tactical levels, were helpful with general ideas, but when it came time to interpret accurately Communist terminology, they were generally not proficient enough for lack of a sufficient intelligence background. The fact was, although they are Vietnamese, Communists, especially North Vietnamese Communists, use a vocabulary which includes several terms whose connotations entirely escape the South Vietnamese layman's ability to comprehend, much less render it in another language.

U.S. Support and the Problem of Leverage

The ARVN logistics system was well established at every level in the field but it was primarily an area-type organization more oriented toward providing support for garrison activities rather than for mobile operations. Major logistic requirements for these activities usually consisted of rice and common types of ammunition which, because of the shortage in transportation facilities and frequent road interdictions by the enemy, were stocked in field depots at a high level of supply. When ARVN units went on operations — generally for short periods of time — their troops usually carried with them their individual allocation of rice and basic load of ammunition. This practice of self-support became a matter of routine in the long run and as a result, very few tactical commanders required their logistical staffs to take part in operational planning. Even if they did, there was not much their supply officer's could contribute except to be alert for contingencies.

As mobile operations were increased in frequency and size during the years following Vietnamization and with the increased participation of all combat arms, logistical support was hampered by severe limitations, especially when the area of operation was far removed from field depots and lines of communication. In such operations, almost all supplies and support assets had to be moved by helicopters and this was the primary reason why ARVN units had to depend on US advisers and through them, on the support provided by US forces. This dependence centered chiefly on airlift assets and certain critical operational supplies such as ammunition, fuels, barrier materials for the construction of fire support bases and other items that the ARVN logistics system either did not carry or could not provide in time to meet requirements.

US advisers were usually solicitous and zealous concerning the logistic support for their units. Naturally, no adviser could tolerate watching his unit fail to accomplish a mission merely because of a lack of supplies or equipment. That was why ARVN units could always depend on US advisers for whatever supplies they needed in any combat situation. And if an ARVN commander for some reason requested more than was required for his combat needs or even for non-combat needs, his adviser usually complied to the extent he felt reasonable, often out of compassion. Thus, to ensure adequate support for combat operations, US advisers usually had to accomplish all coordination activities from planning to actually delivering the support assets or supplies, especially in large-scale operations requiring a sizeable amount of logistical support.

The US advisory effort in the field, therefore, brought about much relief and confidence for ARVN combat units. ARVN commanders were most

U.S. Advisers Briefing ARVN Rangers Prior to Long Range Reconnaissance Mission (Near Cambodian Border, Nov 1970)

gratified by the adequate and timely logistic support that US advisers always provided for their needs. But in a few instances, the solicitude and largesse of US advisers seemed to backfire because certain ARVN units gradually developed a propensity for wasteful use of supplies and over-reliance on the US system. This did not go unnoticed, however, for US advisers subsequently limited themselves to monitoring and following up on ARVN logistic support actions and procedures with the implied goal of requiring ARVN units to learn how to take care of themselves logistically and to develop their own system. No longer would US advisers and units readily and willingly meet every ARVN requirement as they had before except in those emergency cases when the ARVN system was unable to respond.

Despite the gradual and remarkable improvement in the ARVN logistic system and the fact that all logistic requirements were to be handled by it, ARVN units still desired to have an advisory system as backup. This was not because they wanted to remain perpetually dependent but primarily due to the fact that they did not entirely trust their own system which was too inflexible and not responsive enough to meet the fast changing tactical requirements effectively.

US advisers did not command. Nevertheless, they were in a position to influence their counterparts and make them accept their advice and recommendations. There were several ways a US adviser could exert his leverage. As a provider, he might choose to withold the assets required by the ARVN unit to accomplish its mission pending satisfactory compliance with what the adviser thought was desirable. This always seemed to work — for whatever immediate purpose — since the adviser controlled most of the support assets. Additionally, the US adviser, in view of his broad professional knowledge, was apt to win over his counterpart by force of reason or logic.

As a result, during the years of intensive combat, from 1966 through 1968 when US advisers provided substantial support, their influence was undeniably strong especially during combat operations. But when the reduction of US support assets was initiated in early 1969 as a part of the Vietnamization program, whatever leverage US advisers could still use to influence their counterparts became essentially a matter of personal relationship and individuality. Some ARVN commanders genuinely liked Americans and continued to cooperate in a commendable spirit of harmonious teamwork. They felt they still needed the assistance of US advisers whose professionalism and experience was respected and held in high esteem. Others, however, guessing a reverse in wind direction, deliberately left US advisers out of the picture and failed to consult them or even inform them of unit activities. Fully aware of this changing attitude, some advisers became cautious and reluctant to give advice and abstained altogether from critical comments. Obviously, they knew that their counterparts, like most ARVN commanders, were extremely sensitive to criticism and if there was a need to contribute to the accomplishment of certain tasks, these advisers would only offer, tactfully and suavely, constructive remarks lest the rapport and mutual trust be negated.

Experience showed that the adviser who skillfully utilized his leverage with support assets in combination with his personal persuasive logic and reasoning in order to influence his counterpart usually succeeded in improving his working relationship and his counterpart's effectiveness. It was also true that leverage, if based only on the provision of support assets, simply resulted in temporary gains by the adviser who additionally never learned much from a true working relationship. In this case, the adviser ceased to be an adviser and his true role was not being accomplished. On the other hand, the tendency to "let the adviser do it all," in the few cases where it might have existed, seemed to stem from a negative attitude of ARVN commanders reacting to excessive and rough leverage. In general, when an adviser began his second tour of duty, he was an artful master of his job and knew how to make things work effectively.

Observations on Tours of Duty and Relationships

With the exception of key positions at the command level, the normal tour of duty for ARVN advisers as well as for US combat troops in South Vietnam was one year. But not all US tactical advisers in the field stayed on the same job for the entire year. Advisers in ARVN battalions, for example, were rotated every six months if the combat situation permitted. This limited tour policy seemed to benefit the American servicemen in many respects. Its impact on the effectiveness of the advisory effort, however, is a matter worth discussion.

US advisers assigned to ARVN tactical units, especially battalions and regiments, usually worked hand in hand with their counterparts at all times. They lived and fought in an isolated environment which hardly afforded them any material or physical comfort. The constant mental pressure and physical exertion required were not conducive to their maintaining a high degree of efficiency for sustained periods of time. Had they been required to serve for a long or indefinite period of time, certainly their efficiency would have diminished. But the tour was limited. They all knew exactly when they could go home and this was not only an incentive that spurred them to devote all their time and energy to their job but also a tremendous psychological boost for their families.

The good performance of a tactical adviser, however, seemed to depend on a certain continuity and stability of effort devoted to a unit. This would require him to stay at least 18 months with a unit, but two years would have been better. The one-year tour, six-month rotation policy, despite its advantages, did not maintain enough continuity to make the advisory effort as effective as desired. For an adviser's activities were not simply confined to the unit to which he was assigned; they also encompassed the social environment in which the unit operated and to which he was bound. It took an adviser several months to familiarize himself with that environment and by the time he became really productive, it was already time to pack and leave.

When an adviser left a unit, he carried with him a wealth of knowledge which was still required by his teammates. His experience and adeptness were personal and could not fully be transferred to his replacement. The void created by the departure of an adviser was most acutely felt at the small-unit level where advisers were few but problems and voids in knowledge of the local situation were many. Standing operating procedures were helpful to some extent and enabled the new adviser to get

a quick feel of his job but they could not substitute for the experience
and knowledge required to identify and solve the many complex problems.
This was where continuity was needed. This also explained why district
advisers, whose tour of duty was 18 months, were more effective in their
efforts to help local units and the local population. The difference
was obvious; they had more experience and knew more about the local
environment.

Time was also required for the adviser to demonstrate his abilities,
obtain confidence and to establish his influence within a unit. He needed
opportunities to prove himself and to show the ARVN troops what he could
do for them. Only then would his advice be welcomed and his recommendations
heartily accepted. Otherwise he would remain just an adviser whose suggestions were courteously received but not always heeded. In several
instances, a long cooperation and association usually brought about
better understanding, mutual trust and true harmony between the adviser
and his counterpart. And when a relationship evolved from mutual trust
and respect, there seemed to be nothing the adviser and his counterpart
could not work out between themselves for the benefit of the unit.
Experience showed that wherever there was a good working relationship
between the ARVN commander and his adviser, the unit always operated in
a relaxed atmosphere of efficiency and it was easier to bring it to the
desired degree of effectiveness.

An adviser, no matter how efficient he was in his role, could not
substitute for the ARVN commander. But the influence he exercised had
a great impact on the unit's effectiveness. For this effectiveness to
continue undisturbed, a certain stability of command and leadership as
well as advisory effort was required. To the extent that it was possible,
the adviser, just like the ARVN commander, should stay on with the same
unit as long as it was deemed necessary.

Cooperation between US advisers and their counterparts in ARVN
tactical units was usually close except in a very few cases. This relationship was founded on mutual trust and respect. In almost all units, the
adviser acted as an assistant to the ARVN commander. He never transgressed
his advisory role and certainly never thought of taking over command

authority except in a few cases when the situation required. But this happened only in small units.

Command is a difficult art. Besides professional competence, a commander must also possess certain qualities to exercise the art of command effectively. It is the same with an adviser. The role of the US adviser, in view of its relative complexity, was not an easy one.

Certainly there were several dissimilarities between the US adviser and the ARVN commander. Some of these could be found in their approach to leadership, their culture and way of life. Other differences were either technical or procedural; these could easily be eliminated. There were, however, certain differences resulting from human nature that were impossible to reconcile within a short time. Naturally, the keys to success in every human partnership lies in the character and attitudes of the men themselves. Personality, therefore, played an important role in the adviser-counterpart relationship. It was obvious that unless both partners wanted to get involved and unless they subordinated their personal desires for the good of the unit, there was no chance for them to foster a true relationship. But once a good relationship had been established, the enthusiasm with which each strived to work together toward a common goal was apt to induce better cooperation and coordination between their staffs and subordinates. Over the years, this became the rule rather than the exception.

In several instances, US advisers grew impatient with the seemingly sluggish approach to work displayed by the Vietnamese in general. This was understandable. Having a relatively short tour of duty, US advisers tended to try to accomplish as much as they possibly could within that time. An adviser was apt to deluge his counterpart with ideas, plans and programs as fast as he could think of them. To his counterpart, however, it was not always easy to cope with all of them at the same time, because there were certain things the adviser would fail to recognize as difficult or impossible unless he was a Vietnamese commander.

As a result, to enable his counterpart to perform effectively, the adviser would have to assign priorities, to sort out and organize suggestions and find an appropriate time for consultations. If the adviser kept harassing a counterpart with uninterrupted suggestions, regardless of substance, he was apt to discover that he could accomplish very little and that his effectiveness as an adviser was greatly reduced. On the other hand, if he deluded his counterpart with excessive flattery or just left him alone and was too easy going, his advice was apt to be taken lightly even though it was founded upon experience and professional competence.

In general, achievement depended a great deal on the adviser-counterpart relationship. Whether this relationship worked depended again on several things. However, the keys to success were the adviser's personal attitude and his genuine desire to help his counterpart. Mutual respect and understanding were always required. For without mutual respect, nothing could be achieved and no advisory technique could help.

An Evaluation

By early 1973, when the last US advisory teams departed South Vietnam, most ARVN commanders had worked closely with several different advisers. On an average, each tactical commander had experienced some relationship with from 20 to 30 different advisers over the war years.

During the initial period of the war, the United States advisory role was confined to delivering equipment and training ARVN units. As the war escalated in tempo and intensity, advisers became increasingly involved in tactical training and advising ARVN unit commanders on how to conduct combat operations. In this new tactical role, the efforts of advisers initially met with some inertia on the part of some ARVN commanders. These commanders had long combat records resulting from the years they fought alongside French forces. The habits they had developed under French influence were hard to change or modify overnight. They found American training methods too constraining, too conventional and ill-suited to the war conditions in Vietnam. Whereas the French emphasized commando tactics, characterized by rapid movement and hasty raids with little or no combat support, the American way was methodical, careful and thorough, characterized by detailed planning and preparation. In a word, it was by the "book." Intermediate objectives were chosen, fire-plans prepared, and all moves were made step-by-step. When the objective was seized, a careful search was always made for documents; all scraps of paper were recovered and analyzed. To the combat-experienced Vietnamese, much of the American way of doing things was too slow and too "academic." They were complacent with their war records, thinking that they were adequately experienced or at least knew how to fight this type of war. American tactical training, they felt, was something they did not require at that time.[3]

In some respects, the aversion to accepting US advice on tactical matters was not entirely attributable to pride or self-consciousness. In fact, during the early 1960's, most US Army company-grade officers assigned to field advisory duties in South Vietnam had no real combat experience, except for the few career officers who had fought in Korea a decade earlier. In the eyes of experienced ARVN regimental and battalion commanders, the standing and value of these young advisers were not very high. Their role, therefore, was particularly difficult and the range of their effectiveness greatly limited. During this period, US advisers mostly concerned themselves with the utilization of equipment, weapons and equipment maintenance, and assisting ARVN units in technical or logistical matters, but rarely in combat or tactical matters.

The role of US tactical advisers, however, underwent a radical change during the mid-1960's when US combat support assets, especially airlift, helilift and tactical air were introduced into South Vietnam in increasing quantities each year. For the first time in many years, ARVN unit commanders felt vulnerable because of their reliance on US advisers who provided and controlled these combat support assets. The advisory role definitely became more significant and its effectiveness increased visibly when heliborne operations and US tactical air support made their appearance. The outlook and intensity of the war seemed to add more purposefulness and a closer rapprochement to the relationship between advisers and their counterparts.

---

[3] This subject is also discussed in the monograph of this series, <u>RVNAF and U.S. Operational Cooperation and Coordination</u>, Chapter 7.

If the impact of the advisory presence was to be evaluated in terms of the specific contributions it brought to the ARVN war effort, then it can be said that every level of ARVN organization for combat needed advisers for some reason, and the usefulness of advisers varied from level to level. At the battalion level, the role of advisers was particularly important as providers and coordinators of combat support; it was less prominent in intelligence since battalion advisers were not as well versed in the terrain or the enemy situation as the ARVN commanders. The critical importance of combat support planning and coordination, and the weakness of ARVN commanders in these skills, were painfully demonstrated in the ARVN operations toward Tchepone, in Laos, in 1971. US advisers did not accompany their battalions and regiments in this campaign and the optimum employment of US firepower and helilift could not be achieved without them. As we moved up the tactical hierarchy, the need for advisers was more acutely felt in two specific areas: planning and leadership. The basic weaknesses of ARVN units at regimental and sometimes at division level in those areas seriously affected the performance of subordinate units. However, the strength of US advisers whose adeptness in planning and leadership was particularly prominent played a major part in improving these problem areas.

The ARVN trooper by nature was a good soldier, enduring, brave, and resilient in combat. Small unit cadres were also audacious, enthusiastic and easily trained. The problem was that these soldiers and cadres did not always receive the benefits of good leadership. When the performance of a certain unit was poor, chances were the commander had failed to provide proper guidance and take corrective actions. The deficiency was in no way attributable to the men themselves who, like Panurge's herd of sheep, only followed the leader regardless of where he might go. The leverage of US advisers, meanwhile, seemed to be more effective at the lower levels than at the higher echelons where it would have provided better results. At higher levels, the advisory effort tended more toward fostering good rapport than applying leverage to get results. Consequently, it was not altogether responsive to the requirement for assisting ARVN to overcome its shortcomings. These major shortcomings were in all phases of staff planning, in the operation of communications systems for effective command and control, and in realistic personnel policies that would permit the timely elimination of incompetent commanders. It is unfortunate that US advisers at the top echelons of the structure did not push hard enough for improvements in these fields. The advisory effort should have endeavored first to bring about an effective command, control and leadership system for the ARVN before trying to improve the combat effectiveness of small units. If this priority had been established, the entire advisory effort would have been more beneficial.

During the last two years of US advisory presence, 1971-1972, the regional assistance commands seemed to be more suited and more responsive to ARVN tactical requirements. In each corps area, the regional assistance command commander and his staff provided direct assistance and support to the ARVN corps, especially in planning and directing its combat efforts. It was the new direction and emphasis of the advisory effort at this level that were responsible for the marked improvement of ARVN performance in the field despite the fact that US advisers and combat support assets at lower levels were being greatly reduced. The performance of ARVN units during the enemy's 1972 Easter offensive was eloquent testimony to the effectiveness of the regional assistance command concept. It was this emphasis on cooperation and support provided by regional assistance commands to each ARVN corps that helped the RVNAF hold out and avoid defeat and collapse.

In retrospect, our war experience indicates that at the corps level there should have been a strong advisory system at the beginning to work directly with the corps commanders and help them improve their staffs. Each ARVN corps would have been responsible to produce results with the assistance of a limited field advisory system, consisting of the ablest personnel and reaching down to only a few key positions at lower levels. It could have been augmented by a number of mobile training or assistance teams under the direct control of the regional assistance command commander to be used when required to meet ARVN tactical and training needs as they surfaced in each individual unit.

CHAPTER IV

The Intelligence Adviser

A Pioneering Effort

The development of the RVNAF as a modern, westernized armed force began during the First Republic, 1955-1963. During the early years of this period, the intelligence branch, like other arms and services, had to be almost entirely self-sufficient in developing organizational and operational improvements, although its own means and resources were meager and outdated.

The first major problem that the ARVN intelligence branch had to solve was the shortage of trained personnel. There was a need for cadres at every echelon and in every branch of the ARVN and the competition for this limited resource meant that only a nucleus of cadre could be spared for the intelligence branch. The selection of personnel for assignment to intelligence positions was based not so much on actual professional competence or experience as on expectations, sometimes based on hardly more than an estimate of the individual's development potential.

To help the ARVN intelligence branch overcome this problem, the US Army Training Relations and Instruction Mission (TRIM) set about in early 1955 to organize an accelerated two-month intelligence course for ARVN officers. This course was conducted in the Philippines and was the first intelligence assistance provided by the US Army. Most graduates of this course were assigned as instructors to the ARVN Intelligence School in Cay Mai in the Cholon district of Saigon, which conducted its first course for ARVN intelligence officers in November 1955. The only training materials available at that time for the instructors and their students were transcriptions of the notes the ARVN instructors

had taken during their two-month training. The urgent need for more
and better instructional materials led to the assignment of the first
US Army intelligence adviser in South Vietnam; the Cay Mai Intelligence
School was the first ARVN organization to welcome him.

The first American adviser was regarded with considerable awe by
the ARVN officers at the Cay Mai School. Not only was this "first" a
novel event, but the word "adviser" itself created some impressions in
Vietnamese minds that probably would have greatly surprised the American
involved. In Vietnamese minds, "adviser" was associated with the position of "conseiller" which implies some supervisory powers such as enjoyed by former Emperor Bao Dai when he served as counselor for the
first Viet Minh government in 1945. Some derogatory connotations were
also visualized, for it was remembered that in the early 50's, Red Chinese advisers to the Viet Minh were acclaimed by the Communists as their
"prodigious adviser comrades." Thus the position of an adviser, as far
as intelligence officers of the ARVN were concerned, invariably evoked
an aura of authority and of scholarly knowledge, especially since it was
compared with Mr. Ngo Dinh Nhu, the then all-powerful political counselor
to his brother, President Diem.

At the Cay Mai Intelligence School, the man most preplexed by the
event was the commandant himself. He had been summarily informed by the
Training Bureau, General Staff, that a US Army advisier would be assigned
to his school to provide assistance in training. Nothing more was
learned about his mission, functions, authority, or the scope of his
activities. These were the things that the commandant wanted to know
in detail but could not obtain from the General Staff. The first action
he took was to order the establishment of a separate office for the
adviser in the school headquarters compound and he issued positive instructions to all school personnel that only the two assistant-commandants
were permitted to deal with the adviser, and then only in his absence.[1]

---

[1] I was one of his two assistant-commandants.

Despite the commandant's initial misgivings, the adviser's presence was an instant success since through his efforts the school immediately obtained US Army intelligence training texts which it needed so desperately. In general, the entire school staff was favorably impressed by the adviser's activities and the way he conducted himself. His suggestions helped solve the problem of training aids and he tactfully kept an eye on the instruction being given in various classrooms, the performance of ARVN instructors, and how the students reacted and progressed. He make a point of jotting down his observations and comments and drafted them into memoranda for the personal attention of the school commandant. He also played an active role in helping the commandant run the administrative aspects of the school by offering suggestions on the maintenance of vehicles, weapons and other equipment. He accompanied the commandant on the weekly inspections, visiting barracks and student sleeping quarters and even participating in social and ceremonial functions held by the school.

The school commandant was elated. His adviser was truly an adviser; the way he performed his duties left no doubt about his sincere desire to help, to assist. He did not exercise any authority nor did he encroach on the commandant's command duties. The school staff members were greatly gratified by the free English lessons that he conducted and they felt no complications when performing their daily work in his presence. On their part, the students remained intensely curious about the American adviser and tried to learn as much as they could about his role and his relationship with, and attitude toward the school. They were enlightened and pleased with their findings which assisted them several years later when they welcomed US advisers into their own units.

Increasing Commitment

In September 1960, for the first time since the Geneva Accords, the Communists in South Vietnam increased activity in Kontum and openly attacked the provincial capital of Phuoc Binh, 100 miles north of Saigon. These enemy actions took everybody by surprise. It became obvious then that there was a lack of hard intelligence on the Communists; this lack was acutely felt by both Vietnamese and Americans. With the concurrence of the RVN government, the United States agreed to deploy US Army advisers to all ARVN intelligence organizations from the Joint General Staff (JGS) level to corps, divisions and sectors (provinces).

At the JGS, the US intelligence advisory team which was assigned to J-2 in April 1962 was a pioneering effort at this level. The team consisted of nine officers, two of whom served as senior and deputy senior advisers to the chief, J-2. The others were assigned to each of the operating divisions of the J-2: collection, training, interrogation, aerial photo, order of battle, and technical intelligence. The mission assigned to the team was not so much to provide advice to the J-2 personnel but rather to help keep track of and record intelligence data on the enemy situation throughout South Vietnam, especially information pertaining to the enemy's order of battle and infiltration from North Vietnam, as collected by ARVN sources. It did have an advisory role, however, and the US team with J-2 suggested ideas concerning policies and procedures to improve ARVN intelligence activities at all levels in three aspects: organization, training and operations. The team thus functioned in a dual capacity, collecting intelligence data and providing advice at the same time. To the J-2, JGS, the US team was particularly useful in providing training assistance since through its efforts, all intelligence courses, both in-country and offshore, were conducted with regularity and responded effectively to ARVN intelligence training requirements.

What the J-2, JGS needed most from the US advisers at that time was assistance in obtaining modern equipment, especially for imagery interpretation, to replace obsolescent equipment. Another urgent need was for US-produced intelligence information. The US team's failure to respond immediately to these requirements made its advisory effort look suspicious in the eyes of ARVN intelligence officers. But gradually the team's contributions to ARVN intelligence, in terms of agent reports and signal intelligence, became significant.

Unit 300, which was activated in 1962 as a collection agency subordinate to J-2, JGS, was assisted in its operations by the 1st Detachment, US Army 500th Military Intelligence Group. The US Army detachment assumed an advisory role in addition to coordinating its collection activities with Unit 300. The ARVN human intelligence collection system was organized into groups, teams and nets operating at all echelons in the field from corps to subsectors (districts). Agents operated under civilian cover in professions or businesses appropriately selected for each type of objective or operation. These organizations cooperated with US Army intelligence advisers who were deployed to the sector (province) level.

This form of coordination proved very effective. On the one hand, ARVN agents were provided detailed guidance for every step of their operations and they were able to absorb quickly the fine points taught by practical experience. On the other, by operating together, US advisers readily shared the difficulties and challenges met in each specific local environment by ARVN operatives whose successes or failures affected US operations as well. A drawback of the system was the poor credibility of the US cover. Although US Army advisers also posed as civilians, their cover was ineffective. To the highly suspicious Vietnamese population of that time, most American civilians were considered intelligence operatives and those Vietnamese who associated with them were, ipso facto, considered their agents.

By 1962, technical exploitation of materiel was still a novelty within the ARVN intelligence system. Communist materiel and armament during that time were a heterogenous assortment of different types and models making the task of exploitation and classification extremely difficult. In addition, the Communists also employed locally-produced weapons, grenades and mines whose effect was more propagandistic than practical, but whose use created additional work for the technical intelligence branch. The testing and exploitation of enemy materiel and weapons were made easier by the wealth of technical data provided by US Army advisers, especially those pertaining to new Communist weapons. These data proved extremely useful to ARVN units. The advisers also provided professional guidance to the Technical Intelligence Section, J-2, JGS, on the methods used in exploiting technical data from captured war materiel.

In counter-intelligence activities, the US Army 704th Intelligence Detachment provided advisers for the ARVN Military Security Service (MSS). Although the mission and functions of these advisers were similar to those performed by the intelligence advisers in the J-2 system, the US-ARVN relationship in counter-intelligence was more restricted in scope. A major reason for this was that the Military Security Service was also responsible for political intelligence and served as a security watchdog for the regime. The MSS therefore reported directly to the office of the President or to his political adviser, from whom it also received directives and orders. It was obvious in those circumstances that cooperation and coordination in the exchange of information with US advisers were limited to counter-intelligence operations against Communist activities and could not include the full range of MSS domestic intelligence and security functions.

In the area of signal intelligence, a US Army Radio Research Unit (RRU) was deployed to South Vietnam in 1962. The US Army 3d RRU performed as a collection agency for MACV J-2 rather than as an advisory body for the ARVN 1st Signal Exploitation Company which was the sole Vietnamese communications monitoring unit at that time. Nonetheless, this ARVN unit was able to absorb through its close association with the 3d RRU some modern techniques which proved far more effective than those learned from the French.

In general, during the period of the increased US commitment, 1962-1965, although US advisers were deployed throughout the ARVN intelligence system, their relationship with ARVN intelligence counterparts seemed to be cautious, especially during the period of political upheavals leading to the military coup of 1963. The Diem government suspected that the US Embassy was supporting the rebellious Buddhists and that US intelligence agents stimulated them into action. As a result, the relationship between Vietnamese intelligence personnel and US advisers was seriously affected. Understandably, no Vietnamese intelligence official would want to incriminate himself by maintaining too close a relationship with US intelligence personnel who were suspected of plotting against the government. The subsequent political turmoil during

1964 did not help improve this relationship and the Vietnamese continued to be cautious and reluctant to become too closely involved.

At the corps, division and sector levels, however, the US-ARVN intelligence relationship was not affected in any way by political events in Saigon. The extent of cooperation and the directness of the advisory effort in intelligence was most conspicuous in II Corps Tactical Zone following the introduction in September 1962 of a US Army Mohawk OV-1 squadron which operated from Nha Trang and Qui Nhon. This squadron provided valuable assistance in aerial photography to ARVN intelligence since the Vietnamese Air Force RC-45 and RC-47 planes during that time did not have photographic capabilities suitable for use over the Highlands. Objectives for aerial photography were developed by the II Corps G-2 and approved by the corps senior adviser before becoming missions flown by the US Army 23d Special Warfare Aviation Detachment. Most remarkable was the use of these Mohawks in tactical support missions, as suggested by ARVN commanders, since the plane could be equipped with rockets and cal .50 machineguns. Although unorthodox, this use of an observation aircraft was approved by the US advisers in view of urgent and specific tactical requirements.[2]

The Period of Full-Fledged Cooperation

The role of US Army intelligence advisers and the US-ARVN cooperation and coordination in intelligence activities took a vigorous step forward in 1965 when US combat troops were introduced into South Vietnam. The war had entered a new phase and in the face of stepped up Communist attacks and infiltration, United States efforts and capabilities to monitor the enemy situation were inadequate.

---

[2] The Mohawks were disarmed in early 1965 when the US Army Chief of Staff, General Johnson visited Vietnam and discovered the armed Mohawks. He wanted to avoid a squabble with the USAF that might jeopardize the use of US Army armed helicopters.

This was a period of large-scale, division-size combat operations pitting US forces against main force units of the North Vietnamese Army (NVA). In keeping with the force buildup, United States collection agencies and intelligence units were gradually brought into South Vietnam. For the first time, modern US techniques such as the OV-1 side looking airborne radar (SLAR) and infra-red imagery (Red Haze) were put to use. Other airborne detection devices, such as the "people-sniffer," were also employed. Air reconnaissance and aerial photography missions were flown by sophisticated USAF jet aircraft such as the RF-4C and the RF-101. The number of Mohawks increased to 115 by 1968. All these modern assets contributed to improving knowledge about the enemy to an extent never before reached during the war. In signal intelligence, the use of airborne radio direction finding (ARDF) helped pinpoint enemy units with accuracy and continuously keep track of their movements.

Effective as it was in collection, through the use of modern technology, the US intelligence effort during these early months seemed to be somewhat deficient in analysis and lacked depth when it attempted to assess the true nature of the war and the determination of the enemy. This was understandable since never before had the United States faced such a pernicious enemy on terrain which thoroughly favored him and under a form of warfare in which he made the rules. Other constraints in language and culture added to the difficulties faced by US intelligence personnel in South Vietnam. These weaknesses, by contrast, were the very strengths of the Vietnamese who unfortunately did not have the technological capabilities possessed by the Americans. It appeared then that if they joined forces in intelligence work, a perfect union could be achieved from which both would benefit. At the very least, this union could alleviate some of the difficulties encountered by Americans and at the same time would help the Vietnamese attain maturity in advanced intelligence collection operations.

The requirement for cooperation and the concept of mutual compensation were recognized by the Vietnamese and the Americans and led to a substantial increase in US advisory personnel in the field, from corps level to the district, and to the establishment of combined intelligence agencies. The number of US Army intelligence advisory personnel at sector level, for example, increased from three to seven. More important, however, was the activation of four combined intelligence agencies: the Combined Intelligence Center, Vietnam (CICV), the Combined Document Exploitation Center (CDEC), the Combined Materiel Exploitation Center (CMEC) and the Combined Military Interrogation Center (CMIC). The operation of these centers by a mixed Vietnamese-American staff with US-provided modern assets and Vietnamese indigenous resourcefulness greatly enhanced collection and analyses activities and provided effective intelligence data support for MACV J-2, J-2, JGS, and combat units for all allied forces at all levels.

The senior intelligence adviser for an ARVN corps was usually a colonel or a lieutenant-colonel. His counterpart, the corps G-2, until 1971, was almost always a major or lieutenant colonel. Though not seriously impeded by rank discrepancy, the relationship was somewhat affected by it. The corps intelligence adviser regularly provided his counterpart with intelligence data collected by US sources such as ARDF, SLAR, Red Haze, Sniffer and aerial photography. He also made available to the corps G-2 human intelligence gathered from prisoners and ralliers under temporary US custody and certain agent's reports. Information obtained from communications intelligence, however, was not subject to systematic dissemination by US advisers. If and when such information was made available to the corps G-2, it was usually carefully edited and restricted to general information. It was apparent that in this respect, US advisers were bound by national security codes which precluded complete disclosure of this type of intelligence even to an ally in war.

During this period, US intelligence advisers also provided liaison between G-2, ARVN corps and G-2, US Field Forces. As such, they played a key role in all intelligence activities in the corps area. To ARVN tactical commanders, the most valuable and useful intelligence data were those concerning enemy unit locations or movements as detected by ARDF. Fully aware of this fact, US commanders often provided this information directly to ARVN corps commanders. Therefore, one of the corps G-2's major concerns was how to obtain this same data before or at least at the same time as his commander received it from the US Army corps senior adviser. Obviously, no G-2 enjoys being fed intelligence data by his own commander. Thus, for a relatively long time, US intelligence advisers were evaluated by their ARVN G-2 counterparts on the basis of their ability to supply timely, critical intelligence.

But the role of the American adviser was not confined to the exchange and provision of intelligence data. It also encompassed US supply and support of intelligence equipment, and funds needed to operate an effective ARVN humint system. The amount of this support, however, was not equally available to all ARVN units. It depended greatly on each individual senior adviser, his interest in intelligence operations, and his own evaluation of ARVN agent net-effectiveness.

During daily working contacts, US intelligence advisers seldom made professional remarks concerning their counterparts' way of doing their job. Advisory comments, if any, usually consisted of explaining US techniques and procedures which had been found effective. This non-meddling attitude reflected a tactful respect toward ARVN intelligence officers who reciprocated in kind. A mutual respect developed which helped maintain a good working relationship and rapport between the adviser and the advisee.

At the division level, US intelligence advisers earned extra esteem and enhanced their professional standing through direct participation in combat operations with the division operational staff and by giving a helping hand to the division G-2, supplying him with US intelligence data or interceding for the employment of US collection resources. The sharing of the increased intelligence workload occasioned by combat operations resulted in making the rapport between the US adviser and his counterpart closer and more firmly founded.

In contrast to tactical units, the ARVN territorial commands at province and district levels had much more complex intelligence organizations which made the role of the US intelligence advisers many times more difficult. At the provincial level, for example, the intelligence structure encompassed a vast array of committees and units operated by different agencies, such as the provincial security committee, the provincial intelligence-operations coordination committee (PIOCC), the Phoenix committee, the province intelligence and security platoon, the province reconnaissance unit (PRU), etc. Each committee in which the sector S-2 participated was oriented toward a different set of objectives and problems and involved such different resources and intricate procedures that it would take an adviser a long time to familiarize himself with his task and the local intelligence activities. Most US intelligence advisers at sector level were army officers whose professional background sometimes consisted solely of an intelligence officer basic course at Fort Holabird, Maryland. Their professional experience was consequently minimal and whatever knowledge they had was primarily technical or procedural. Naturally, the advice they provided was based on the US Army manual on combat intelligence, FM 30-5, and often had little applicability to improving intelligence effectiveness at the sector level. The problems faced by the sector were usually beyond the scope of US Army field manuals.

The problems faced by US intelligence advisers at the district level were even more difficult and made their advisory role more demanding. As an adviser attempted to have a closer look at the intelligence problems at the grassroot level, he came to grips with so many complexities inherent in the enemy's infrastructure that it usually took him months to understand the basics. He learned to differentiate, for example, between a resident guerrilla and an unattached guerrilla, between a tax collecting agent and an econo-finance cadre, a liaison-communication cadre and a simple messenger, between front organizations and sympathizers, etc. Meanwhile the district resources and assets available for the collection of intelligence were severely limited. The district S-2 was usually a young second lieutenant or aspirant fresh out of school and still groping around in his job. What little guidance and supervision that both the S-2 and his adviser received from above came mostly from the sector headquarters, which was usually too preoccupied with its own problems to devote much time to district intelligence affairs. For both the ARVN and US systems, guidance and support seemed to stop at the sector (province) level. The result was obvious. Left to themselves in a totally strange environment, US intelligence advisers in the districts could do little more than learn from experience and try to adapt as rapidly as possible to the new environment.

Intelligence cooperation and coordination at the central level were entirely different from those in the field. They constituted an effort which was more of a co-worker partnership than an adviser-advisee relationship. Most indicative of this relationship was the way the four combined intelligence centers referred to above were organized and operated. In each center there were separate United States and Vietnamese elements organized along the same functional lines and almost paralleling each other but under separate commands. But section by section, personnel of the two elements sat together and worked together. Although the work schedule was separately established by each element, it was usually the same since both elements had the same tasks and worked toward the same objectives. The advantages of this co-working system were apparent; it accelerated and enriched the exchange of data and enabled ARVN personnel, through exposure to US work methods and practice, to learn new techniques and a modern approach to their profession. For example, ARVN intelligence personnel learned from their counterparts how to develop an activity pattern analysis for a certain area, how to keep track of the situation in a Communist base area, how to use automatic data processing to store and retrieve intelligence data, how to exploit and copy these data when required, how to test new materiel captured from the enemy, etc. As a result, and with the assistance of modern US technology and assets, the production and dissemination of intelligence became more methodical and faster and since intelligence was made available to all units on an equal basis, the professional relationships among American and ARVN commanders and staffs at all echelons were greatly enhanced.

At the four combined intelligence agencies, US personnel usually outnumbered their counterparts. Nonetheless, their working relationship was generally good from the very start and caused no problems over the years. This happy and productive cooperation was possible for two reasons: First, the relationship was based on a formal agreement reached between MACV and the JGS, which determined the procedures for cooperation covering a wide range of subjects, such as the sharing of office space and facilities, guard and security duties, the authority of each element commander, and the approach to be used in problem-solving. Second, and more important was the exemplary spirit of cooperation displayed by the top intelligence officers of both sides, the MACV Assistant Chief of Staff J-2 and his counterpart, the ARVN chief, J-2, JGS. On his initiative, for example, Major General William E. Potts, US Army, ACS/J-2, MACV held regular meetings in which he briefed the MACV commander, the Chief of the JGS and his Chief of Staff and J-2 on the current enemy situation as viewed from the US side. This innovation in US-ARVN intelligence cooperation set the tone for the pervasive spirit of cooperation at all echelons. It also provided the opportunity for General Abrams, COMUSMACV, and General Vien, Chief of the JGS, to discuss in detail the current enemy situation, trends and intelligence estimates for the future.

Anatomy of a Relationship

The formal MACV-JGS agreement on combined intelligence activities served as a useful basis for coordination and cooperation. It provided the RVNAF a number of basic guidelines regarding the American advisory role which had been mentioned only summarily in a JGS memorandum in April 1955. In April 1958, the JGS published another memorandum intended as a "reminder" to ARVN unit commanders concerning their duties and responsibilities toward American advisers. Both documents only indicated briefly what ARVN commanders should do to provide support and assistance to US advisers but failed to tell them how to work with their advisers to obtain maximum results. As a result, each ARVN commander had to figure out for himself how he would approach the delicate problems of the relationship, learning as he went from his own experience or from others.

By and large, the attitude of each Vietnamese commander toward his adviser depended on his own enlightened experience and education. It was largely a matter of personal improvisations, never the subject of formal guidance. By contrast, every US adviser was briefed and aided by handbooks on the role he was going to assume, on the country where he was to live, its geography, history, social customs and manners and on the specific branch or unit with which he was going to work.

In addition to this general background, the US adviser sometimes even had advance knowledge on the very person he was going to advise, his biography and his character as reflected by the remarks or comments of his predecessor.

Despite the hospitable and accommodating nature of Vietnamese in general and all the preparatory work that US advisers accomplished prior to their assignment, the relationship between them seemed to be affected by certain unfounded prejudices or misconceptions, especially during the early years of US direct participation, instilled perhaps by superficial reports of the communications media—movies and television in particular. The fact was, due to cultural differences and the language barrier, Vietnamese were generally inhibited and almost never took the first step in dealing with foreigners. Whatever contacts they maintained with US advisers were made primarily by commanders or responsible staff officers since they were the only persons qualified both by the requirement of their jobs and a certain ability to speak the English language.

The cultural inhibition of ARVN personnel seemed to be a reason why some US advisers complained about the lack of enthusiasm and the apparent lethargic approach to work on the part of the Vietnamese. Whatever their merits, critical remarks along these lines certainly did not improve adviser relationships. In defense, the Vietnamese usually argued that US advisers served only one year, enjoyed a good life and were not immediately concerned about family affairs or anything other than their jobs. As a result, they reasoned, the Americans were able to devote all their energies to their short tours while they themselves had to live with the war for all their lives.

One year was indeed short as a tour of duty since it included the unproductive time spent in familiarization with environment and job, usually about three months. In some instances, an adviser would be transferred to another job even before completing his one-year tour. As a result, it was impossible for some ARVN commanders to work with any particular adviser long enough to develop a fruitful relationship.

The commander of one combined intelligence agency once observed that during the period of a year he had had six different US counterparts. This high turnover rate for advisers seriously affected the combined effort, especially since it was a long-range effort requiring a certain continuity in job relationship. Some ARVN commanders even found, to their dismay, that what had been agreed previously by a certain adviser was not necessarily palatable to his successor. As a result, both sides often abstained from committing themselves to any long-range undertaking. In view of the nature of intelligence work, which required steadiness and continuity, a longer tour of duty for those advisers assigned to intelligence duties would have been advisable. Eighteen months would have been reasonable but two years would have certainly been better for the sake of the combined effort. I was especially fortunate that my counterpart, Major General Potts who had completed previous tours in Vietnam, was held in his position of MACV J-2 for almost four years. This is a good indication of the emphasis placed on the importance of the intelligence program by General Abrams.

Although US intelligence officers were uniformly well versed with what they were supposed to do as advisers, there were greatly diverging personal approaches or techniques, especially in the exchange of intelligence data with ARVN counterparts. This was most noticeable at the sector and division levels. Some operated on a broadly conceived approach to their duties by striving to meet ARVN essential requirements by all means even when this involved bending some rules or regulations. They could always manage to do this, for example, by direct voice communication. Others, however, tended to be overcautious. For example, the cautious ones always made a point of checking with superiors before releasing any piece of intelligence or only supplying it upon request and after the counterparts had learned about it through another source.

Because of this cautiousness, the general belief among ARVN intelligence officers was that their advisers often withheld information from them for some unknown but possibly sinister reason or another. Several ARVN intelligence officers indeed suspected that in early 1968, their advisers were unwilling to release intelligence reports concerning the enemy's preparations for the general offensive. They reasoned with the dangerous conviction that by withholding this vital information, the US apparently wanted to quickly solve the war through a major ARVN defeat. This misapprehension naturally dissolved with time but a certain suspicion still persisted among some ARVN intelligence officers that under certain circumstances, US advisers were not free to exchange essential information with ARVN ounterparts.

Some ARVN units were also convinced that certain United States intelligence reports were solely disseminated to US advisers to the exclusion of their counterparts, especially when the tactical situation became imminently dangerous. It was then that the attitude and countenance of the senior adviser and the intelligence adviser were apt to have a decisive psychological impact on their counterparts. It was as if US advisers were some kind of guardian angels without whom all hell would break loose. The examples were few but convincing enough. The evacuation of US advisers from the forward CP of the ARVN 22d Infantry Division at Tan Canh early in the morning of 23 April 1972, minutes before enemy tanks and troops overran the CP, was a deadly blow to the morale of the ARVN defenders. Then, in Quang Tri, the disorderly retreat of the 3d Infantry Division, which took place even before any orders were given, appeared to be the only sensible thing to do once US advisers had been hastily extracted from the CP.

Normally, when an adviser was assigned to an ARVN intelligence unit, the ARVN counterpart usually tried to evaluate him, not on the basis of the courses he had attended but in the light of intelligence duties he had previously assumed and the length of time he served in these assignments. Much of what he later offered as advice would be weighed on the basis of his professional experience.

As for the ARVN staff and personnel, company-grade officers, NCOs and privates alike, those who did not have the chance to be in close touch daily with the adviser, what really counted in their eyes was the latter's behavior toward their commander and how he treated them. If he spoke some Vietnamese, something that most US advisers tried to do, the troops were certainly delighted and the ice would be broken, if only because his weird accent brought them some amusement. The same was true with his counterpart even if the latter could speak English. In most all cases, however, the adviser's Vietnamese proficiency did not carry him beyond an exchange of courtesies.

In general, most US advisers were defeated in their effort to use spoken Vietnamese in work discussions. This was understandable, first because Vietnamese, being a tonal language, was phonetically difficult for most Westerners to master in a short time. Then, the eagerness of the Vietnamese to practice their English—which most of the educated spoke with some degree of proficiency—really discouraged the US advisers to carry on his Vietnamese language practice. For an American intelligence officer to be really effective in his job, especially when it required a profound knowledge of the Vietnamese Communists, the mastering of Vietnamese was essential. But then not every US Army officer had the time or inclination to develop this ability and in view of the variety of intelligence objectives, only a few truly proficient in the language were required.

Outward appearances were sometimes a matter of importance to ARVN personnel. Experience showed that in combined intelligence agencies, ARVN personnel usually watched US advisers come and go to see if proper military courtesy was rendered to higher ranking ARVN officers. To them, this was a way to find out for certain whether US personnel considered their ARVN counterparts as rank-for-rank equals and whether they had any respect for the ARVN in general. Concerned about equality and discrimination as they were, ARVN personnel usually felt gratified when they could share every facility, whether at work or at rest, with Americans on an equal footing. The examples given by US personnel always worked on their counterparts. For example, in a jointly-shared facility, if US troops did house cleaning every morning by themselves, ARVN personnel automatically joined them and usually tried to perform just as well.

In general, in their relations with US advisers or co-workers throughout the years, ARVN personnel usually came to the same generalizations as they judged their counterparts. They were convinced that US personnel were:

1. Very punctual, always neatly dressed, highly disciplined, and respectful of orders.

2. Responsible and professionally competent.

3. Sociable and compassionate.

4. Tactful for the most part. They were well aware that advisers did not command.

5. Very well trained, especially the technicians and specialists.

Other qualities that ARVN personnel found common among US intelligence advisers were: they usually monitored events in minute detail and promptly reported them to superiors; they were also willing to help their counterparts overcome difficulties, especially those related to resources needed in the performance of their tasks and this assistance was always swift.

The traits that the Vietnamese attributed to intelligence advisers were perhaps similar to those found among all advisers, regardless of their branch or specialty. However, objectively speaking, intelligence advisers were more successful in their role than most others. This was perhaps due to the fact that the intelligence advisory effort was undertaken in a most tactful but very effective manner in which the adviser acted both as a co-worker and an adviser. This dual approach to advisory assistance made both adviser and counterpart understand each other better since they shared a common task and worked toward the same objective in a similar environment. As a result, the advice given was more realistic, more essential to the common task and apt to be more willingly accepted. This approach also made the advisory effort a two-way, mutually-benefitting enterprise since it compensated for the inherent shortcomings found among advisers such as constraints imposed by culture, language, a short tour of duty and lack of continuity.

During the course of cooperation and coordination, certain sensitive problems concerning the authority of each partner were all solved in a rational and formal manner, thus averting possible conflicts and disagreements. The differences that remained and occasionally arose were usually resolved with relative ease due to a similarity of intelligence concepts, procedures and organizations and more importantly, to a spirit of genuine cooperation built on mutual assistance and respect.

As a result of this assistance, ARVN intelligence improved markedly with every passing day and proved responsive to the requirements placed on it by the need to know more about the enemy even during the post-cease fire period when the US advisory role was terminated. The spirit of cooperation and coordination, despite this, was maintained up to the very last moment when South Vietnam collapsed.

CHAPTER V

The Logistic and Technical Adviser

Significant Milestones

When the first US field advisers were deployed to major units and military schools of the Vietnamese National Army in early 1955, the Vietnamese Army logistic system still functioned under the aegis of French officers and NCOs who assumed most of the key command and staff positions. The Vietnamese Army logistic system was then at its embryonic stage. It functioned as a separate organization but its young cadre only served in an assistant capacity.

In 1956, the French High Command was dissolved. In its wake, the French Expeditionary Corps and all French cadre of the Vietnamese Army logistic system departed in haste. It was only then that the US Temporary Equipment Recovery Mission (TERM) was established and the Vietnamese Army logistic system began to receive US advisory assistance through TERM. *(Chart 8)*

A senior US Army colonel of the Quartermaster branch was introduced to the Chief, G-4, General Staff. He was to work with this staff division and assist in developing a workable logistic support system for the Vietnamese Army. An office was immediately installed for him within the G-4 compound, staffed by a Vietnamese NCO who spoke good English. The adviser's office became part of the G-4 staff division in all respects, and its occupant became known to the Vietnamese personnel as the "Adviser-Colonel." The adviser-colonel seldom stayed in his office. He came and went with unpredictable irregularity, sometimes showing up every day, sometimes appearing only once every two or three days. But the G-4 staff knew that he was extremely busy and worked with total dedication.

Chart 8 — Organization, Temporary Equipment Recovery Mission, 1956

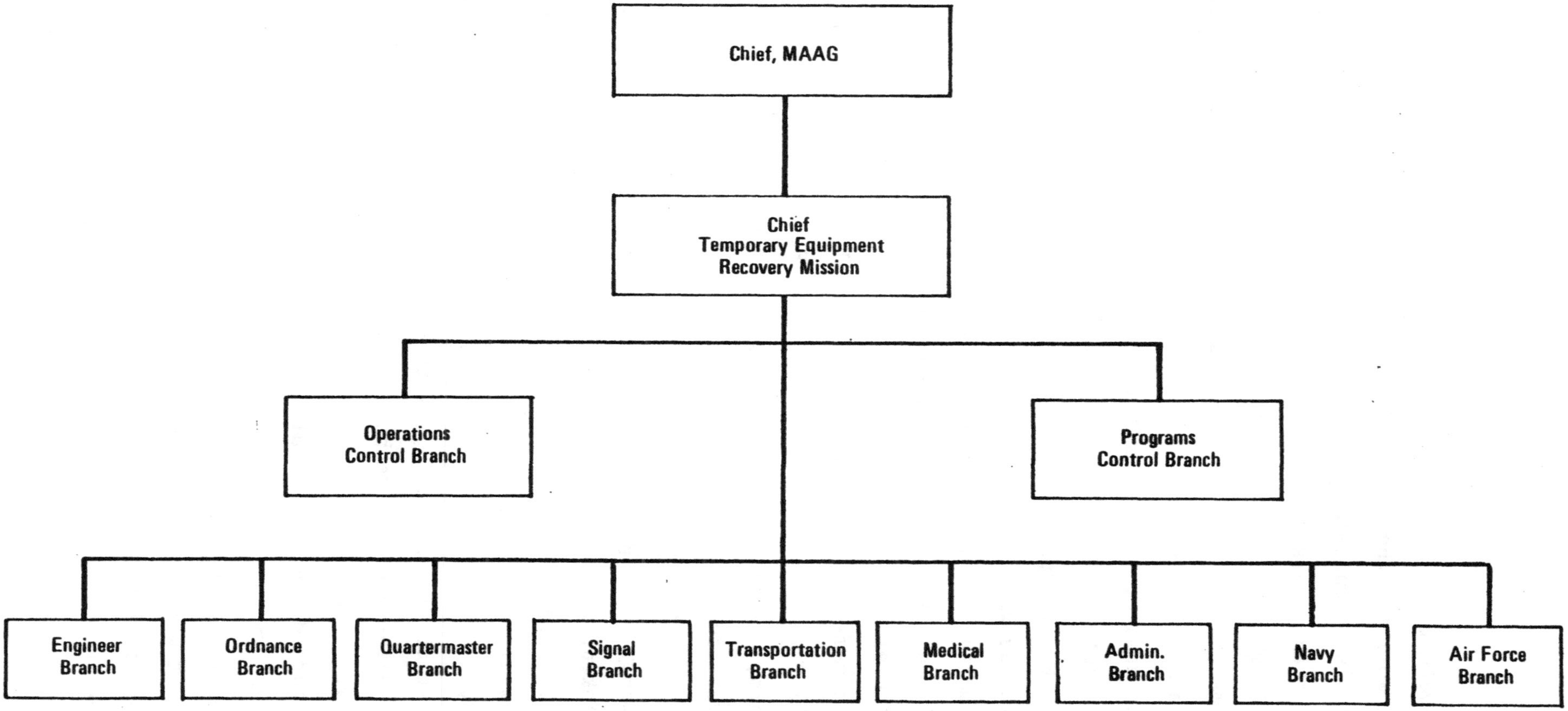

```
                    Chief, MAAG
                         |
                      Chief
              Temporary Equipment
                 Recovery Mission
                         |
        ┌────────────────┼────────────────┐
   Operations                         Programs
  Control Branch                   Control Branch
        |                                |
  ┌─────┼─────┬─────┬─────┐       ┌─────┼─────┬─────┐
Engineer Ordnance Quartermaster Signal Transportation Medical Admin. Navy Air Force
 Branch  Branch   Branch        Branch    Branch      Branch  Branch Branch Branch
```

97

Every time he came to his office, he brought something new and a lot of work for the G-4 staff. At first, there were stacks upon stacks of manuals, pamphlets, and assorted publications. Then came unsigned, typewritten memoranda containing certain recommendations that he suggested might improve the organization and operation of the system. Sometimes, there were pictures taken of glaring deficiencies in preventive maintenance and storage, accompanied by still more memoranda, usually unsigned, but sometimes bearing his signature. He and Vietnamese logisticians held many discussions, always through the intermediary of the NCO-interpreter.

It was with a deep sense of appreciation that Vietnamese logisticians welcomed the growing pile of manuals and memoranda because they responded exactly to what he had always sought: a new direction for the Vietnamese logistic effort. Months of hard work for all of us would follow each time he came. We were gratified but felt greatly frustrated by our own inability to understand the language. He seemed to share our eagerness to learn, not only the new things but also the language through which they were to be learned. He cheerfully gave us English lessons in the afternoon after duty hours. Communication between us therefore improved with every passing day as we progressed. The first difficult steps had been taken; they were in the right direction. With his devoted help, we felt confident we could overcome any obstacles that lay in the way of our new direction toward progress.

By the end of 1957, the logistical structure of the Army of the Republic of Vietnam (ARVN, as it became known to all US advisers) had been realigned to the technical service concept then being used by the US Army. Standing operating procedures for the new system were prepared and enforced. At technical services, TERM officers helped in the task of inventorying, storing and maintaining equipment and supplies that the departing French forces had left behind. Excess and unserviceable equipment were turned in to TERM for disposal. And in the reorganization task undertaken under the General Staff G-4's supervision, technical service chiefs received the same kind of advisory assistance that had benefited G-4. The eagerness to learn, to improve on the part of most technical service chiefs was to a great extent influenced by the exemplary close cooperation between the G-4 division and its US advisers. It gave impetus to the progress being made throughout the system.

Because of stepped up activities, the MAAG began in 1961 to attach technical advisory teams to ARVN base depots to assist their commanders in the operation and control of stock and storage. Each advisory team, whose members included civilian technical representatives (techreps), was considered an element of the base depot organization. Its mission was to train ARVN depot personnel in addition to working as specialists or technicians themselves. At each base depot, US advisers were paired off with ARVN section chiefs with whom they shared the same office, usually adjacent to the depot commander's.

The pair-off concept applied to work as well as to recreation. During coffee-breaks, for example, US advisers and their counterparts retired to the same officers' club or cafeteria on the base for refreshments. They usually contributed to the operation of these facilities by donating PX items as gifts such as coffee-makers, paper cups and plates, napkins, etc. Sometimes they also lived in quarters close to each other on the base. For all practical purposes, they displayed an admirable spirit of teamwork.

The only thing that usually caused disagreement between advisers and counterparts was the amount of aid equipment to be requisitioned. ARVN officers frequently complained about the excessive cutbacks made by US advisers in their requisitions; the adviser would usually cite the limitations in the aid budget without disclosing the figures, except in a few instances to prevent hard feelings.

From 1962 to 1965, with the activation of Area Logistics Commands (ALC) and in keeping with increased activities of ARVN field support units, US logistical and technical advisory teams were deployed to ALCs, field depots and direct support units. Technical advisory teams were directly controlled by the ALC's senior adviser; they served both as the senior adviser's technical staff and as advisers to ARVN logistical units. Logistical and technical advisory teams shared the same cantonement with the ALC and ARVN technical service units. In each instance, the senior adviser was provided a separate office but his staff shared office space with ARVN personnel. This greatly facilitated communications and made daily work more effective and productive. While logistical advisers were primarily concerned with planning and staff work, technical advisers would mainly look after stock control, maintenance shop activities and the preventive maintenance performance within troop units. Staff and command visits augmented by "end use inspections" were the normal operating procedures of US advisers, whether performed separately or with the participation of ARVN counterparts. Each end-use inspection was followed by written reports but staff and command visits normally resulted only in oral reports accompanied by discussions.

As of 1965, following the direct participation of US combat forces and the activation of the US 1st Logistical Command and US Army, Vietnam (USARV), the logistical advisory responsibility was transferred from MACV J-4 to USARV headquarters, in keeping with the service component principle. As a result, advisory teams working with ARVN technical services reported to USARV instead of MACV J-4. The problem with this new arrangement was that it did not exactly correspond to the way the Joint General Staff (JGS) of the Republic of Vietnam Armed Forces (RVNAF) was organized and operated. The JGS was both a joint service and an Army general staff. Consequently, the commander of the Central Logistic Command (CLC) which was activated in 1966 to replace G-4, was both Deputy Chief of Staff for Logistics of the JGS and the ARVN. In this capacity, he received advisory assistance from two US headquarters, MACV and USARV. For all practical purposes, however, the MACV logistical liaison team which had been attached to the JGS since the early days continued to function as an advisory team for the CLC; the only difference noticeable was the augmentation of its staff with personnel.

As was the case with most other ARVN agencies, the senior logistic adviser was accommodated in a separate office adjacent to the CLC commander's but his staff members were scattered among the CLC divisions, particularly the Supply and Maintenance Division, the Movement Control Division and the Base Development Division whose operations required the permanent presence of US advisers since they dealt with the coordinated employment of both Vietnamese and American assets. In 1968, the sole responsibility for providing advisory assistance to the ARVN was assumed again by MACV J-4.

Also, as of 1965, in each of the five logistical support areas, there were US field logistical support units under the control of the US 1st Logistical Command which supported US combat units under US Field Forces. Although these field support units were not responsible for providing advisory assistance, they contributed a great deal in helping to expand the ARVN logistical support system. In particular, at the beginning of the Vietnamization program and during the following years, 1969-1972, US general and direct support units under the 1st US Logistical Command provided, through the intermediary of US advisers, on-the-job training for a large member of ARVN personnel from support units of the same or corresponding level. This training task focused on the operation and maintenance of new types of equipment and the effort was intended to prepare RVNAF to cope both with the increasing requirement for specialists and the receipt of new equipment from US combat units when they were phased out as a part of the Vietnamization program. American POL units for example received and trained ARVN field depot personnel in the operation of 5,000-gal tank trucks and fuel pumping stations. US general support units received and trained ARVN Ordnance direct support units' personnel in the maintenance of M48A3 medium tanks and 175-mm guns while ARVN engineer direct support units' personnel received training in the maintenance of road building machines and bulldozers such as DC-6 and DC7E, Rome plows and 75-ton rock crushers. ARVN signal direct support units' personnel, meanwhile, learned on the job how to maintain new types of field radio sets such as the AN/GRC-122, -106, and AN/TRC-35.

At US logistic support units, which were to transfer their operational responsibility, bases, and facilities, such as fuel pumping stations, river groups (LCM-8/LCU), floating cranes, transportation, terminals at Saigon, Da Nang, Qui Nhon, and Nha Trang, integrated communications terminals and relay sations, ARVN personnel were authorized, upon completing training, to stay and work at the US bases until they eventually took over.

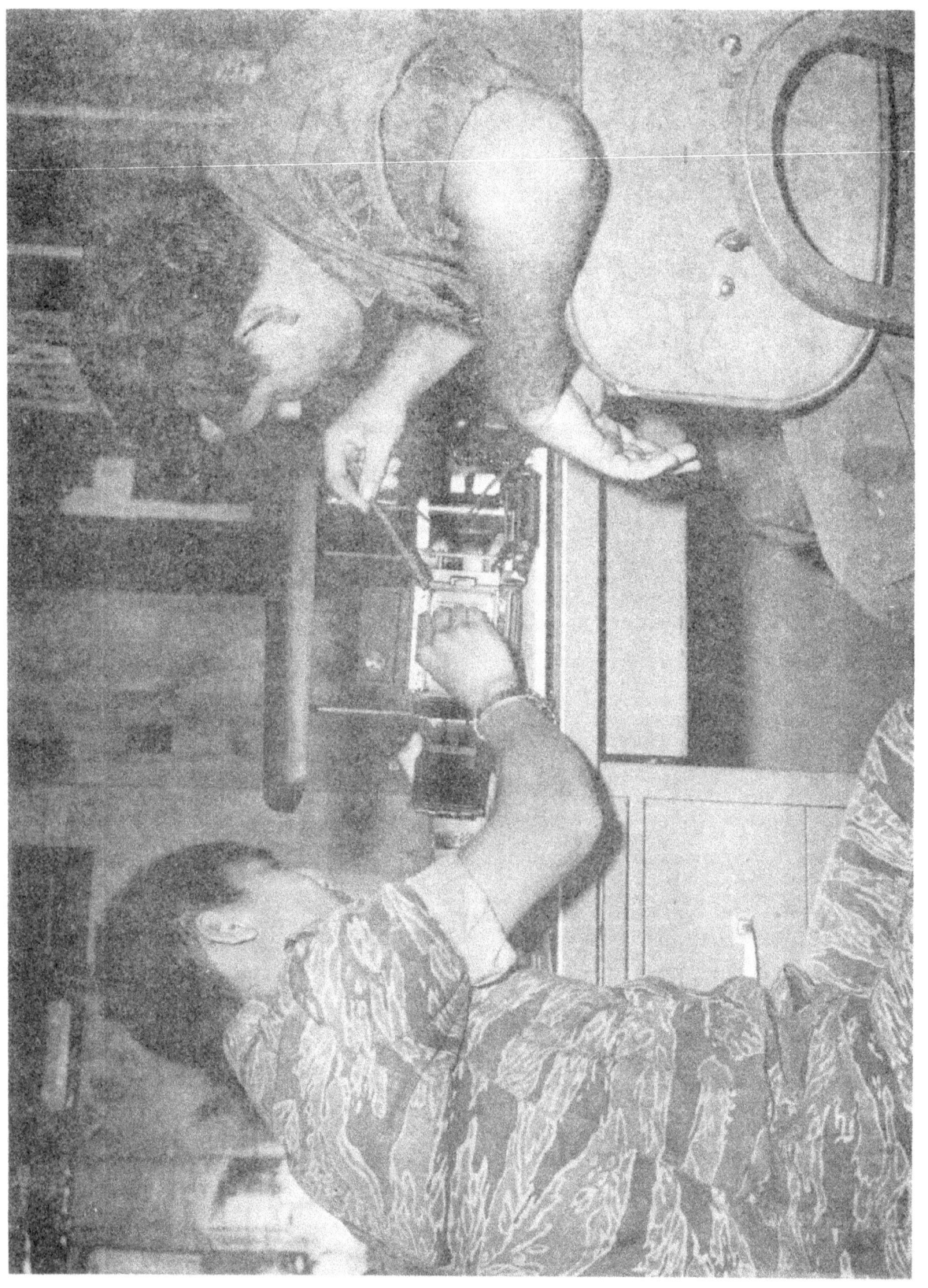

On-The-Job Training Provided by U.S. Photography Technician (Oct 1970)

In addition to providing on-the-job training for ARVN personnel, US Army logistic support units were also models of functional efficiency for ARVN unit commanders. For area logistics commanders in particular, the US Army Support Commands at Da Nang, Qui Nhon, Nha Trang, and Saigon provided them the opportunity to learn staff planning and asset management through liaison visits. US transportation battalions also provided ARVN transportation groups the opportunity to learn through combined operations how to organize truck convoys efficiently and how to manage efficiently their assets. Additionally, US Army logistic units provided effective advice to assist ARVN units in solving their temporary difficulties in supply and transportation especially for the support of combat operations.

As of 1970, in keeping with the gradual redeployment of US forces and the progress made by ARVN cadres and specialists, US logistic and technical advisers were reduced at the Area Logistics Command and unit levels. As a result, a US technical advisory team had to work with several ARVN technical service units at the same time and the team chief was no longer assigned to any particular unit but rotated among the units he advised. The team still kept a home office but this office was now installed at the direct support group or field depot headquarters or at the ALC advisory group headquarters. US advisory teams working at the central base depot echelon were little affected by the redeployment plan, however.

To keep pace with the momentum of Vietnamization, ARVN logistic units, with the assistance of US logistic and technical advisory teams, feverishly worked with US advisers and units concerning plans for the reception and operation of integrated communications, calibration, lines of communication and ports.[1] By the end of October 1972, preparatory work for the turnover of these systems accelerated to an even more hectic pace in view of a possible cease-fire agreement

---

[1] The operation of major base depot maintenance facilities requires the use of advanced test, measurement and diagnostic equipment. This equipment must be precisely calibrated to be of any use. Intensive training of RVNAF personnel was necessary to prepare them to take over this vital function. For more on this subject, see pp 112-114, RVNAF Logistics, a Report in the Indochina Refugee Authored Monograph Program, by Dong Van Khuyen.

This agreement, however, did not materialize until three months later, on 27 January 1973. In full implementation of the agreement, all American advisers and military specialists were withdrawn from South Vietnam during the following two months. The US Defense Attache office (USDAO) which was activated on 28 January 1973, took over the MACV compound but not MACV advisory functions. Its responsibility was to manage the continuing Security Assistance Program in coordination and cooperation with the RVNAF. Its role was that of a co-worker, not an adviser. Due to strength limitations, imposed by the Paris Agreement, USDAO had to rely on American civilian contractors to perform certain management tasks. With the objective of facilitating cooperation, a small number of USDAO personnel and most contractor personnel were assigned to those RVNAF agencies responsible for establishing military aid requirements such as the National Materiel Management Agency (NMMA) and the Logistic Data Processing Center (LDPC) where they helped translate these requirements into a dollar program. Although they did not have advisory responsibilities, members of the USDAO and personnel representing contractors were always provided necessary management data by the ARVN agencies with which they enjoyed a close relationship. In contrast to the practice of US advisory teams, USDAO personnel and employees did not make regular visits to ARVN logistical units in the field, but they frequently received reports on ARVN activities through US consular personnel posted in each of the military regions. USDAO officers occasionally visited ARVN logistic installations in the Saigon area and in the field, sometimes as members of the tours conducted for foreign military attaches. Like the foreign attaches, they also brought along cameras and mixed well as a group. The big difference was that they asked more informed and intelligent questions and were more systematic. Despite the formal relationship occasioned by the new circumstances which prohibited the Americans from acting as advisers, ARVN logisticians placed their total confidence on USDAO officers and treated them as if they were advisers. In difficult moments, they could always count on frequent visits by USDAO officers, and this further bolstered their confidence in continued United States assistance.

Civilian Technicians and Specialists of the U.S. Army
Materiel Command as Advisers to the Army Arsenal, 1972

The Base Depot Upgrade Program

During 1969, among the major tasks tackled by ARVN logisticians in an effort to improve logistical operations was the modernization of three major base depots, the 80th Ordnance, 40th Engineer and 60th Signal. This upgrade effort was aimed at increasing in-country rebuild capabilities and curtailing overseas rebuild programs. As part of the Vietnamization plan, the base depot upgrade program was a complex enterprise involving many areas of endeavor and many different agencies and organizations. To be successful, the program needed to be carefully studied and developed prior to implementation.

Major General R. Conroy, MACV-J-4 and I, as CLC commander and his counterpart, agreed to establish a combined US-ARVN committee to study the program. Chaired by Colonel McNair, senior ordnance adviser, the committee included several US and ARVN signal and engineer officers as permanent members and a few specialists of the US Army Materiel Command. After initial guidance given by both the MACV J-4 and myself during the first meeting, the committee settled down to work at the office of the senior ordnance adviser. Every month the committee reported in a joint session to General Conroy and myself concerning progress being made and received additional guidance. After three months of work, the results of the study were submitted, with our endorsement, to the Commander USMACV and Chairman of the JGS for approval.

When the program was implemented in 1970, the combined study committee was transformed into a program management committee which continued to utilize the same successful staff procedures: combined staff meetings for review of progress and joint action to obtain desired results. The committee was disbanded in early 1972 when modernization objectives had been achieved.

Funded at US $17 million, construction at the three base depots included new warehouses, rehabilitation of the existing warehouses, a refrigerated storage system, a drainage system, latrines, utilities, and road and open storage surfacing. The entire upgrade project cost US $25 million and included machinery installed in 1970 and 1971.

The program transformed the old, run-down facilities into modern industrial plants that were similar to those in the most advanced countries. Under the tutelage of the American adviser-specialists, the ARVN technicians, military as well as civilian, trained hard and learned the skills they knew they would need when the Americans departed.[2]

The ingredients of success in this program were hard work and a sincere desire to cooperate. On their part, US advisers were motivated by a desire to help the RVNAF acquire modern rebuild facilities. ARVN officers also fully devoted themselves to the task and were driven by an eargerness to learn at every stage of the program. Finally, the success of the program could be attributed to the harmonious atmosphere of cooperation in which every problem was studied and every decision made as a combined action.

Path-Finder I and Path-Finder II

During the years 1968 and 1969, ARVN logisticians were greatly encouraged from the results obtained through the reorganization of logistical support along functional lines for the infantry division. This was followed by the consolidation and automation of the RVNAF supply system through the establishment of the National Materiel Management Agency (NMMA) and the Logistic Data Processing Center (LDPC), both of which constituted the new Republic of Vietnam Automated Materiel Management System (RAMMS). Elated by this progress and in view of the eventual turnover of US logistical bases and facilities to the RVNAF, I was convinced that this was the time to reorganize the whole RVNAF logistical system along functional lines. During a meeting with Major General Maples, then MACV J-4, I outlined my idea and obtained

---

[2] For more on the depot upgrade program, see pp. 109-112, RVNAF Logistics, op. cit.

his concurrence for planning purposes.

At the request of MACV J-4, a group of specialists from the US Army Materiel Command came to Saigon with the specific mission of studying the feasibility of my reorganization project. The group formed a committee which became known as Path-Finder I. After two weeks of study and observation, the committee submitted its findings to MACV J-4 and the CLC. The report concluded that my proposed reorganization was entirely feasible in view of the success obtained at the division level and the availability of modern facilities which were soon to be transferred to RVNAF. It recommended the consolidation of supply base depots into three general depots to be located at (1) Da Nang, for the support of MR 1; (2) Qui Nhon, for the support of MR 2, and; (3) Long Binh, for the support of MR 3 and MR 4. At the same time, technical service field depots were to be deactivated. The committee also recommended a standardized form to be employed by direct and general support units for the purpose of evaluating and reporting achievements.

Path-Finder I's assessment and recommendations were considered rational and useful, particularly with regard to the reporting of supply activities. Both MACV J-4 and the CLC approved the use of the new reporting form and directed that the functional reorganization be planned in detail pending an appropriate opportunity for implementation.

The opportunity arrived sooner than expected because of the accelerated redeployment of US logistic agencies from South Vietnam. To implement the reorganization, Major General Jack Fuson, MACV J-4 and I agreed to establish a combined US-ARVN committee known as Path-Finder II. The committee's missions were to (1) continue the studies and review the recommendations made by Path-Finder I; (2) review the entire ARVN supply system and procedures with particular emphasis on weak areas; and (3) recommend improvements in order to bring about maximum efficiency with existing facilities.

The Path-Finder II committee was chaired by Colonel Vu Van Loc, assisted by Colonel H. W. Sheriff from the Office of the Deputy Chief of Staff for Logistics, Department of the Army. It included as members several ARVN technical service officers, MACV staff officers and American civilian specialists in supply, storage, logistic planning, communications and automatic data processing. The committee established an office at the CLC and spent the first four weeks visiting and holding seminars in ninety logistical units across the country from the sector level to the JGS. Each month, the committee held a meeting with ARVN technical service chiefs; General Fuson and I attended as co-chairman. The meeting was intended to review progress and provide guidance for the work being done. After three months of intensive work, during which the ARVN and American logisticians worked side-by-side, the committee submitted its final report on 16 October 1972; it concurred with all Path-Finder I recommendations and presented a total of 21 recommendations of its own concerning organizational and management improvements. All recommendations were approved by MACV J-4 and the CLC.

The ARVN logisticians, who were to be charged with implementing the Pathfinder improvements, had learned much during this 90 days of intensive study of logistic organization, doctrine and operations. In intimate contact with experienced American logistics specialists, they learned by exchanging views, observation, and by sharing in the preparation of the final report.

The US element of Path-Finder II left South Vietnam upon completion of the report but the ARVN committee members were retained and given the responsibility for implementation of the improvement program until it was completed near the end of 1973. The most significant achievements were centralized and automated management under CLC, the creation of divisonal logistics battalions and the consolidation of technical service field support units, all under the functional concept.[3]

Two notable differences between the Base Depot Upgrade program and Path-Finder II mentioned above pertained to the chairmanship of the Joint committees and in program management during implementation. In

---

[3] For more on Pathfinder, see pp. 139-141, RVNAF Logistics, op. cit.

Path-Finder II, the chairmanship was assumed by an ARVN officer; his deputy was an American officer who, despite an equal rank, was more senior in terms of professional experience and age. This was perhaps a unique instance during the entire process of cooperation between US advisers and ARVN logisticians. Normally, a US officer would serve as chairman or at least co-chairman of such a committee since US officers were in general more professionally experienced and knowledgeable than their younger counterparts. The merits of this unique arrangement, which was encouraged by the MACV J-4 himself, were self-evident. Responsibility helped ARVN logisticians meet the challenge and reach maturity with the backing of experienced, knowledgeable US technicians. As a result, ARVN committee members effectively managed this project until final success even though US advisers were no longer at their side. Path-Finder II was a resounding success during both the study and the implementation phases.

Observations of the U.S. Logistical Advisory Effort

Over the years, the US arrangement for advisory command and control underwent several changes as a result of the military situation, US authorized strength, and the organization of US combat forces and logistical support in South Vietnam. Apart from a gradual expansion in strength and deployment, the logistic advisory organization was at first placed under the MAAG, then under MACV control. For some time, US advisers were separately controlled by each service component: Army, Navy, Air Force, but finally control was unified under MACV J-4. Each change was made with the apparent purpose of streamlining command and control on the United States side. But the final arrangement seemed not be be in keeping with the objective for better and more effective advisory service. To ARVN logisticians, what really mattered was whether or not the arrangement provided for better and more effective support for the RVNAF. The question was: Were the RVNAF better served if US logistical and technical advisers were placed under the Commanding General of USARV or MACV J-4?

A definite advantage resulting from US advisers being placed under USARV was that field support and assistance were swifter because most US Army logistical facilities were deployed in close proximity to ARVN logistical units. Therefore, any intercession on the part of US advisers for the benefit of ARVN units, regardless of the purpose, would be direct and made easier by the fact that advisers operated within the same USARV structure. However, this arrangement seemed to be incompatible with the relationship between MACV and the JGS. First, there was no Vietnamese counterpart to USARV. The JGS was in fact both a joint staff and an Army general staff. The Deputy Chief of Staff for Logistics, JGS, therefore, performed the combined duties of J-4 of the joint staff and G-4 of the Army general staff in addition to being commander of the Central Logistics Command. In this capacity, he had to work with MACV J-4 and USARV G-4 at the same time instead of a single agency. The coordination and monitoring of all military assistance activities, as far as the JGS was concerned, were not facilitated by this dual arrangment. And in case a transfer of responsibility was required when USARV and US logistical units stood down for redeployment, the transition was apt to cause delays and discontinuity to logistical support activities.

On the other hand, the consolidation of all logistic and technical advisory efforts under MACV J-4, although not conducive to better support in the field, was fully compatible with the JGS organization in that it provided for a single agency responsible for co-ordinating and monitoring military assistance activities and ensured continuity in the face of eventual changes in US force structure and deployment.

Regarding advisory strength and the diversity of specialties required for the advisory effort, there was an opinion that since all requirements were initiated by the US and not actually based on RVNAF estimates, there may have been an excess in some areas of US technical advisers. That was only partially true. It was true that estimates of US advisory strength and specialties were all made by MACV (or the MAAG) and that the JGS indeed never formally asked for any specific number of advisers or specialties. But it would be wrong to say that this had never been discussed nor had any agreement been reached between

MACV and the RVN leadership concerning general logistic advisory requirements. The fact was ARVN logisticians were unable to determine the RVNAF needs in terms of advisory strength and advisory specialties for the simple reason that they had neither the experience nor the knowledge in these matters. If MACV had asked what kinds of US specialists the RVNAF would require for assistance in operating and maintaining the new M-48A3 medium tank, for example, the best that ARVN logisticians could have done was to state in very general terms that assistance in supply and maintenance would be required at all echelons, nothing more. As to a specific MOS and how many of them would be required, ARVN logisticians always considered that only the MACV staff would have both the knowledge and the experience to provide this information. As a result, specific estimates and requirements for advisory assistance were always provided by MACV.

Could there have been an excess of technical advisers? I doubt it. Being on the receiving end of US military aid and advisory assistance for over twenty years, through periods of relative calm as well as intense fighting, my colleagues and I only found a shortage, never an excess, of advisers. As has been said, for many years it was impossible for ARVN logisticians to determine the type and number of advisers required, however, it was equally true that in time, they learned to estimate their own needs in categories of specialists. Consequently, during the period 1973-1975, they contributed effectively in establishing, in cooperation with USDAO, programs for the replacement and reduction of American specialists working under contract with ARVN logistic agencies.

The effectiveness of advisers depended in a large measure on how long they stayed in their jobs. This was especially true of logistic and technical advisers. The one year tour was definitely too short for these advisers to acquaint themselves with the environment, the procedures, the human relations aspect of their assignment in order to effectively contribute their experience and know-how to the task of helping improve the RVNAF logistics system. It is my personal opinion that, now having to face the same harshness and hazards as their tactical colleagues, logistic and technical advisers would have contributed much more to the

RVNAF if their tours had been longer, 2 years at the ALC level and 3 years at the central level. But perhaps this would have placed too much of a strain on their families. A balance, therefore, should have been struck between the results desired in South Vietnam and the personal sacrifices.

The success of giving advice or receiving it is an art that depends a great deal on personal virtues and the individual's approach to human relationships. Professional competence and experience did not always make a good adviser if he was not at the same time a man of tact and good manners. Irascibility and haughtiness would not solve problems, but only make them worse. The key to success depended on flexibility, restraint and understanding. A good adviser was neither too passive nor too aggressive. He would accomplish little if he waited for his counterpart to come to him for advice and only provided it when asked. On the other hand, if by overzealousness, he flooded his counterpart with a cascade of problems, real or imagined, and aggressively told him to do this and that or tried to do everything by himself, his good intentions would be defeated. For unmeasured aggressiveness sometimes gave a counterpart the impression that he was being spied on or under scrutiny or surveillance. His self-preservation instincts would prevent him from cooperating wholeheartedly or worse, push him into rebellion and he would refuse to cooperate and let the adviser do it all.

From my experience in dealing with advisers, I think that discussions between advisers and counterparts would lead nowhere if, in the heat of debate, the advisers adamantly stuck to their positions and by criticizing the arguments of their counterparts, sought to impose their own solutions to the problem at hand. The best approach to convince counterparts in this case was tactful persuasion. If the discussion was in deadlock, the advisers could always suggest postponement and further study of the problem by both staffs. After taking time to reconsider all arguments and in the absence of immediate pressure, the counterpart would readily accept what they had earlier rejected.

To all Vietnamese and most Asian people, face is important and it is difficult to convince a RVNAF counterpart if he feels he would lose face by yielding. A useful rule of thumb for advisers was that they should never impose ideas or preconceived solutions. What they should do was to tactfully induce their counterparts to become cognizant of the problem and through suave discussions and cool persuasion, lead them to willing agreement.

Daily personal contacts between advisers and counterparts were the best and fastest means of getting things expedited at the lower levels. At higher echelons, periodic and even impromptu meetings also served well the advisory effort. But written memoranda often proved the least effective, chiefly when they were signed by a higher authority. Experience shows that these memoranda were usually received with nonchalance and some irritability by ARVN commanders despite the good words and well thought-out ideas. But if correspondence was a must to place important recommendations on record or to confirm some verbal communication with a view to keeping higher commands informed, the contents should have been thoroughly discussed with the counterpart and prior agreement achieved if possible. Only in this way, would the counterparts gladly and willingly comply with the ideas and recommendations contained in the official letter. The important thing was to avoid taking the counterpart by surprise with the unexpected.

During the first few years of the advisory effort, however, written memoranda were the only working instrument for US advisers. It was a transitional period during which ARVN logisticians were still not familiar with the American language and methods. In these circumstances, written suggestions and recommendations became necessary and useful. But as ARVN officers became proficient with the language and thoroughly familiarized themselves with American doctrine and techniques through US manuals or courses at US service schools, they preferred to deal with advisers directly rather than through written communications.

Personal contacts between the US senior adviser and his counterpart at either one's office also provided a good opportunity to discuss the problems of leadership or efficiency concerning the counterpart's subordinates. Since this was a delicate matter, it could not be the subject of an exchange of letters but kept confidential and informal between the two principles. Most subjects of leadership brought up by US advisers usually pertained to commendations of meritorious ARVN personnel, weaknesses of ARVN commanders, misuse of equipment, inefficient control, and of supply pilferage.

With regard to personnel commendations, US advisers were extremely straightforward in recommending promotions or awards for those ARVN personnel they considered particularly deserving. As to the question of an ARVN commander's weaknesses, the subject was usually tactfully brought up with the implication that it was up to the ARVN to decide. US advisers usually abstained from recommending disciplinary measures or relief from command as a remedy but despite their customary hands-off policy, they usually kept a close eye on ARVN-initiated measures to correct situations until there was a significant improvement or the officer in question improved or was replaced. US advisers had to contend with the fact their suggestions to remove some unworthy commander were seldom acted on immediately. The ARVN procedures for removal involved lengthy investigations and the faulty commander was always given a chance to improve. Only when improvement failed to materialize were disciplinary measures taken which might include removal from office.

Problems of equipment misuse and lack of control were usually discussed by US advisers and substantiated by photos or local and foreign press articles. These cases involved such irregularities as private use of military vehicles, pilferage at ports or sale of military gasoline. Particularly during the years of US force redeployment, US advisers complained about widespread vehicle thefts from American units, mostly utility vehicles and prime movers. They sought to enlist the cooperation of ARVN logisticians and Vietnamese authorities to curtail military vehicle thefts and gain more effective control of the commercial vehicles used by US forces. The most important statement on this subject was by a high-ranking US adviser during one of our meetings:

> Losses and pilferages during the course of clearing up a war are a normal thing. This is true of any war anywhere. I only ask that you do your best to help stop this vice and return to our forces whatever lost items you happen to find. But if there is nothing you can do, then Vietnamese authorities should be alerted to keep these lost materiels from being sold abroad. In this way, you can help both curtail the drain of foreign currency and contribute toward restoring the national economy.

The subjects of misuse, abuse or theft of military property were only briefly raised by US advisers and never discussed at length. US advisers also deliberately avoided using the term "corruption" in conversations. It was as if they felt the allusion to corruption was untactful and might hurt ARVN logisticians' feelings. But it was true that ARVN logisticians were never self-conscious about the subject whenever it was brought up. Indeed, they always admitted, without irascibility, the existence of corruption as an inevitable social vice occasioned by a long, destructive war and general impoverishment. They always appreciated the concern of US advisers about this debilitating vice that they themselves and the RVNAF in general tried hard to combat and eradicate. So it was with full cognizance of the problem, with candor and openness that ARVN logisticians discussed corruption with US advisers and even asked for their cooperation in combating it. During the intensive anti-corruption drive, US advisers were always kept informed of investigative results and disciplinary measures being taken. But US advisers seemed to make a point of never making allegations nor helping identify any corrupt individual on the basis of hearsay or rumors. In fact, they abstained altogether from providing names.

Some advisers were too reticent about reporting what they believed to be instances of misuse or misdirection of equipment or supplies. On the other hand, others saw it as part of their mission to observe and report on how US-supplied military assistance was being employed and they tactfully reported irregularities to their counterparts. In cases where they believed the counterpart might himself be involved, the proper course would have been to see to it that the counterpart's superior was made aware of the matter. In all instances where allegations of this nature were made, prompt and fair investigations were ordered by the ARVN authorities and appropriate action followed.

Field visits regularly conducted by US advisers and ARVN counterparts were by far the best and most effective means of getting things accomplished. Such "pair-off" visits not only helped US advisers, and ARVN counterparts to obtain a clear understanding of unit activities, achievements and problems, but they also provided excellent examples of cooperation and inspired confidence among subordinates by the extent of concern and solicitation with which US advisers helped ARVN units overcome difficulties, especially with the supplies that only US advisers could provide. Apart from joint visits, US advisers frequently made separate visits to ARVN units where they were also warmly welcomed.

Other effective devices of advisory assistance were monthly or quarterly full-fledged staff meetings during which the senior adviser, his ARVN counterpart and staff members of both sides reviewed progress made by units, discussed shortcomings and decided on actions to be taken. These meetings helped pinpoint and analyze ARVN weaknesses and place emphasis on measures required for remedy or improvement.

With regard to important and extensive problems requiring careful study and research, experience revealed that full cooperation under the form of combined study committees worked far better than if the problem was tackled separately by each side. The question of who chaired the committee was insignificant as long as principles and working methods were jointly established and approved. Reciprocity and mutual respect were the keys to success in these ventures and were consistently applied to every phase of the project, whether it was progress review or providing guidance for the next step. If a committee chairman was required, I felt this position should be assumed by the side who was actually responsible for implementing the project. This not only made sense politically, it was also psychologically sound since once given the primary management responsibility, ARVN officers were naturally inclined to work harder, and were more deeply involved in obtaining success. They were also able to learn more, make progress and gain self-reliance which after all was exactly what the advisory effort sought to achieve.

A prerequisite of good management was the adequacy of information. By contrast with US advisers who were usually supplied with all required information concerning ARVN logistical activities either by ARVN logistical units or through their own system, ARVN personnel were usually denied management information by the US side. Vietnamese logisticians resented this fact but could not explain it to themselves except by assuming that the Americans were bound by security regulations which forbade them to disclose certain management data to ARVN counterparts. A case in point was information related to the Military Assistance Program and other special programs of military aid. ARVN logisticians were usually kept in the dark as to annual appropriations and quarterly allocations to each technical service. As a consequence, ARVN logisticians were unable to make timely decisions and take appropriate actions in keeping with authorized capabilities. In time, they developed the idea that US resources were inexhaustible and tended to request far more than was actually needed. They did so with the sure expectation that the advisers would cut the requests to fit the program.

During the post-cease-fire period, 1973-1975, the need for management data required by USDAO and the CLC became more acute since they were both held responsible for justifying military aid requests and had to be prepared to face eventual cutbacks. The type of information that had previously been supplied by US advisers was no longer available. As a result, USDAO depended on ARVN logisticians for information. Since military aid was a matter of life and death to the RVNAF, USDAO felt that there should be very close cooperation and that we should share the responsibility for results obtained. Consequently, USDAO gave ARVN logisticians all the management data required. This cooperation took the form of a management data center installed at both USDAO and the CLC during the second half of 1974 with the objective of exploiting all data pertaining to the RVNAF and US military aid. The center became a meeting place for the US Defense Attache and the CLC commander to discuss and solve the many problems occasioned by US military aid cutbacks. The success with which USDAO and the CLC kept the RVNAF adequately supplied on the battlefield, although not at a level comparable to previous periods, could be attributed to the adequacy and timeliness of management data supplied by both sides.

Some Lessons Learned

United States advisers were assigned an exalted but most difficult task. To succeed in this task, they had to perform it with tact and diplomacy. On the other hand, making full use of each adviser's service was not easy either. It required the same ingredients for success from the Vietnamese.

In addition to human relations and cooperation, two factors seemed to affect the effectiveness of the US advisory effort to a certain degree: language and culture, and standing operating procedures concerning US advisers. But despite its limiting effect on communication, the problem of language was effectively solved through the use of interpreters and a constant effort by ARVN personnel to learn to speak English. Language, therefore, was eventually no big problem. The understanding of local customs and manners naturally helped US advisers establish good rapport with Vietnamese counterparts. The same could be said of Vietnamese officers if they knew American customs and manners. If both were able to understand each other culturally, then mutual respect and affection would develop naturally.

As previously mentioned, during the 20 years of benefiting from the US advisory effort, the RVNAF published only two short memoranda, in 1955 and 1958, concerning the relationship of US advisers and ARVN officers. From 1958 on the US-ARVN relationship was the subject of no further directives or instructions. This was indeed an omission of great consequence which gave rise to many unsettled complaints by both sides. Some ARVN commanders thought that US advisers spied on them while some US advisers contended that ARVN commanders deliberately withheld information concerning their units. But these complaints would have been infrequent had a comprehensive set of instructions been published by the JGS telling each ARVN officer exactly what to do and how to benefit from the program. It was indeed regrettable that this subject was neglected.

The fact that most US officers selected for advisory assignments had to attend an orientation course in the US prior to reporting overseas was an excellent means to prepare them for advisory duties. But US logistic advisers could have benefited even more if a similar but shorter course had been conducted in Vietnam under the CLC sponsorship. Such a course would have greatly enhanced the US adviser's knowledge in terms of Vietnamese culture, the RVNAF logistic structure, operations, and dissimilarities with the US system. Such a course would have made US advisers thoroughly conversant with current programs and problems and the most effective techniques to be used. It certainly would have made the US advisory effort more successful.

An orientation program for advisers such as this could have been jointly prepared and updated by MACV J-4 and the CLC. Lectures on important subjects could have been given by the MACV J-4 and the CLC commander or by both ARVN and US staff members. If properly conducted, such a program would have had a tremendous effect on the RVNAF logistical system since it emphasized the ARVN interest in the advisory system and inspired a strong cooperative spirit among ARVN logisticians.

Before terminating his tour of advisory duties, each adviser should have been required to write and end-of-tour report to record with candor his own assessment of performance and results and the strengths and weaknesses of the unit he had advised with particular emphasis on special areas for improvement. This report should have been made available to his successor who could have used it as a basis for continuing what had been achieved between him and his counterpart. Copies of this report should also have been sent to MACV and the JGS to serve as confidential documents on which to base actions and plans for future improvement. Such end-of-tour reports were indeed made by all senior advisers upon their depature from South Vietnam but unfortunately they were not made available to the JGS.

In conclusion, the logistical advisory system as it was established for the benefit of the RVNAF was extremely effective and entirely responsive to our requirements. Despite a difficult task, logistical

advisers always accomplished their missions and duly earned the respect
and enthusiastic cooperation of ARVN logisticians. The allegation that
US advisers acted as policemen only existed among a few near-sighted
ARVN commanders who invariably were either incompetent or lacked
confidence. In any case, the major offense of US advisers in the eyes
of Vietnamese was perhaps an overanxious propensity for immediate
results and overzealousness. US advisers were indeed indispensable
to the RVNAF as long as we depended on US war materiels. The quantity
and categories of advisers of course could vary according to the progress
and experience gained by ARVN logisticians, but the RVNAF could not get
along without American military aid budget managers and supply and maintenance managers at the central level whenever new types of equipment entered
the RVNAF inventory.

CHAPTER VI

The Pacification Adviser

The U.S. Response to Insurgency

Only one year after the Geneva Armistice was signed in 1954, which allowed South Vietnam to stand on its own pending reunification, the Communists initiated subversive activities. As early as July 1955, signs of security deterioration were appearing in the provinces of Quang Tri and Quang Nam. In October of the same year during the country-wide referendum, many polling stations were targets of sabotage.[1] Then in 1957 there was a significant increase in guerrilla operations, assassinations, kidnappings, and sabotage directed primarily against GVN officials in the countryside. By the fall of 1959, the insurgents seemed to have gained the upper hand despite all security measures taken by the Government of Vietnam; their actions gradually became bolder. In September 1959, they ambushed two companies of the 23d Infantry Division in the Duc My area and in early 1960, they launched attacks against the rear base of another division located in Tay Ninh. It was obvious that GVN control was eroding and the cities were being isolated from the countryside where the Communists seemed to be able to operate freely.

In the face of this mounting crisis, US officials in Saigon began to show more concern for security in the rural areas and improving GVN representation and control. The US Ambassador, together with the Chief, MAAG and other senior officials of the "Country Team," developed a

---

[1] This referendum resulted in a vote of confidence for Ngo Dinh Diem and the rejection of Bao Dai as chief of state.

Counterinsurgency Plan outlining the political, military and economic efforts required to help the GVN combat insurgency. Many reforms, mostly political and social, recommended by the US-conceived plan unfortunately were ignored by the Diem administration. Militarily, however, the GVN was eager to accept an expansion of the US advisory effort and increased military aid. The US Military Assistance Advisory Group immediately placed new emphasis on counterinsurgency training and began attaching field advisers to ARVN battalions on a selective basis. At the end of 1960, the MAAG also initiated training and support for the Civil Guard and People's Militia. In addition, US Special Forces teams undertook the training of the newly-created ARVN Ranger companies. It was very obvious at that time that the US was increasing its commitment in South Vietnam.

After President John F. Kennedy took office in January 1961, his new administration increased support for the RVN in the face of stepped up Communist aggression. The formation of the National Liberation Front (NLF) which was announced in Hanoi in December the previous year left no doubt as to North Vietnam's ultimate objective in the South. Soon after the visit of Major General Edward G. Landsdale to South Vietnam in January, the United States Government created an interdepartmental action group known as Task Force, Vietnam, with the mission of studying, planning and coordinating actions for the support of South Vietnam against the Viet Cong. In Saigon, a corresponding task force was also established; it included all members of the country team.[2]

The security situation throughout South Vietnam, meanwhile, continued to deteriorate. During a twelve-month period ending in May 1961, there were well over 4,000 GVN officials at the grass-roots level killed by Communists. In September, during an attack against the provincial city of Phuoc Thanh, the Communists employed a concentrated force of several battalions. It was obvious that the war of insurgency being

---

[2] Major General George S. Eckhardt, Command and Control, 1950-1969, Vietnam Studies (Department of the Army, Washington, D.C.: 1974) pp. 20-22.

waged by the Communists in South Vietnam had taken on a double aspect: that of guerrilla warfare augmented by conventional attacks. To assist in countering this double crisis, the GVN instituted the strategic hamlet program, its first politically-cohesive pacification effort to combat insurgency and restore control over the countryside. At the same time, a mission to South Vietnam headed by General Maxwell D. Taylor recommended a further increase in US advisory effort and combat support, continued expansion of the RVNAF, and support of the GVN strategic hamlet program. These proposals provided a new direction and emphasis to the US military effort during the following years. To improve command and control of the expanding effort, the United States established the US Military Assistance Command, Vietnam (MACV) and assigned General Paul D. Harkins as its first commander on 8 February 1962.

At this time it appeared that United States support for RVN in terms of advisory assistance for pacification and security was operated by and channeled into two uncoordinated systems: civilian and military. The US Ambassador received from the US State Department policy guidance as it pertained to political and economic problems while the MACV commander was responsible for military matters and reported to the Commander-in-Chief, Pacific (CINPAC). However, as the senior US representative in South Vietnam, the US Ambassador had the overall responsibility of coordinating and supervising all American efforts, military and civilian. His relationship with the MACV commander was one of coordination, consultation and information; all disagreements between the two were to be referred to Washington.[3]

Until the overthrow of President Ngo Dinh Diem in November 1963, the strategic hamlet program received only modest support from the United States on the civilian side. At the start of Operation "Binh Minh" (Sunrise), which launched the program in March 1962 in Binh Duong

---

[3]Ibid, p. 29.

Province, for example, the United States Operations Mission (USOM) initially supplied only $300,000 for support of resettled families. Another type of contribution was the printing by USIS of a small pamphlet depicting the new "Good Life" in strategic hamlets. But military support for the program was much more significant in that it nearly doubled the force structure of territorial forces, so vital to the maintenance of security in the provinces and districts, to a total of 108,000 in addition to providing them with proper training and equipment. However, the political instability that immediately followed President Diem's overthrow in late 1963 almost shoved the pacification effort into complete disarray.

In the face of this setback and increased Communist subversive activities, the US decided to revitalize its support and dispatched a new team to South Vietnam composed of Ambassador Maxwell D. Taylor, Deputy Ambassador Alexis Johnson and General William C. Westmoreland. Together with the Directors of the US Agency for International Development (USAID, Formerly USOM), the Joint US Public Affairs Office (JUSPAO, which absorbed USIS in its organization), and the Office of the Special Assistant to the Ambassador (OSA or CIA), the new team formed what was known as the "Mission Council." Like its predecessor, the Task Force, the Mission Council served as an advisory body for the US Ambassador. At about the same time, MACV also established a new staff division, the Rural Development Support Division to respond more efficiently to support requirements for pacification.

The deterioration of security throughout South Vietnam reached such proportions in late 1964 that the US introduced combat troops for the ground war and in 1965 began a sustained bombing campaign of North Vietnam. Consequently, the immediate danger of South Vietnam's collapse was averted and with improvement in the military situation, there was a need for further consolidating US activities in support of pacification. When Ambassador Henry Cabot Lodge was reassigned to Saigon in early 1966, he placed Deputy Ambassador William J. Porter in charge of coordinating all pacification support activities. In Washington, President Johnson appointed Mr. Robert W. Komer as his special assistant to look after the "other war" in Vietnam. Later in the year, the US Embassy created the Office of Civil Operations (OCO) in an effort to consolidate the activities of all US civil agencies in support of pacification. On the military side, MACV elevated its Revolutionary Development (RD) Support Division into a Directorate and assigned a general officer as director. Also, to increase civil-military coordination, another general officer was assigned to the office of Deputy Ambassador Porter.

CORDS Organization and Operations

As the fighting escalated, it became obvious that progress in pacification depended primarily on the military effort; it was impossible to pacify a rural area in the face of an enemy battalion. Its prospects of success necessarily depended on effective coordination of civil and military operations. Recognizing this need for an unified effort, President Johnson in early 1967 placed the MACV commander in charge of all pacification support activities, a move which was announced by the new US Ambassador, Ellsworth Bunker, in May 1967. The Office of Civil Operations was merged with the MACV RD Support Directorate to form the Office of the Assistant Chief of Staff for Civil Operations and Revolutionary Development Support (ACS/CORDS), headed by a civilian. At the same time, Mr. Robert W. Komer, Presidential Assistant, was appointed Deputy Commander MACV for CORDS with ambassadorial rank. *(Chart 9)*

The advent of CORDS and the new arrangement for command and control within MACV represented a unique effort especially tailored to the requirements of the war being fought. Perhaps this was a major test to see whether civilian and military elements could mesh together in an integrated effort designed to provide support for a special aspect of the war. An unprecedented arrangement, CORDS quickly solved and eliminated all problems which usually characterized civilian and military organizations working together.

The CORDS organization also reflected a certain flexibility of response in the face of complex requirements occasioned by the pacification task. Its staff elements were in charge of supporting almost all

Chart 9 — CORDS in MACV Command Channel

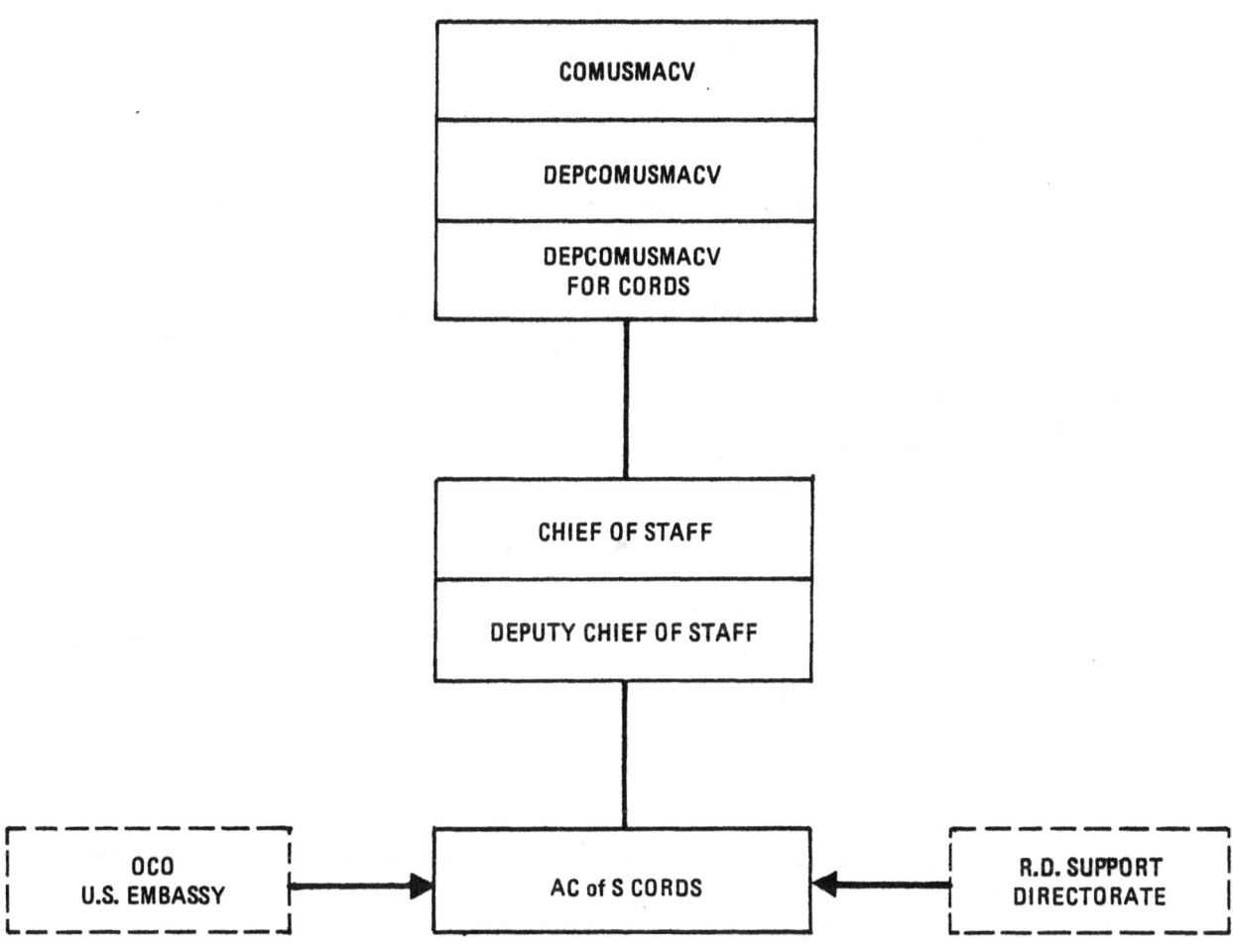

the major GVN programs associated with pacification. Other specialized areas such as economic development, agriculture, farm credit, land reform, etc. continued to be supported by USAID. *(Chart 10)*

At the corps tactical zone level (military region after 1970), a similar arrangement was instituted. The senior advisers — III Marine Amphibious Force and Field Forces I, II commanders and the commander, Delta Military Assistance Command — were each assigned a civilian Deputy for CORDS and their CORDS staff organizations were also a mixture of civilian and military personnel under the control of his Assistant Chief of Staff for CORDS. *(Chart 11)*

The Deputy for CORDS was responsible for the establishment and implementation of all plans and operations in support of the GVN pacification program, including civil operations conducted by US units within the CTZ/Region. The Deputy Senior Adviser assisted him with problems concerning the ARVN forces employed in pacification support.

The Division Tactical Area (DTA) or Special Zone (SZ) was a level immediately under the CTZ/Region in the pacification support structure. However, its role was tactically oriented and mostly confined to providing regular force units for the support of pacification. In 1970, the DTA was abolished and as of that time ARVN infantry divisions no longer played a direct role in the conduct of pacification. As a result, US tactical advisers assigned to ARVN divisions were not as active in pacification activities.

By far the most important and extensive organizations for pacification support was the US advisory effort at the province and district level. As early as 1962, following President Kennedy's decision for increased emphasis, US military advisers were deployed to all provinces at the same time as USOM field representatives. The need for increased assistance in restoring security during the following year led MACV to test-assign US advisers to the 13 districts surrounding Saigon in April 1964 as the Hop Tac pacification campaign was launched in this area. Results produced by this pilot program proved so encouraging that two months later, the US Secretary of Defense, Robert S. McNamara, concluded that more districts should have advisers. By the end of 1965, when the

Chart 10 — Organization, Office of the Assistant Chief of Staff for CORDS, MACV

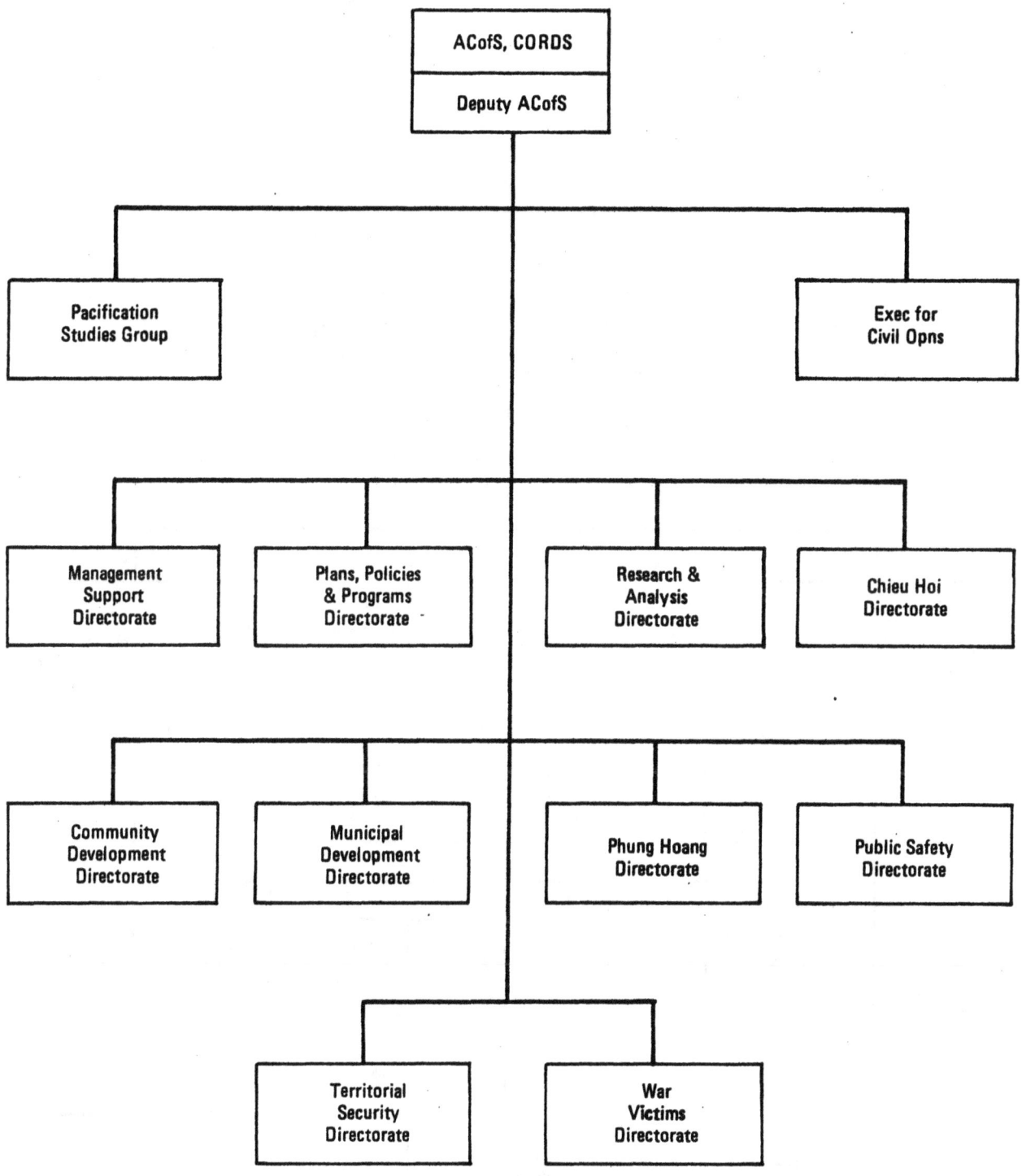

Chart 11 — Organization, CTZ/Region CORDS

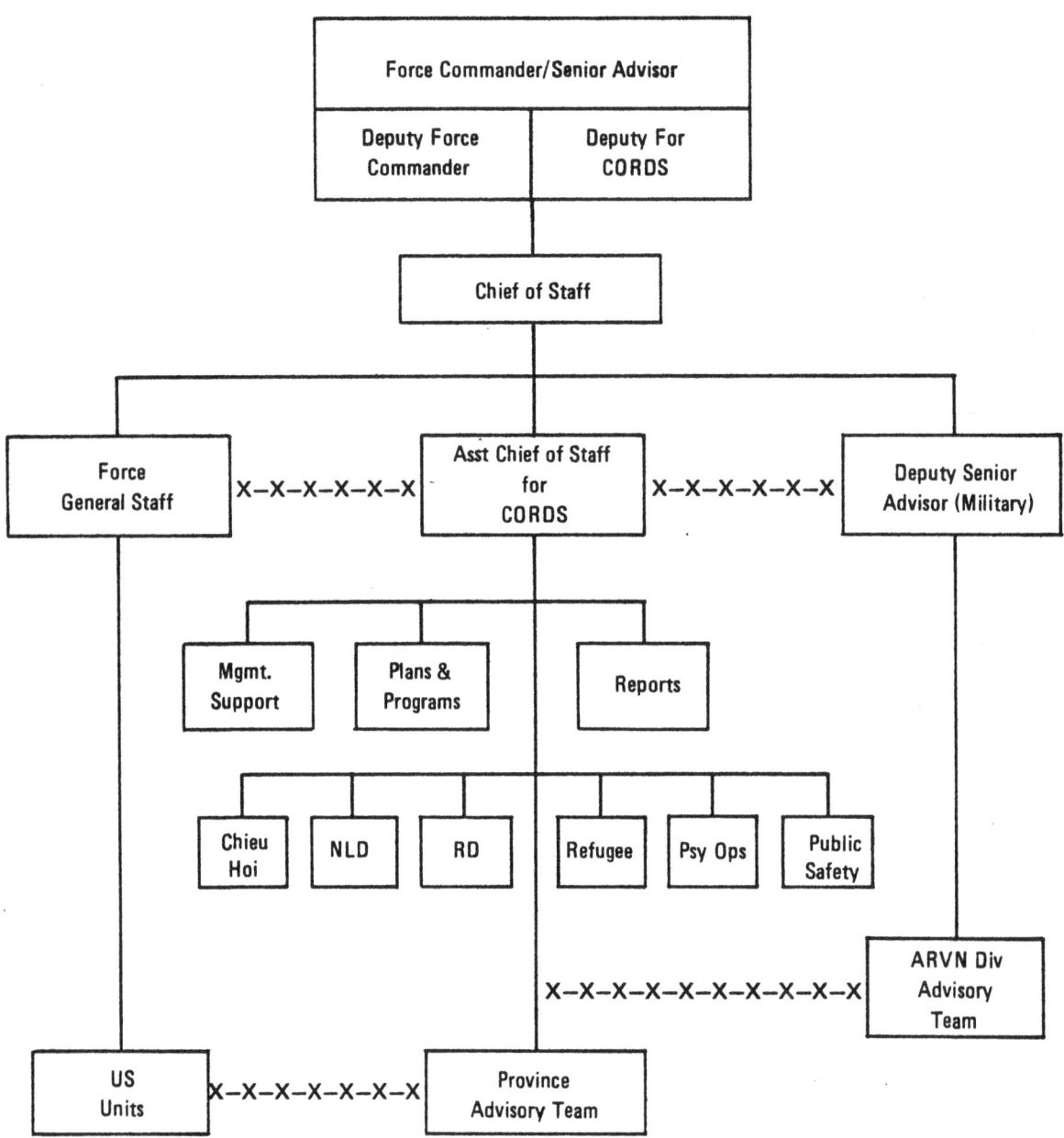

X–X–X   Coordination — Military and CORDS matters.

RVNAF assumed the primary role of pacification support, the total number of US advisers had increased substantially in provinces and districts.

With the advent of CORDS in May 1967, the US civilian and military advisory efforts at the province and district levels began to consolidate into a single organization. The province senior adviser could be a military officer or a civilian. If he was a military officer, his deputy would be a civilian, and vice versa. Although he was the senior adviser to the Vietnamese province chief, the specialized advisers who made up his staff were authorized, each in his own area of interest, to make recommendations to the province chief. At the district level, most senior advisers were military officers. When ARVN regular force units operated in a province in support of pacification, their US advisers were operationally controlled by the province senior adviser. *(Chart 12)*

By the time the CORDS organization was well established throughout South Vietnam, the total US pacification advisory strength included about 4,000 military personnel and 800 civilians. By mid-1967, these figures increased even more but the additional strength was devoted to the task of advising and training the Regional and Popular Forces (RF and PF, formerly Civil Guard and People's Militia, respectively). Most of the additional advisory spaces were used to create a total of 353 Mobile Advisory Teams (MAT) whose mission was to train RF and PF units. Each MAT was authorized two officers, three non-commissioned officers and one interpreter; it was tasked to train from three to six RF companies and an additional number of PF platoons. The training provided by these MATs emphasized small unit combat tactics and pacification support. At the same time Mobile Advisory Logistic Teams (MALT) were also organized to help improve logistical support for the RF and PF.

In addition to field advisers attached to provinces and districts and mobile advisory teams, the US pacification advisory effort also included training advisers assigned to RF and PF training centers across the country, and by extension, the Marine squads that participated in the Combined Action Program in I Corps area and the US Special Forces personnel who advised and trained the Civilian Irregular Defense Groups (CIDG). The accomplishments of the Combined Action Program and the CIDGs will be discussed later in this chapter.

Chart 12 — Advisory Relationships, Corps, Province and District Levels

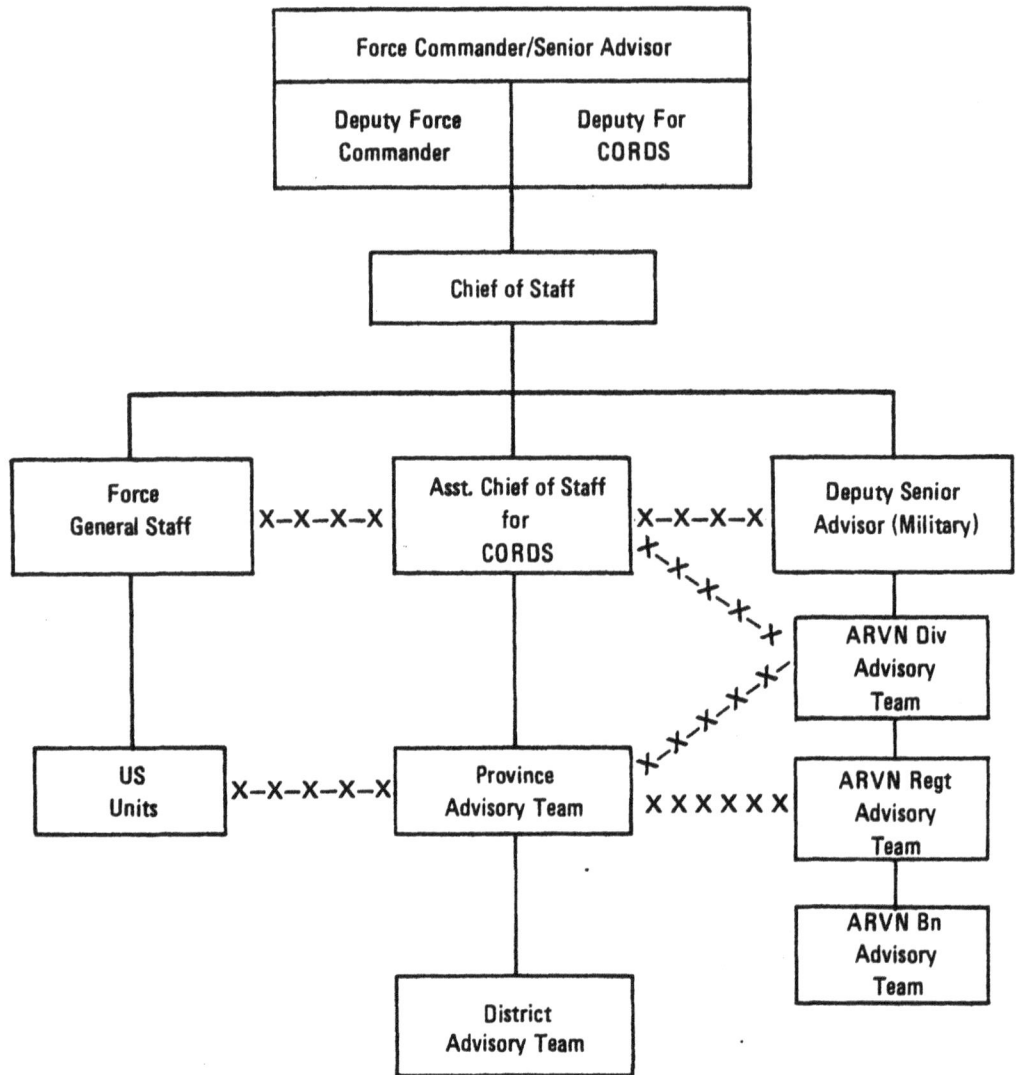

X—X—X—X Coordination — Military and CORDS matters.

XXXXXXX Operational Control when unit assigned on RD direct support mission.

MAT in Action:
On a Firing Range with PF Troops (Long An, December 1970)

MAT Members Checking Targets After PF Troops Practice Firing the M-16 Rifle (Long An, Dec 1970)

A First-Aid Class for PF Troopers by MAT Member (Dec 1970)

MAT Member as Adviser to Vietnamese NP Field Force
(Da Nang, 1970)

By 1969, total US advisory strength in South Vietnam was about 16,000, including 1,000 civilians. By mid-1969, US Army advisers alone numbered about 13,500, including 6,500 in CORDS organizations; 95% of these pacification advisers were assigned to field duties outside Saigon, to provinces and districts and to mobile advisory teams. This was perhaps the greatest emphasis ever devoted by the US in support of the RVN pacification program.

After the cease-fire of 28 January 1973, as US military units were phased out, MACV was dissolved and replaced by the US Defense Attache Office (USDAO) whose mission was to continue to manage the Security Assistance Program for the RVN. The CORDS organization was terminated at the same time as the United States advisory effort. Those CORDS functions related to economic affairs and development were transferred to USAID. To supervise and coordinate civilian operations across South Vietnam, the US Embassy created the Office of the Special Assistant to the Ambassador for Field Operations (SAAFO).

At each of the military regions, a US Consulate General was established which absorbed all the residual elements of regional CORDS. At the district level, all advisory teams were redeployed after the cease-fire. The province advisory teams, however, were consolidated into 20 area offices after the removal of military personnel. Each area office was responsible for civil operations within from two to four provinces except for the more important provinces such as Binh Dinh which was covered by one area office. But area offices were subsequently disbanded and finally the US presence in each RVN province was reduced to a small "civilian liaison team."

Relations and Contributions

American aid and assistance provided to South Vietnam immediately after 1954 effectively assisted the nascent nation in overcoming its initial difficulties. With this aid, South Vietnam was able to resolve many of its economic problems, especially those concerned with the resettlement of nearly one million North Vietnamese refugees fleeing South.

These accomplishments, coupled with a considerable reduction in internal dissention, gave the new administration of Ngo Dinh Diem a solid basis of popular consent. And after regaining political stability by defeating rebellious sects and setting aside the difficult problem of reunification for the moment, the RVN was well on its way toward healing the wounds of war and developing its national economy.

To achieve its national goals, the RVN desperately needed US economic and technical assistance. Through the United States Embassy in Saigon and its specialized agencies, the US systematically channeled aid required into programs undertaken by the GVN ministries. However, North Vietnam was determined that its foe south of the 17th parallel would not develop too rapidly. Subversive and sabotage activities directed from the North increased throughout South Vietnam. To counter this growing Communist threat, the Ngo Dinh Diem government implemented certain anti-subversive measures involving some degree of participation by the total population. But US support did not become deeply involved in such political programs as People's Action, Communist Denunciation and even in developmental projects such as Agrovilles and Land Reform. It was obvious that during this time, the emphasis of US aid was more economic than military.

Indeed, owing much to American financial and economic aid, the RVN was able not only to overcome its budgetary deficits but also to initiate several economic development projects. As a result, productivity in rice, rubber and several secondary crops and cattle breeding was slowly but consistently on the rise. Rice production in 1959, for example, reached the 5 million ton mark, doubling the figure of 1954. At the same time, roads, canals, railways, and ports were rehabilitated or reconstructed to assist in providing a strong economic infrastructure.

On the other hand, in cooperation with the Vietnamese General Staff, the MAAG devoted its efforts to building, training and modernizing the Republic of Vietnam Armed Forces. Predicated on its experience of the Korean War, the US provided support for a conventional 150,000-man force, predominantly army and composed of well equipped infantry divisions. All organization, equipping, and training efforts were directed toward the objective of countering an overt, conventional invasion from North Vietnam.

By the early 1960's, the Communist subversive threat had become so critical that the United States increased its assistance to the RVN. To help the RVN fight the unconventional war, the MAAG agreed in mid-1960 to support and train Ranger companies and subsequently Ranger battalions. In Saigon, the Country Team under the US Ambassador's direction, developed a Counter-Insurgency (CI) plan which was perhaps the first cohesive and determined effort aimed at meeting the insurgent challenge. Among other things, this CI plan recommended a 20,000-man increase in the RVNAF force structure and some reforms in the security-keeping apparatus of the RVN.

The Counter-Insurgency plan was approved by Washington as soon as President Kennedy took office in early 1961. The ARVN was therefore increased to 170,000. Also, in keeping with the plan, the US provided support for an authorized 68,000-man Civil Guard and a 40,000-man People's Militia (these forces were eventually redesignated Regional and Popular Forces, respectively). Subsequently, the US signed with President Ngo Dinh Diem a Treaty of Amity and Economic Relations and sent Vice President Lyndon B. Johnson on an official visit. In rapid succession, two fact-finding missions, one led by Dr. Eugene Stanley and the other by General Maxwell D. Taylor and Dr. Walt W. Rostow, confirmed the US determination to pursue its economic and military support for the RVN along the lines suggested by the CI plan. More US advisers were assigned to ARVN units and the revitalized territorial forces. By the end of 1961, all the RVN provinces had received an advisory team, to include civilian advisers.

In 1962, the revised CI plan became the Comprehensive Plan for South Vietnam. Its principal goal was to support the Strategic Hamlet program which had been conceived by the Diem administration in late 1961. With increased American aid, and the development of strategic hamlets, the general security situation throughout South Vietnam by the end of 1962 had taken on a brighter outlook.

But the prospects were soon darkened by the Buddhist uprising in the summer of 1963 which led to the coup of 1 November 1962 in which President Diem was killed. During the rapid succession of military governments which followed, South Vietnam was edged into a period of utter political instability and turmoil which found the Strategic Hamlet program disrupted and finally neglected. The countryside, therefore, was plunged again into insecurity despite US advisory and assistance efforts.

As the situation deteriorated, US authorities in Saigon became more concerned with pacification but it was impossible for pacification to make desired progress as long as the regime remained shaky. The "Victory Plan" which was implemented in 1964 did not achieve any significant results. Also, the Hop Tac pacification campaign around Saigon was not fully successful because of the lack of interest among GVN pacification authorities. But the US experiment of assigning advisers to districts did prove successful and soon developed into an extensive program.

During the years following 1965, while US combat troops were pouring into South Vietnam, US authorities also endeavored to help the GVN solve its pacification problems. But during the initial period of US buildup and subsequent intensification of the fighting, most resources were devoted to the military effort which outwardly overshadowed the "other war." However, as the GVN regained political stability when Generals Nguyen Van Thieu and Nguyen Cao Ky were installed in power, pacification became again a matter of national priority with the creation of the Ministry of Rural Construction. During the Honolulu Conference of February 1966, RVN leaders expressed their special concern over pacification and the US promptly gave its commitment for additional support. Under the US-inspired idea of Revolutionary Development, the Ministry of Rural Construction (also called Revolutionary Development) headed by Major General Nguyen Duc Thang set about organizing cadre teams and establishing a large training center at Vung Tau for training personnel. At the same time, USAID channeled substantial funds into "New Life" development projects and also began helping the National Police activate its Field Police forces. Major General Edward G. Landsdale was designated by Ambassador Lodge as senior adviser to General Thang for the revolutionary development effort.

As US and RVNAF forces were gaining the upper hand in military operations across the country, US authorities also kept the pressure on the GVN to emphasize its pacification effort more vigorously. At the Manila Conference in October 1966, South Vietnamese leaders were willing to commit up to 60% of ARVN infantry battalions to the task of pacification support. The Combined Campaign Plan for 1967 (AB-142), translated this idea into action and formally assigned the primary mission of pacification support to the ARVN. Subsequently, ARVN infantry battalions underwent special training courses in pacification support in order to be able to carry out this mission more successfully.

Concurrently, on the US side, a significant effort was made to consolidate advisory and support activities. First, the Office of Civil Operations was created in late 1966. It was soon superseded by CORDS, a new civil-military organization which was made an integral part of the MACV command structure in May 1967. With the advent of CORDS, Vietnamese authorities found it easier to coordinate and cooperate. As US support for pacification was unified under a single-manager system, its relationship with the GVN pacification structure also became closer and more responsive.

Inspired by this move, the GVN instituted a system of interministerial Revolutionary Development (later redesignated Pacification and Development) Councils throughout the governmental hierarchy down to districts. At the central level, the fact that the council was chaired by the Prime Minister and later by the President of the Republic himself emphasized the national priority and duly gave pacification a strong incentive for progress. By mid-1969, the pacification and development (PD) councils at every level down to province were effectively assisted by centers for the coordination of PD which served as permanent staff organizations in charge of plans, coordination, and evaluation of pacification operations.

In retrospect, from the Vietnamese point of view, US contributions to pacification in South Vietnam were immense and all-incompassing. They covered all areas of endeavor and included every aspect of support, from financial and material to ideological and technological. Their impact on the program was far-reaching at all levels, in all areas of effort, and much of this credit must be given to the US pacification adviser.

By far the most important and outstanding among US contributions was the expansion and upgrading of the Regional and Popular Forces which in time made up over one half of the RVNAF total strength and became as modernized in armament as the regular forces. This achievement was directly attributable to CORDS authorities who untiringly worked toward developing the RF and PF and providing them adequate support. Upgrading the combat effectiveness of these forces was also a prominent program conducted with dedication by US advisers at provinces and districts and in RF/PF training centers. For many years, US mobile training teams — MATs and MALTs — tenaciously devoted themselves to their difficult task under the most spartan conditions and in the roughest areas of South Vietnam. Other cohesive efforts such as the Marines' Combined Action Program in MR-1 and pair-off or combined activities programs in MR-2 and MR-3 also significantly contributed to the marked improvement of territorial forces, the mainstay of security and pacification.

The next significant US contribution to pacification was the sizable expansion of national police forces which ranked among the most important elements of pacification. With USAID support, the national police developed into a formidable force, 121,000-man strong by 1972. Its combat elements, the field police units which were created in 1966, became the main operational force against the enemy infrastructure. Police advisers who were assigned to practically every aspect of policy operations, constantly strived to develop this para-military force into an effective instrument for the identification and destruction of the VC infrastructure.

Many other contributions made by US advisers directly or indirectly to the pacification effort were equally signficiant. They included civilian or para-military forces that US advisers helped activate, train and provide operational guidance; RD cadres; Provincial Reconnaissance Units (PRU); Census Grievance Teams; and more significant, the Civilian Irregular Defense Groups (CIDG).

The idea of forming RD cadres, a Communist-inspired concept, was adopted by US advisers and implemented with the backing of the CIA. The first RD cadre groups, characteristically enough, were activated in late 1965 with locally recruited youths in the province of Binh Dinh, a former stronghold of the Viet Minh for many years. US advisers also helped activate and train the Truong Son or Montagnard RD cadre. Two RD cadre training centers were established with American funds, support and advisers, one in Pleiku for the Truong Son cadre and the other in Vung Tau, the bigger of the two. The Vung Tau RD training center later became a national center for the training of village and hamlet administrative cadres. By 1968, total RD cadre strength including the Truong Son cadre numbered 50,000 but after 1970 this figure decreased when the Ministry of RD was dissolved.

Census grievance teams and provincial reconnaissance units were entirely an American creation. They were organized with the purpose of polling popular attitudes toward the GVN and carrying out unconventional activities required for the identification and elimination of the Communist infrastructure. PRUs were eventually placed under the control of the National Police to obtain desired results. Their members included some carefully selected personnel who were recruited from Communist ralliers.

The CIDG program was a substantial US effort to help organize and train Montagnards for the defense of border areas that dated back to the early years of the insurgency. These groups were a para-military force created in 1961 by the US Embassy with the purpose of rallying the support of and controlling the Montagnard tribal groups living in the central highlands and border areas. In 1962, US Special Forces detachments assumed the responsibility for training CIDGs but the program was turned over to MACV control as of 1963. Over the years, the CIDGs expanded considerably in strength, reaching a record high of 42,000 in 1968. Although they were a para-military force, CIDGs were well trained, well equipped and well supported. They also included in their ranks a number of ARVN deserters seeking higher pay and more adventure. In view of the traditional suspicion of Montagnard motives and the connection of a few CIDG units with the rebellious FULRO movement, the GVN was always concerned with this para-military force and even suspected the involvement of some US advisers in the CIDG rebellion which erupted in Ban Me Thuot in 1964. But as a combat force, the CIDGs contributed significantly to

the control of enemy infiltration routes along the border. This was
one reason why the GVN did not oppose the presence of this separate
military force which it did not initially control. To resolve the political sensitivity of this problem, MACV eventually transferred the CIDGs
to GVN control. CIDG troopers subsequently became rangers or regional
troops and were integrated into the RVNAF.[4]

Throughout the years of the war in South Vietnam, US forces undoubtedly contributed much to the pacification effort, directly or indirectly,
through tactical operations on the ground, in the air, or at sea and
by providing combat support to ARVN forces such as helilift, gunships,
medical evacuation, and helping destroy and clear enemy base areas. As
to US advisers, although they did not participate significantly in all
pacification activities such as the People's Self Defense Force program,
there were specific areas of pacification which could not have been successfully undertaken by the GVN without their assistance and contributions.

The Phoenix program was an excellent example. Eliminating the enemy
infrastructure had been a major concern and objective of the GVN since
the beginning of insurgency. But the program had lacked cohesiveness,
purposefulness and an efficient organization. At the instigation of
US authorities associated with CORDS, the Phoenix program was initiated
with a view to consolidate and provide a more effective effort against
the VCI. But even after Phoenix was established at the central level,
it would have been extremely difficult to activate in the provinces and
districts had it not been for the contributions made by US pacification
advisers in terms of facilities and resources. For the PIOCC and DIOCC,
for example, US advisers in addition to their regular duties even had
to supply the typewriters and typists. Despite assistance and guidance
provided by US advisers, the National Police, primary executor of the
program, did not appear to be effective enough for the task at hand.
A major shortcoming was the lack of specialized cadre, chiefly in the

---

[4]The primary role of CIDG, strike-forces and border security, is discussed on p. 51.

Special Police branch which was responsible for collecting information and identifying members of the enemy infrastructure. All efforts at solving this and other shortcomings of the program were never completely successful.

Other pacification-related programs such as Chieu Hoi and most particularly, refugee relief and resettlement, and land reform benefited substantially from US support and the work of US advisers. The Chieu Hoi (Open Arms) program was rather a slow starter in the RVN anti-subversive effort because of the rigid anti-Communist stand adopted by the Diem administration which outlawed Communism altogether and also because of the lack of resources. The program became a full-fledged effort only after 1963 when through US advisers, the GVN learned that the Philippine amnesty policy had produced handsome dividends. The RVN Chieu Hoi effort made excellent progress after 1967 when a ministry was created to give it cohesive direction. In this effort to win over the enemy, the Joint US Public Affairs Office (JUSPAO) made substantial material contributions, helped print and drop leaflets, conducted broadcasts and provided money for the ralliers. The US also provided funds for the establishment of Chieu Hoi centers and vocational training courses. As a result, the number of enemy personnel rallying to the GVN side increased steadily and reached an all-time high (47,000) in 1969. Over the years of its existence, the program resulted in a total of over 200,000 ralliers, which was a remarkable return for the costs involved.

But US contributions were even greater in the relief and resettlement of refugees and the land reform program. As the fighting intensified in 1965 and during the following years, the number of refugees also increased manyfold. With its meager resources, the GVN was unable to handle this growing influx of refugees in a satisfactory manner without US support. The direct participation of US combat troops in the war led US authorities to take a greater interest in the refugee problem. With increasing financial and material aid from the US government and private US charity organizations, the GVN built camp facilities, and brought relief to and helped resettle millions of refugees. The biggest inflows of refugees happened during 1968 and 1972, the years of Communist general offensives, reaching a record high of nearly four million in 1972. US financial contributions amounted to approximately $100 million every year but were gradually reduced after 1971. Still, they made up about 80% of total GVN budgetary outlays for refugee relief and resettlement.

The land reform program which was regarded as an unprecedented and most resounding success was partially the product of studies and research conducted by US experts who advised the GVN. The resulting "Land to the Tiller" act which was proclaimed on 26 March 1970, sought to distribute about 1 million hectares (2.47 million acres) of farmland to landless farmers within a period of 3 years. Three years later, this objective had been met on schedule. The GVN paid out a total of 15 billion piasters in cash and another 82 billion piasters in bonds to land owners. The rapidity with which this ambitious program was successfully implemented was largely attributable to the effective assistance provided by US expert-advisers in the areas of land survey and cost computation. In addition, the United States provided over $500 million for the entire program, and more importantly, made certain that its advisers at the province and district levels helped guide the land distribution and compensation effort to success.

Aside from these more conspicuous achievements of pacification attained with US money and advisory assistance, there were imperceptible but no less beneficial contributions that helped the RVN administration and armed forces improve their day to day operations and bring more scientific knowledge to bear on the conduct of national affairs. The progressive reforms in management and administration achieved throughout the RVN governmental hierarchy were but one of many examples. By exposure to American methodology and procedures, GVN officials learned how to apply modern management techniques to their own operations. And to keep up with the rapid pace of American business practice, GVN agencies naturally had to adjust their own routine so as not to be left behind in the race toward common objectives. The constant stimulation and encouragement of US advisers were largely responsible for this marked improvement. As a result, the traditional functionary lethargy of colonial times was deeply shaken and gradually gave way to a much more efficient bureaucracy in every aspect.

The same learning and adaptation process was the major reason for improvement in planning by the military staffs at the JGS and field levels. Several years had elapsed since the CI plan of 1960 and the Comprehensive Plan for South Vietnam of 1962 were published before the RVNAF conceived and developed a program worth calling a national plan. The first cohesive planning effort, the Victory Plan of 1964, although militarily oriented, led the way toward comprehensive planning on a national scale for the years that followed. Successive Combined Campaign Plans, initially drafted by the MACV staff and subsequently by the JGS, gradually bore testimony to the improving RVNAF planning capabilities. Without the cooperative guidance of US advisers, this improvement would never have been achieved. Beginning in 1968, pacification planning came of age and was perfected with every passing year. The most notable national-scale product was the Four-Year Community Defense and Local Development Plan, 1972-1975, an effort which was entirely Vietnamese but bearing the indelible mark of several years of US contributions.

Another very significant contribution by the CORDS staff and US pacification advisers that radically improved the assessment of pacification progress was the modern evaluation system which used scientific analytical methods and advanced operations research technology. The problem included the requirement to effectively manage and evaluate complex pacification operations conducted under scores of programs and encompassing 44 provinces, 250 districts, over 2,000 villages and 10,000 hamlets, all with the participation and support of hundreds of thousands of troops, policemen and cadres. It was obvious that only scientific management methods and timely reporting procedures could help our Vietnamese leaders fully understand the situation throughout South Vietnam and make appropriate decisions. Responding to this critical requirement, CORDS experts and advisers carefully and methodically developed several evaluation and reporting systems, all in apparent cross-connection with one another and covering almost every area of pacification-related activities: PSDF, Chieu Hoi, National Police, Refugees, RD Cadre, Information, Self-Help projects, land reform, Communist terrorism, and Territorial Force Management. A pacification data bank was established in Saigon to store the

experience of several years of performance. Among the systems used to
assist in the evaluation of territorial forces was the MACV originated
Territorial Forces Evaluation System. The advisers furnished the data
for this system which provided ARVN commanders with reasonably valid
assessments of progress and shortcomings in the territorial forces.
But the most noteworthy and more important was perhaps the Hamlet
Evaluation System (HES). Despite some adverse criticism, this system
proved the best and most valuable tool ever devised for the purpose of
efficiently managing a program as complex as pacification. Not only
did it contribute to a better evaluation and management of pacification,
it also taught our Vietnamese pacification authorities more about their
overall program.

I have presented in general terms and from the Vietnamese point of
view some of the most discernible contributions made by United States
advisers to the pacification program in South Vietnam. Most of these
contributions, although made at top levels, had a major impact in the
field. But at the field level, there was another aspect of US contributions, more human and personal in nature, where the United States
pacification adviser was personally assisting his counterpart in solving
daily problems.

At the corps level, US contributions were more evident in that they
complemented admirably the inherent shortcomings of ARVN commanders and
staffs with regard to pacification. Long the participants of a continuous, armed but predominantly ideological conflict, many ARVN field
commanders had become, strangely enough, strictly professional, mili-
tarily-minded soldiers. Although there was nothing wrong with this, it
seemed that the many lessons learned concerning pacification during both
the First Indochina War, 1946-1954, and the years of counter-insurgency
in South Vietnam were all forgotten by them. Most ARVN field commanders
acted as if they were totally detached from the problems of pacification
and concerned themselves solely with military matters. The truth was,
after fighting alongside US units, ARVN commanders and their staffs had
become more professional in an orthodox manner and had successfully
mastered the modern tactics of conventional warfare, but they were

woefully inadequate as contestants of the "other war." For one thing, pacification demanded much more than the ability to use conventional military techniques and tactics. It required from military commanders a strong awareness of the political and socio-psychological problems involved in winning the battle of the "hearts and minds" or at least an attitude favorably disposed toward these problems. Consequently, under such leadership, ARVN Corps staffs were hardly prepared to tackle the complex tasks of pacification without constant assistance and guidance from a well qualified US adviser.

Another glaring deficiency was the ARVN Corps staff's weakness in the ability to conduct addquate planning for the military support of pacification and the review of provincial pacification plans. This weakness was attributable to the fact that most ARVN Corps commanders were neither demanding enough nor endowed with planning habits. Inevitably, when staff studies or evaluations were desired ARVN staffs were not qualified to produce desired results. Some attributed this to the lack of training and the inadequacy of an educational system which did not emphasize research and analysis. Regardless of the reason, it appeared that most ARVN officers were not prepared for the planning task nor were they required by their commanders to think and plan ahead. The presence of US advisers, however, immediately assisted in correcting this shortcoming. Initially in many cases, they drew up plans for the benefit of the ARVN staffs who simply adapted them for ARVN purposes. But through constant exposure to and learning from US advisers, ARVN staffs gradually improved and became entirely self-reliant when US advisers were no longer available. This is one example of the productive aspect of a close personal relationship which existed at those levels of the ARVN hierarchy requiring staff work and planning. *(Chart 13)*

With respect to operations and management, US advisers also assisted in filling most gaps found on the Vietnamese side. Because of close cooperation with US advisers and commanders, ARVN commanders were able to discharge their duties in a more satisfactory manner. Thanks to accurate reports such as HES and periodic evaluations of pacification, ARVN commanders had a clearer view of the situation and could better

Chart 13 — Advisory Relationships, ARVN Hierarchy

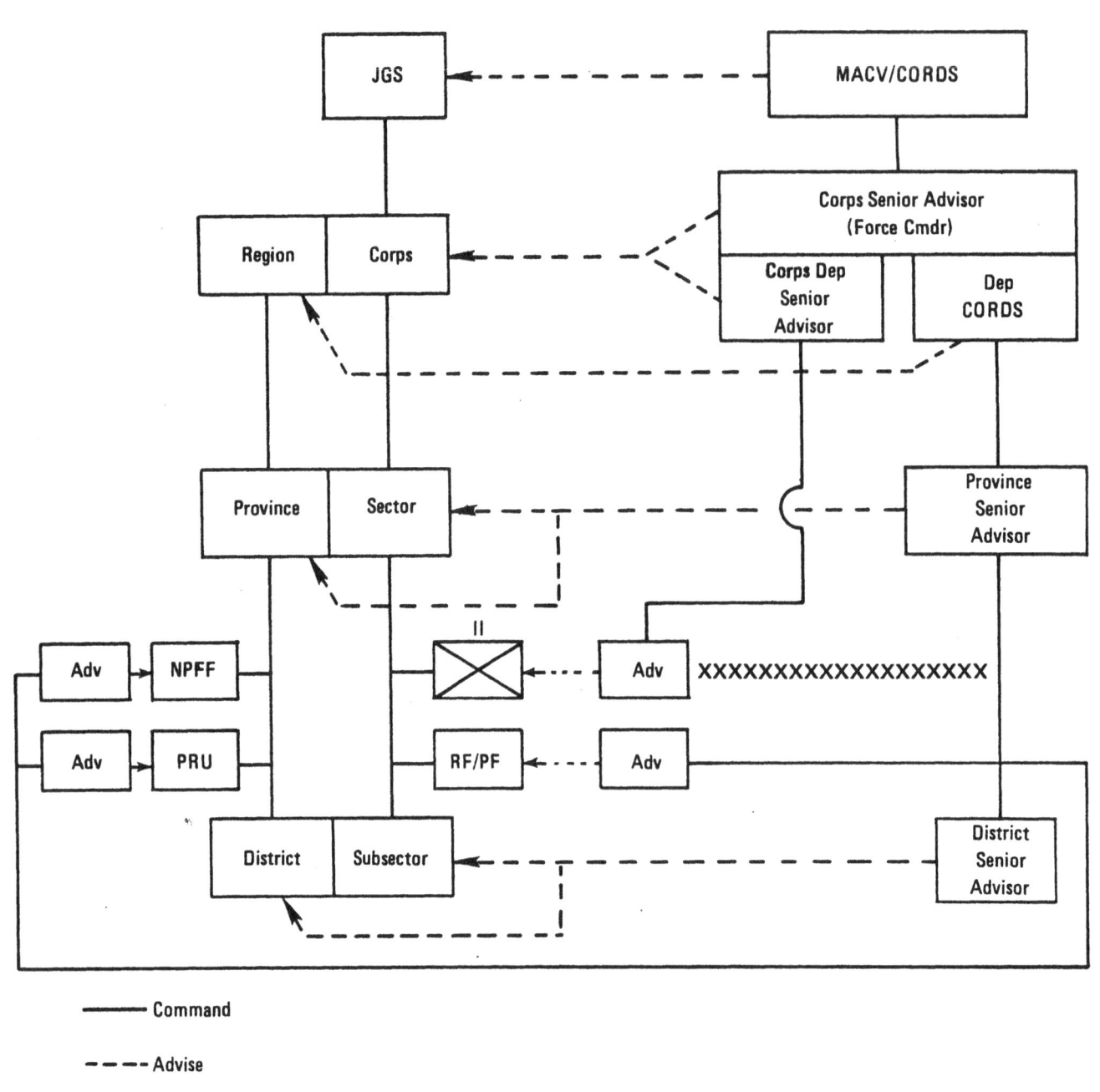

determine what actions to take. This was the result of mutual support and the exchange of information between CORDS and the Corps Center for Coordination of Pacification and Development. Regional CORDS staffs were usually creative and always planned ahead for every foreseeable requirement. Therefore, they sometimes seemed to lead the way for their ARVN counterparts by presenting them with drafted plans to include recommendations for consideration.

For the pacification program, the province and the district were the key levels in the command and control structure. The success of the entire program depended on the success of the Vietnamese and their advisers at these two echelons. The district was the lowest level to have the benefit of US advisers. The province was the level which was responsible both for planning and execution. In terms of US-RVN cooperation, it seemed that the lower the level, the closer the relationship. Indeed, it seemed that the province chief, the district chief, and their advisers were always together and it was a rarity when a province chief or a district chief was seen making visits without his adviser. Their close cooperation was reflected in every phase of pacification activities to include staff planning, determination of objectives and requirements, employment of forces and assets, follow-up, evaluation and field inspections.

The Vietnamese province chief was usually a senior, combat-experienced officer. Several of them stayed in office for many years. Therefore, they were very familiar with their provinces and were highly capable as leaders and administrators. But the province senior adviser, except for those few who came back for a second or third tour of duty, was seldom familiar with the local environment and since the majority of them were military officers, they would usually confine themselves to military matters. By and large, however, the province US advisory staff, especially provincial CORDS, was usually much more capable than the sector staff or the provincial bureaucratic staff. The reasons for this were the same as mentioned above. In addition, at the province-sector level, staff members were for the most part Regional Force officers and the few regular officers who served at that level were usually the unwanted black sheep

of the ARVN family. The employment of forces and resources at the
province level was also a very complex task in view of its extensiveness.
Finally, the province chief was usually busy with his many responsibilities
and could not devote enough time for any particular area of major interest,
whether it be military, political, social or economic.

At the district level, the situation was even more difficult. The
district staff was usually limited and inexperienced. It was routine
to find that the more remote district headquarters would always have the
most problems with pacification. Apart from a few experienced and capable
field-grade officers, most district chiefs were young officers. Although
their youth provided a certain enthusiastic, gung-ho approach to their
jobs, they were usually not qualified for the task of managing a sizable
pacification apparatus comprising an average of from 3 to 6 RF companies,
40 PF platoons, and a few thousand PSDF, not to speak of hundreds of
village and hamlet officials, RD cadre, policemen, and other people's
organizations. A district chief, like his superior at the province,
was faced with myriad tasks, from combat operations, hamlet security,
to Phoenix activities and developmental projects in every imaginable
area of endeavor. The presence of district advisers, therefore, was
most useful. District advisers were usually military officers but
performed the dual role of military and civilian advisers. Many district
advisers succeeded in developing an excellent rapport with the local
population; they were well liked and respected.

In general, the presence of US pacification advisers at the province
and district levels effectively increased the local government's capabilities of managing complex tasks, and made the employment of forces
and resources more effective for the pacification effort. The presence
of US advisers at these levels also indicated that support from US forces
was readily available on call, whatever the purpose. Finally, until
they were removed from the scene, US advisers constituted the main source
of stimulation, incentive for better performance and more devotion by
all Vietnamese concerned with the pacification program.

Some Lessons Learned

United States involvement in Vietnam spanned two long decades, progressing from providing materiel and economic aid to active participation by its own combat troops, all for the purpose of helping South Vietnam counter Communist aggression. In terms of pacification and development, the progress made by the RVN over the years had its ups and downs depending on the tempo of the hot war and United States interest and emphasis concerning the other war. If there were depressing periods such as the first insurgent war years, 1960-1961, the hopeless deterioration of 1964-1965 and the tense months during 1968 and 1972, there were also brighter times when pacification seemed to have firmly stood on the pedestal of glorious success. The short-lived Strategic Hamlet program, 1962-1963, for example, despite its shortcomings and modest US support really reflected the way for effective counterinsurgency. For some time, it succeeded in depriving the Communist fish of some of its water, but it was only a modest achievement. The next period 1966-1967 saw the military initiative and advantage firmly held by US-Free World-RVNAF combat forces who gradually drove enemy main force units across the border and prepared the stage for pacification to proceed. But four long years had elapsed during which the other war seemed to have been completely forsaken. Pacification was given a new and positive start in 1967 and its momentum was accelerating when the enemy chose to launch the Tet general offensive of 1968. This major effort by the enemy again delayed the pacification program. However, new hopes were restored in 1969 and during the following years, conditions in the countryside radically improved and prospects for the future were never so bright. Under the protective shield of military advantage, the total pacification effort was making rapid progress throughout all of South Vietnam. What lessons then could be learned from our experience? What in fact were the merits and demerits of the advisory effort at the field and local levels which were the main battlegrounds where the pacification war was fought?

First and foremost, the United States organization for pacification support, CORDS, proved to be an elaborate, efficient structure which was resourceful and flexible enough to meet all requirements, current and foreseeable, generated by the double war in South Vietnam. The commander, USMACV, who exercised exclusive control of all combat assets for the miltiary war, also had at his disposal the resources with which to fight the other war which was more political and socio-psychological in nature. From the Vietnamese point of view the consolidation of command and control over both military and civilian resources under the USMACV commander was a sound and productive concept. Our experience seemed to indicate that although under military control, CORDS had enough flexibility and delegated authority to meet all requirements effectively.

Next, the ubiquitous US advisory presence in all provinces and districts was a most realistic and effective response to an emergency situation in which the enemy had made inroads into practically every corner of the countryside. When the United States brought in combat troops, the so-called "war of liberation" waged by the Communists had entered its phase of mobile warfare. Most of the South Vietnamese rural areas had by then become cancerous tumors in which the Viet Cong infrastructure cells were eating away at the GVN control body. The best that a conventional military force could do under such circumstances was to push back and defeat the predators, the NVA main forces units. But the scavengers — the VCI and the guerrillas — were still there. To join in the battle of clearing the countryside, restoring security, and reestablishing control, the presence of US advisers at all local levels was indeed a vital necessity. As has been said, the ARVN basic weakness in leadership and staff work, particularly in connection with the pacification effort, could have only been offset by the US advisers whose involvement rapidly turned the tide in favor of the GVN.

A common observation among ARVN commanders and province and district chiefs was that a US adviser in pacification was really effective only when he began his second tour of duty. It was true that generally speaking, most advisers needed a certain familiarization period after arriving in the country. This period of time depended on the nature of the assignment and the environment. Not only was Vietnam a totally alien country, the nature of the war being fought there was also unfamiliar to American military experience. While US officers assigned to staff duties were able to perform satisfactorily as advisers during their short first tours, it appeared that senior advisers at all levels and key positions could have contributed much more to the common effort had they stayed longer in a single tour or better still, returned to the old scene for additional tours. A pacification adviser's role was usually all encompassing. To be truly efficient and productive in every aspect of that role, a living experience was required. One year was certainly not enough to acquire that experience.

Before his assignment, a US officer selected for pacification advisory duties had to undergo a brief orientation course on Vietnam. He was given a fast glimpse of Vietnamese history and culture and the war at the grass-roots level. This preparatory work was useful for all advisers. But for advisers assigned to the pacification program, especially those expected to have contact with the local population, it was not enough. Pacification advisers at the province and district levels should have been required to speak the language too, because this was the only means of obtaining an insight into the local problems of pacification and developing the kind of rapport with the local people that was conducive to success. Although US advisers could usually communicate with their counterparts in English, they were always at a disadvantage when meeting with the local population and GVN officials in villages and hamlets. Experience showed that even with a smattering of conversational Vietnamese, a US adviser could always establish instant rapport and affection. The ability to speak the language, therefore, was a most effective tool of winning the battle of the "hearts and minds."

Finally, because of constant exposure to the local population who for the most part lived under the most spartan conditions, there was a requirement for US advisers to be modest and self-effacing in their way of life and work. Not only were the Vietnamese extremely sensitive to the presence of foreigners, they were also self-conscious about their condition. The reputation of the American adviser among them was made even more difficult by vicious slanderings of Communist propaganda. Although not every adviser was expected to live as a Vietnamese, it certainly helped him mix with people more easily if he cautiously concealed the material opulence of the American way of life. With his counterparts, it was important that he exercise tact and persuasion instead of leverage to get things done, because no Vietnamese could stand a loss of face. The best approach for any adviser was to mention a problem, let his counterpart think about it and in the process, inject suggestive ideas as to how he thought the problem could best be solved. After this process was completed the adviser should then let the Vietnamese voluntarily initiate actions as if they were his own ideas. In this way, a counterpart would be more inclined to listen to his adviser since his authority as a leader was not impaired.

In general, apart from a very few exceptions, all US advisers assigned to the pacification program at all levels discharged their responsibilities in a most admirable way. Many were highly respected and well liked. Over the years, several individual relationships developed into lasting personal friendships. Taken together, all of these individual performances contributed to the overall success of the US advisory effort, especially with regard to pacification. Credit for much of the success of pacification, in the final analysis, must be given to US advisers with a special tribute to those at the district and province levels.

CHAPTER VII

The Training Adviser

A Monumental Achievement

Lieutenant Colonel Robert Murphy, a crew-cut, dark-tanned tall man with a Texan drawl and in khaki shorts reported to the Inter-Arms School of Thu Duc in February, 1955. A lone figure among the dozen or so French instructors who still remained there, he really did not know where to begin. He did not speak French and the commandant of the school did not speak English. A young Vietnamese instructor who spoke English well was called upon to help them eliminate the language barrier, but the communication process was slow. However, only a short time later, Colonel Murphy accompanied Vietnamese instructors in the field where he demonstrated, using sign language, marksmanship techniques and the correct use of the Garand M-1. Thus was the beginning of a long training assistance program which would terminate eighteen years later. Colonel Murphy was one of the first US training advisers assigned to the nascent Vietnamese National Armed Forces and a pioneer for the many Americans who would subsequently assume similar responsibilities.

Less than a year before, when all troops of the 3d Military Region had regrouped from North Vietnam after the Geneva Armistice, the Vietnam National Armed Forces numbered about 210,000 men, including nearly 40,000 regular troops. Predominantly army, this force consisted basically of infantry battalions, some of them grouped into larger tactical formations, the mobile groups, a French organizational concept.[1] Most of the Vietnamese mobile group and battalion commanders came from the

---

[1] There were two mobile groups, the 31st and 32d.

French Union forces where most had started as non-commissioned officers. Only a few had graduated from the first Reserve Officer Candidate School activated when the partial mobilization law became effective in 1951. These few young officers of the new generation later became key leaders of the armed forces and the nation, but regardless of their origin, they had been trained by French cadre and had learned the military doctrine and tactics of the French Expeditionary Corps.

During this period the basic infantry armament of the Vietnamese National Armed Forces consisted of World War II vintage and older weapons of assorted types from America, France and England. Combat Support assets were few, ineffective and included 105-mm howitzer battalions and four armor squadrons which were equipped only with AM-8 scout cars and half-tracks. At this time the Air Force and Navy were insignificant, embryonic forces, numbering about 4,000 men each, equipped with a few trainers and transports and small landing craft and river boats, all turned over by French forces.

The first task given the Training Relations and Instructions Mission (TRIM) created under MAAG was enormous since it involved reorganizing, refitting and re-training a sizable military force in accordance with US Army doctrine and tactics. First priority was given to trimming down this force to a manageable and supportable peace-time level of 150,000, a move that received strong opposition from the Vietnamese General Staff which was hard-pressed with problems of surplus auxiliary troops and operations against dissident sects. A second priority involved a longer range process of upgrading the battalion-based Army of the Republic of Vietnam (ARVN) into a modern force composed of major, self-supporting units, capable of assuring internal security and countering an overt invasion from North Vietnam. Influenced by lessons of the Korean War, the Chief MAAG, Lieutenant General John W. O'Daniel and his staff advocated the activation of divisions tailored to the local environment and requirements. His opinion was not fully shared by several key members of the Vietnamese General Staff who thought that a more flexible type of unit, such as the mobile group, would be more responsive to the kind of war that would probably be fought should aggression occur. MAAG's insistence on the division prevailed but a compromise was reached with the activation of "light" divisions, a stripped-down version of the "field" or regular division. The search for the optimal division continued into the following years, and finally, after many tests and trials, the 10,500-man infantry division was selected in 1957 as the major unit for the ARVN.

After this basic pattern for organization had been established, subsequent force structure increases simply added more combat support assets to the infantry division, activated more divisions and their tactical control headquarters, the corps. As reorganization progressed, ARVN units also became uniformly equipped with standard US equipment and armament and trained in US Army doctrine and tactics. In 1961, as insurgent activities increased, the United States began to introduce combat support assets, mainly airlift and helilift, to augment ARVN mobility and limited tactical air support of combat operations. Support and training assistance for the Republic of Vietnam Armed Forces (RVNAF) increased most significantly when the auxiliary Regional and Popular Forces (formerly Civil Guard and People's Militia) became eligible under the Military Assistance Program (MAP) as an integral part of the RVNAF. And in keeping with subsequent increases in military aid under various improvement and modernization plans, the RVNAF gradually expanded, both in force structure and in combat support assets, reaching a total strength of 435,000 by the end of 1964.

This expansion and modernization trend accelerated significantly following the Tet offensive of 1968, resulting in new weapons for the RVNAF arsenal and the addition of several new units to the force structure. But this trend was accelerated most dramatically by the momentum provided by the Vietnamization program, officially announced in 1969, which ultimately brought the RVNAF total strength to 1.1 million by the end of 1972. By this time, the RVNAF had become the largest and most modern military force in Southeast Asia, equipped with over one million M-16 rifles and M-60 machineguns, over 1,500 armored vehicles, including M-48 medium tanks and over 1,500 pieces of artillery, including long range 175-mm guns. The Vietnamese Air Force in the meantime had

U.S. Adviser Instructing ARVN Troops on Helilift Procedures (March, 1962)

ARVN Paratroopers in Combat Assault Training, 1966

increased in strength to 61,000, equipped with over 1,700 aircraft of all types, including about 500 UH-1 helicopters. The Navy had also expanded its strength to 41,000 and controlled about 1,600 ships and craft of various sizes.

During these eighteen years of dramatic development, the RVNAF had been transformed into a modern combat force, total strength increased more than fivefold and new organizations, doctrine and operational techniques adopted. In terms of human effort and material support, this achievement surpassed anything the United States had contributed to any country since the end of the Korean War. Throughout this period the United States training adviser played a major role and made a most significant contribution to the RVN Armed Forces. As a former Division G-3, Corps G-3 and the last J-3 for the RVNAF Joint General Staff, a position I held for seven years, I was personally involved daily in the improvement and effectiveness of the RVNAF and will present from the Vietnamese point of view an evaluation of the US training adviser as he performed his challenging assignment.

Organization for Training and Training Support

To accomplish its mission during the continuous process of expansion and modernization of the RVNAF, the ARVN school system grew and developed considerably over the years. From a skeletal frame of small service schools and local training centers, this system developed into a complete array of modern facilities accommodating well over 100,000 students at any one time. RVNAF training facilities fell into three major categories: (1) military and service schools, of which there were 33; *(Map 1)* (2) national and regional training centers (for ARVN and territorial forces, respectively), of which there were 13, *(Map 2)* and; (3) divisional training centers, of which there were 14, to include the Airborne Ranger Group Training Center.

This extensive system of schools and training centers was under the control and supervision of the RVNAF Central Training Command (CTC). This major command was established in 1966 to replace our Training Bureau in an effort to consolidate training functions and provide better training support. The CTC was advised and supported by the MACV Training Direc-

Map 1 — Location, Military Academies and Service Schools

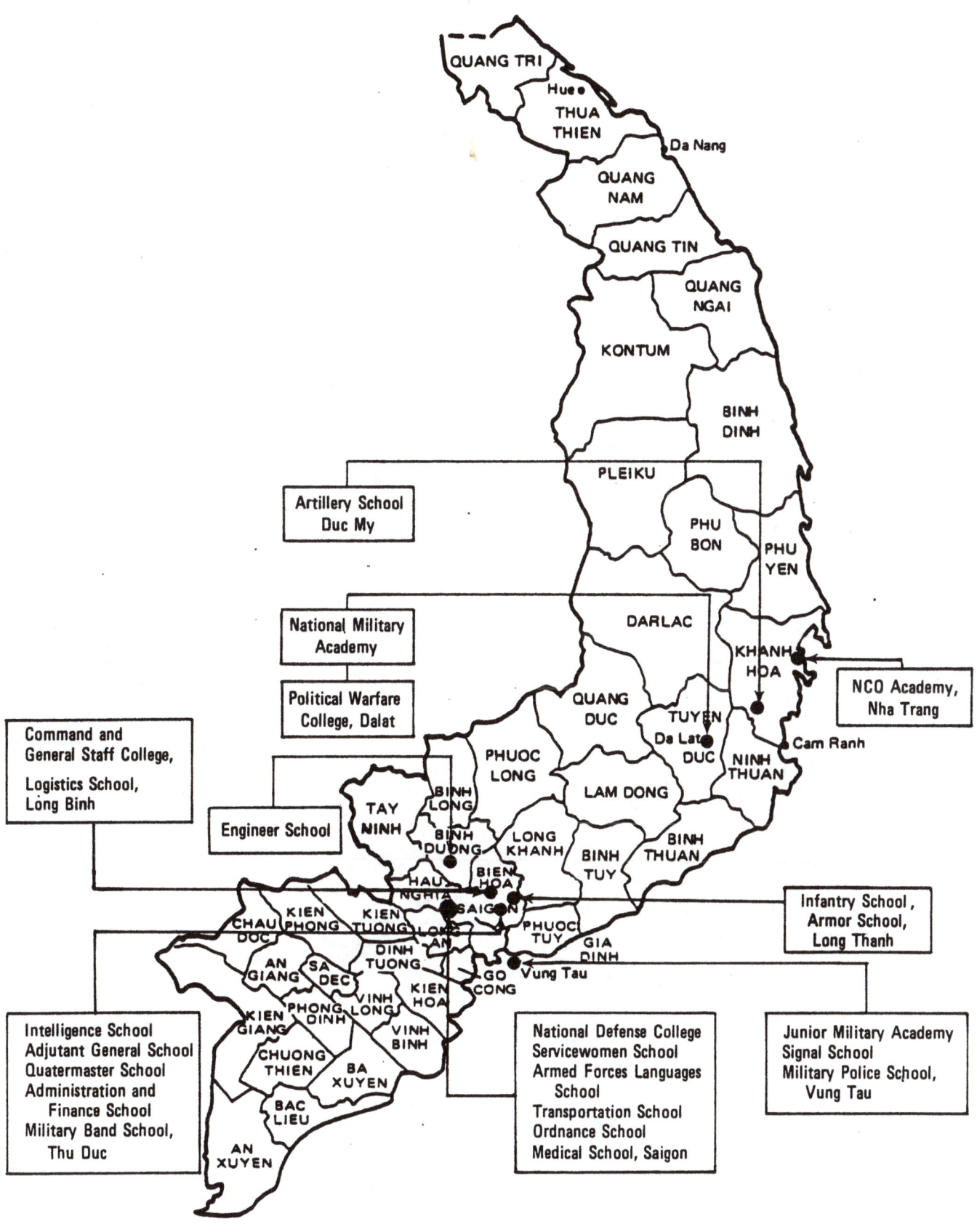

163

Map 2 — Location, National and Territorial Force Training Centers

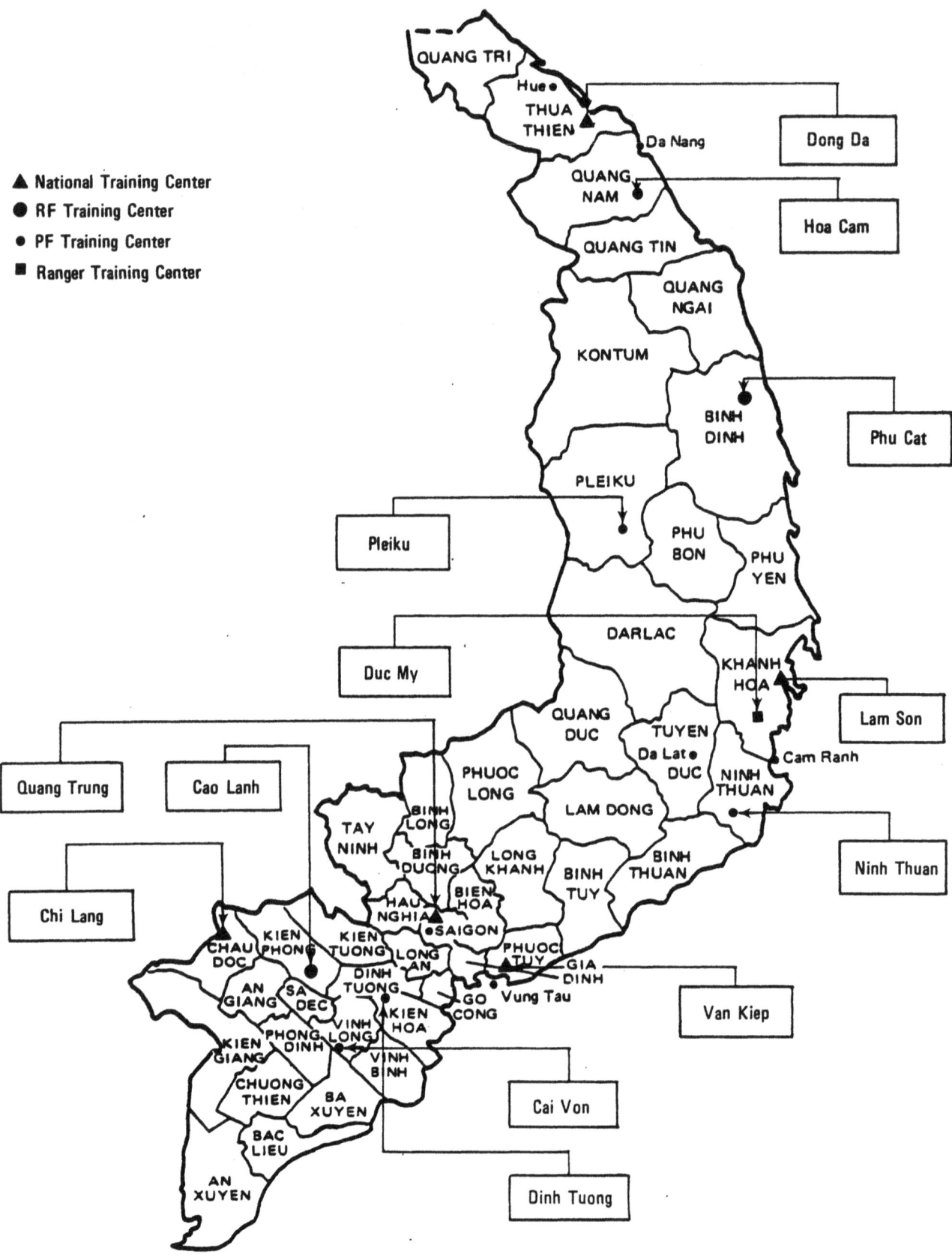

164

torate whose staff divisions paralleled the major supervisory functions performed by the CTC except for direct advisory and training support for the Armor, Artillery and Ranger Commands. *(Chart 14)* The CTC training support functions were performed by two permanent committees, one for Doctrine and Manuals and other for Battlefield Studies in addition to a Training Aids Center, which were all part of its organization. *(Chart 15)*

The CTC commander was responsible for all matters pertaining to training and training support in the RVNAF, including (1) plans, policies and programs for the training of RVNAF regular and territorial forces, combat arms and services and para-military forces; (2) development and modernization of training facilities; (3) preparation of ARVN military doctrine, manuals and training materials for the school system; (4) research of combat experience and development of tactics; (5) conduct of special training courses as required, demonstrations and field exercises, marksmanship competition; and (6) programming of offshore training courses and selection of students.[2]

The Director of Training, MACV was the principal adviser to the Commander, CTC and coordinator of the United States training advisory effort. To assist the latter in performing his duties, the Director of Training, MACV, was responsible for: (1) providing advice and assistance in the development of an effective military training system for the RVNAF, to include evolving doctrine and training literature, annual training ammunition requirements, training budget and facilities development programming; (2) planning, preparing, and executing the Army portion of the military assistance training programs; (3) coordinating training matters involving combined US and RVNAF participation and exercising coordinating authority over the MACV advisory effort on RVNAF training matters, and; (4) providing advice and assistance in the organization, training and utilization of the Armor, Artillery and Ranger Forces.

---

[2]The commander of CTC exercised control and supervision over most training centers and schools. Exceptions were made in cases where the center or school was commanded by an officer senior in rank to the CTC commander. In these cases, such as the Thu Duc Training Center and the CGSC, the commandants reported directly to the Chief, JGS. Nevertheless, the CTC commander supported and inspected these facilities on behalf of the chief, JGS. The source of the information on the CTC was an interview with Lieutenant General Nguyen Bao Tri, the last commander of CTC.

Chart 14 — Organization, MACV Training Directorate

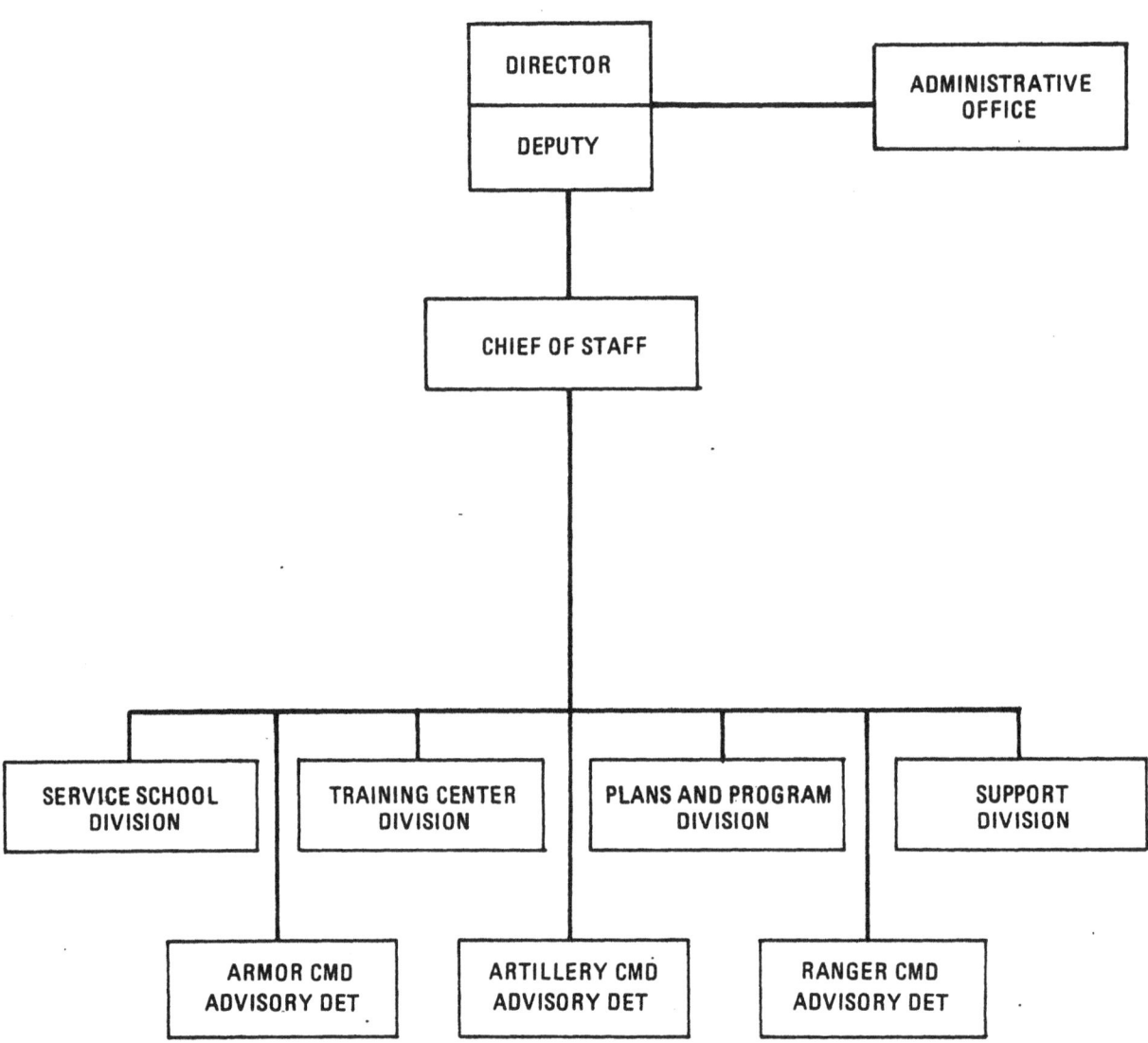

Chart 15 — Organization, Central Training Command

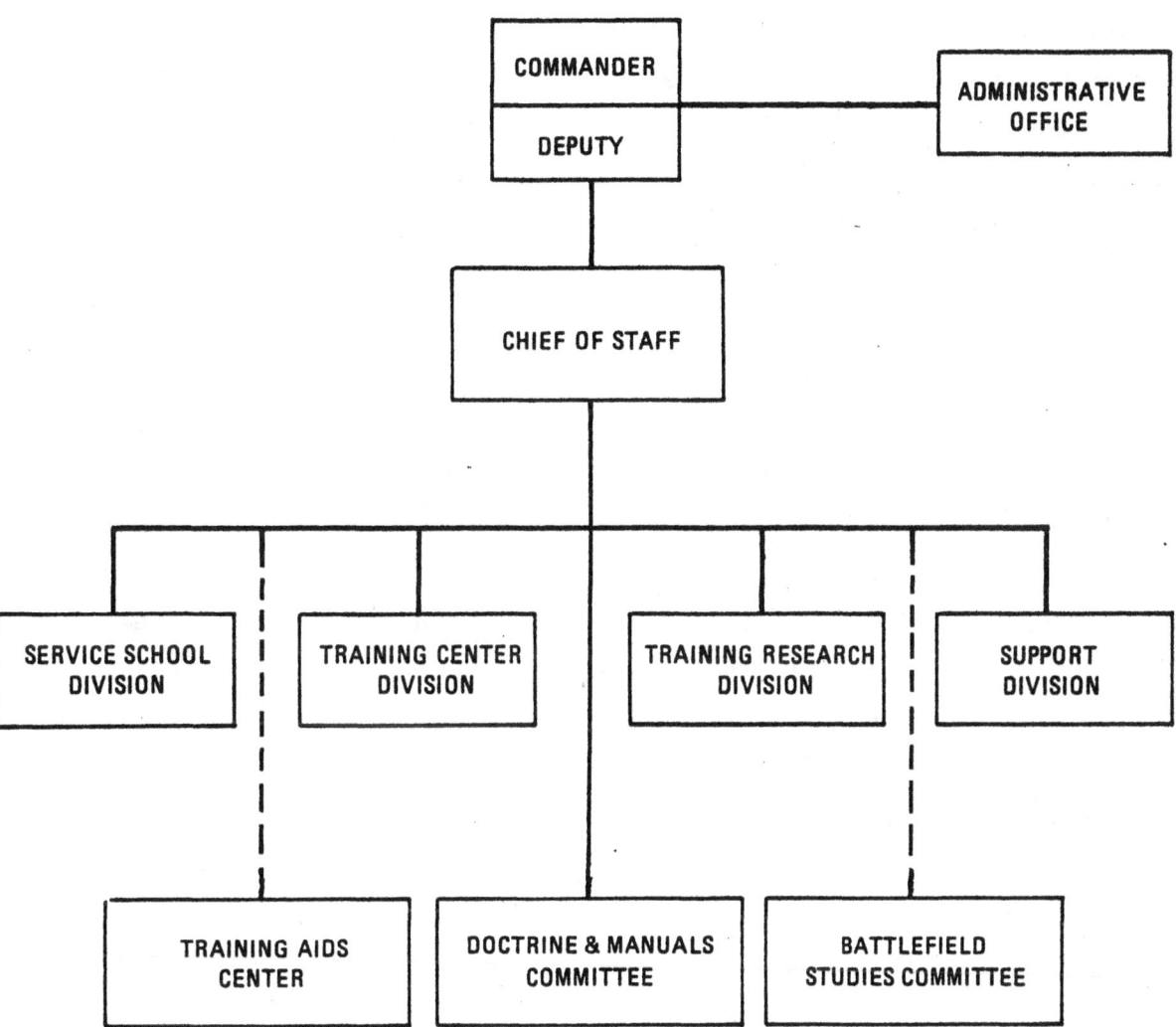

167

For the convenience of advising the CTC and coordinating the US training advisory effort with RVNAF training activities, the MACV Training Directorate was located adjacent to the Central Training Command in the Joint General Staff compound from where it exercised coordinating authority over US advisory teams, fixed and mobile, detached to ARVN service schools and training centers. In full cooperation and coordination, the CTC and MACV Training Directorate jointly developed plans, policies and programs for the training of both ARVN regular and territorial forces and for the development and improvement of ARVN training facilities. At the schools and training centers, US advisory teams assisted ARVN commandants in preparing and conducting training programs and monitored the progress and results achieved.

Training Advisory Activities

The training of leadership cadre and specialists for the Vietnamese Armed Forces began in earnest in early 1955 in conjunction with the reorganization process. In order to familiarize ARVN officers and NCOs with US Army doctrine, operational techniques and methods, an effort was made by TRIM, then CATO, to send selected personnel (English proficiency was the primary requirement) to US service schools beginning in July 1955, except for intelligence students who attended special courses in the Philippines. At about the same time, a Command and Staff course was initiated by US advisers at the 1st Training Center (later redesignated Quang Trung) for Vietnamese field-grade officers with the objective of introducing more senior personnel to US doctrine and tactics.

One of the major problems for the training advisory effort during this early period was language. Except for a very limited number, the only foreign language most ARVN officers spoke was French, and that with varying degrees of proficiency. The selection of students for US service schools, necessarily based on English proficiency, was very limited. The first contingent of ARVN officers who attended US service schools during the second half of 1955, for example, totaled only a dozen. To provide training for a greater number of ARVN officers, it was decided in early 1955 to send officer-interpreters to some US service schools such as the US Army Infantry School at Fort Benning, Georgia, the Signal School at Fort Monmouth, New Jersey and the Artillery School at Fort Sill, Oklahoma. Concurrently, US advisers attached to Vietnamese schools and major units began giving English lessons on an improvised basis and with the encouragement of the MAAG, a large scale effort was made by the Vietnamese General Staff to conduct English courses at the Language School, established in 1957. The period from 1955 to 1969, therefore, was devoted primarily to training instructors for the ARVN school system since it received priority assignment of ARVN officers returning from US schools. During this period, over 5,000 ARVN officers and NCOs received training in the United States in addition to 952 others who were given short orientation tours.

Next to the need of introducing US Army doctrine and tactics to the ARVN leadership, and training instructors for the ARVN school system, there was a requirement to expand and improve the ARVN school system which had been established, equipped and turned over by French forces. When French representation departed in 1956, there were only six major training facilities for the entire Vietnamese Armed Forces, including the Military Academy of Dalat and the Inter-Arms School of Thu Duc. With US support and adviser assistance, only two years later the number of ARVN training facilities had increased to 18.

The next decade, 1958-1968, saw a rapid expansion of the ARVN school system whose facilities increased manyfold. This expansion was made possible by US funds channeled into the Military Assistance Service Funded/Military Construction Program (MASF/MILCON). The year 1968 was a significant milestone of this construction program since, in keeping with the rapid increase in force structure, the RVNAF were provided funds to proceed with the large-scale building of training centers not only for the ARVN but also for the RF and PF. By the time the program was completed, there was a RF and PF training center for almost every province of the RVN, and the total ARVN-RF/PF training center system throughout the country was capable of handling up to 12,000 students at any one time, a six-fold increase over the capacity of the previous decade.

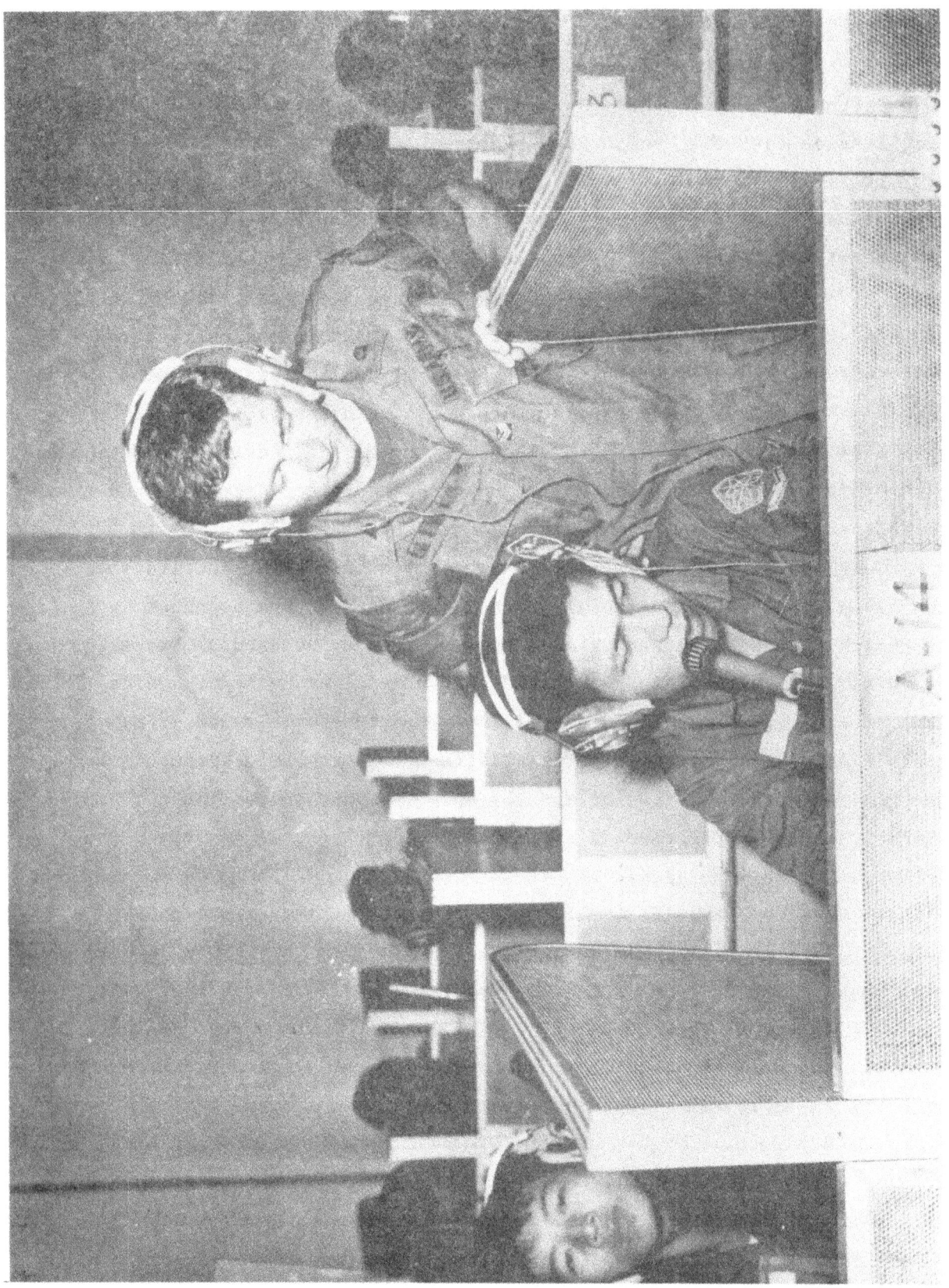

Assisting Students at the RVNAF Language School (Dec 1970)

To assist RVNAF in handling this upsurge of training activities, US training advisory personnel in the field were increased accordingly with particular emphasis on infantry unit and leader training. By 1966, for example, of the eight advisory detachments assigned to ARVN service schools, the more heavily staffed were those at the Thu Duc Infantry School and NCO Academy in Nha Trang. But the US training advisory effort was most significant at the eight ARVN National Training Centers where emphasis was placed on ARVN basic individual and unit training. The largest advisory detachments were those attached to the Lam Son and Quang Trung National Training Centers which also handled the largest contingents of recruits. For the training of the RF and PF, an equally significant advisory effort was expended at the six RF leader and unit training centers and 38 combined RF/PF or PF training centers where US advisory detachments varied in strength from two to 14 personnel. At each of these schools and training centers, the role of US advisers was particularly important. They advised faculty members and instructors on training techniques, assisted them in organizing instructional materials and conducting classes, and provided them with the stimulus needed to inspire cooperation and diligence among students. Although not always directly exposed to the students, US training advisers invariably earned their respect and affection. They were particularly held in high esteem by the Vietnamese private soldiers and NCOs.

Programs of instruction were also subjected to extensive revision by US training advisers and the MACV Training Directorate to provide updated currcula for over 650 various courses. Most noteworthy of this combined MACV-JGS effort was the establishment in 1970 of a five-year training program for the entire RVNAF and the joint budgetary planning and programming for its support. In addition, a sponsorship program was initiated whereby ARVN service schools became directly affiliated with their counterparts of the US Army. The Dalat National Military Academy, for example, was affiliated with its American sister, the US Military Academy of West Point where one Vietnamese cadet was accepted for the first time in 1970.

In 1970, MACV Training Directorate initiated a new program for the continued improvement of all training centers. This plan consolidated the training base by merging some under under-utilized facilities and instructor staffs in order to reduce expenditures and turn National Training Centers into more modern facilities. The MASF/MILCON program provided a fund of US $28 million for this program which was completed in late 1972. In 1971, MASF/MILCON funded the construction of the Infantry School at Long Thanh at a cost of US $7 million. Upon completion in early 1973, this new facility became the home of the Infantry School whose basic mission was to train reserve officers. The old training complex at Thu Duc was used to accommodate other requirements such as the Quartermaster, Finance and Administration, Adjutant General, and Intelligence Schools.

Among ARVN service schools, the most celebrated was the National Military Academy at Dalat whose concept and construction received full support from General Westmoreland, US MACV commander. New construction, which was completed in 1966, provided modern facilities for the academy to replace old French-built barracks. As a major science and engineering institution, the academy was equipped with the most modern laboratory facilities which even the University of Saigon did not have. The cadets who graduated from the Academy's four-year curriculum, instituted in 1966, received a Bachelor of Science degree in addition to an officer's commission and a solid military background. The institution of the four-year curriculum, patterned after West Point, gave the Dalat Military Academy a standing equal to other modern academies in the world. In fact, rated as one among the best in Asia, it became a source of pride for the RVNAF and a showcase for foreign dignitaries and visitors. Much credit for this accomplishment must also be given to the US training advisers assigned to our military academy. A detachment or team of six officers, one warrant officer and two enlisted men was authorized by MACV to assist with almost every requirement to include academic, military and the cadet regiment. It was obvious to all Vietnamese that these personnel had been carefully selected, were thoroughly familiar with academic programs and the procedures of West Point and were highly

The National Military Academy at Dalat:
A Significant Contribution of U.S. Advisory Effort

The Cadets of Dalat NMA:
A Source of Pride for the RVNAF

dedicated and professional in every respect. They held the admiration and esteem of the staff, faculty and cadets and were always most helpful in anticipating and solving any problem.

In early 1968, with the full support of General Abrams, the National Defense College was established. It was the first military school at the national level created with a one-year curriculum and devoted entirely to the study of national defense and national security activities. The first class began in May 1968 with 21 high-ranking military officers and civil servants. Students were selected from candidates among outstanding colonels and general officers and high-ranking civilians earmarked for key positions affecting national security. Guest lecturers for the National Defense College included high-ranking US general officers and officials, top Vietnamese university professors and cabinet ministers. As one requirement for graduation, students had to submit individual research papers on national defense matters. Some of these papers turned out to be the best studies ever made on these important subjects.

The US training advisory effort took a vigorous step forward as US forces began to redeploy in accordance with the Vietnamization program. The goal to be achieved, according to General Abrams, was to expand and improve the RVNAF to the extent that they could "hack it" alone. As a result, MACV endeavored on the one hand to increase US advisory strength and select the best qualified officers for advisory duties on the other. By 1970, advisory strength, especially for the training effort, was filled 100%, as compared to 55% during the pre-Vietnamization period. Among these training advisers, whose total strength reached 3,500 by the end of 1971, about 90% had received combat experience in Vietnam.

To accomplish the objective of improving combat effectiveness of RVNAF so that they could gradually take over from US forces and also to provide for a smooth redeployment, MACV implemented three major programs: (1) on-the-job training, (2) combined operations, and; (3) mobile training.

The on-the-job training program was primarily designed for ARVN technical and logistical units which, under the Vietnamization program, would take over the operation and maintenance of US logistical facilities, including ports, terminals, bases, communications systems, and transportation assets. Under the code name "Operation Buddy," the program was initiated by the US Army 1st Logistical Command and its subordinate support commands and units. To ARVN logisticians at that time, however, the code name was unknown. Faced with the redeployment of US units, they were only preoccupied with the transfer of assets and the problem of how to provide adequate technicians and specialists to operate and maintain the modern facilities.

Operation Buddy was built on the principle that each US technical or logistical unit would sponsor a counterpart ARVN unit and train its specialized personnel until they were fully qualified. Under this program, selected ARVN personnel were sent as apprentices to US units where they would be provided on-the-job training by US specialists. For those ARVN units which were to take over operational responsibilities such as signal operating battalions, their personnel were allowed to stay on the US premises where they practiced their future jobs until they were able to handle them effectively. Later, when each facility was transferred, it often appeared as if it had always been under ARVN control. The smoothness with which the transition was accomplished from US to ARVN control testified to the success of this program. Due to the magnitude and importance of the program, an on-the-job training division was jointly established by the CTC/JGS and MACV Training Directorate to monitor, coordinate and evaluate OJT activities being conducted by US units. The program was terminated in late 1972. By this time the RVNAF had become almost totally self-reliant, operationally and technically.

To enhance the combat effectiveness of ARVN units to the extent that they could assume more of the tactical burden and eventually replace US forces, MACV initiated the concept of combined operations and increased this emphasis as soon as Vietnamization was officially proclaimed. This concept was implemented by US Field Forces under different names but the programs they sponsored were essentially the same. The US I Field Force, for example, launched combined operations with II Corps units under the "Pair-Off" program while the US II Field Force cooperated with III Corps in the Dong Tien (Progress Together) program. Regardless of program names, combined operations were the most pragmatic and most effective technique for training through actual combat on a large scale.

The concept behind these programs consisted of pairing off US and ARVN major tactical units within the same area of responsibility where they jointly planned and conducted operations in mutual support of each other. The operational headquarters of US and ARVN units were either co-located or located in close proximity to each other. Their subordinate elements either operated alongside each other or were cross-attached, sometimes even down to the platoon level. Through constant exposure to US conduct of operations and combat tactics, ARVN units were able to learn much in the areas of operational planning, estimates of the situation and combined arms tactics, especially heliborne operations and tactical air support. The results brought about through these programs were self-evident. In 1970, III Corps units were able to operate successfully in Cambodia without US advisers.[3] Again, in early 1971 I Corps forces launched Operation Lam Son 719 into lower Laos with only heliborne and tactical air support from US XXIV Corps.

The mobile training concept was implemented by the MACV Training Directorate under an extensive program for the benefit of Regional and Popular Forces whose principal mission was to ensure territorial security, a prerequisite for the process of pacification. As of 1967, when the pacification program was pushed vigorously forward, the role of RF and PF became even more important and in view of their basic weaknesses, there was an urgent requirement to improve them in all aspects, to include administration and logistic support. Because of the sizable number of RF and PF units, whose aggregate strength in time made up about 55% of the total RVNAF force structure, and their scattered deployment throughout the country, mobile training and advisory teams were the most affordable means to obtain desirable results within a limited time.

---

[3] Some US advisers accompanied ARVN units in initial phases of the Cambodian operation, but all were withdrawn prior to 1 July. ARVN units remained in Cambodia until November 1971.

Mobile training teams, each consisting of from three to ten US personnel, were provided by US Field Forces. Each team was responsible for a certain number of RF companies and PF platoons in a certain area. Its members rotated among these units and trained them until, according to the team's evaluation, they performed satisfactorily. Despite the extensive efforts of MTTs, these territorial forces still needed more improvement to qualify as combat worthy.

Another program of mobile training, initiated by MACV Training Directorate, was based on the MTT experience but undertaken on a larger scale and modified to suit the diverse requirements of territorial forces. It was the Mobile Advisory Teams (MAT) discussed in Chapter VII.

The mobile advisory effort was emphasized during 1969 and also expanded to assist district governments in enlarging their control. By the end of 1970, when RF and PF units had greatly improved in terms of combat effectiveness, the MATs were still maintained to help coordinate activities between territorial and para-military forces such as the PSDF, National Police, RD cadres, etc. In addition, the MATs also contributed significantly to the development of villages and hamlets under the pacification program.

Aside from US Army programs undertaken by MACV Training Directorate and US Field Forces, the Marines also made a significant contribution in I Corps area toward improving the Popular Forces through their unique Combined Action Program (CAP). From 1966 to the time US Marine units were totally redeployed, the CAP expanded considerably in all five provinces of I Corps area. The CAP concept united a US Marine squad with a PF platoon to form a combined platoon. Marine squad members lived together with PF troopers in a village for an extended period of time up to six months until the PF platoon was capable of defending the village by themselves. Operating together under the concept of mobile defense, PF troopers learned a great deal about the most effective small unit tactics under the Marines' tutelage. The success of this program was undeniable.

Training ARVN Rangers How to Use Compass to Bring In A Helicopter for Landing (Oct 1970)

Advisers Looking On As Ranger Student Successfully Guided Helicopter On Landing Pad (Oct 1970)

Another major contribution made by the US advisory effort was the training of ARVN Rangers, and the organization, training, and continued development of the Civilian Irregular Defense Groups (CIDG), which were not a part of the RVNAF until 1969. These major efforts began as early as 1960 when US Special Forces took under their tutelage the 65 ARVN Ranger companies that the GVN formed for counter-insurgency purposes. Training by US Special Forces and US civilian specialists was conducted at three training centers at Song Mao, Hoa Cam and Duc My. Concurrently, US Special Forces also devoted their effort to organizing, arming and training Civilian Irregular Defense Groups (CIDC) composed of ethnic Montagnards for the defense of the central highlands and the control of its approaches. Beginning in 1961, CIDGs were deployed to base camps along the border for the control of Communist infiltration routes. By 1968, total CIDG strength had reached 42,000, totally equipped and supported by the US. As of 1969, CIDGs were gradually turned over to RVNAF control. Their members either became Rangers or regional troopers. With this manpower, the RVNAF were able to activate 25 Border Defense Ranger battalions. This brought up the total Ranger force structure to 45 battalions deployed to all four corps areas under the control of 15 group headquarters. The individual training advisers of the US Special Forces were highly professional officers and enlisted men who demonstrated the utmost in professional talent and devotion to duty.

Observations and Comments

In general from the Vietnamese point of view US advisers assigned for duty at ARVN service schools and training centers were apparently selected with great care and they all instilled a good impression on ARVN staffs, faculties and students. Their outward appearance alone inspired discipline and studiousness. Tall, healthy, invariably handsome in their starched uniforms and shining boots, they conveyed the perfect image of neatness and military elegance, a far cry from the usually carefree French instructor of former times in ill-fitted shorts and civilian shoes. Simply by looking at them, the average ARVN student was struck by admiration and an ardent desire to imitate. This alone produced a good effect on the students. Another good habit of US training advisers was their punctuality which directly accounted for the cutback in tardiness among ARVN instructors.

Most training advisers were endowed with broad professional competence; they were entirely knowledgeable in their special areas of interest. The difficult points in instruction or questions raised by ARVN instructors were all explained carefully by advisers who always made a point of being precise and never ad-libbing. If they were in doubt of something they always took time to consult manuals or associates and invariably came back with the correct answers. This intellectual probity exerted a good influence on our ARVN instructors who gradually ridded themselves of the poor habit of improvising answers in classrooms, apparently to save face.

In my opinion the most resourceful and effective training advisers were those of the US Special Forces who developed the CIDGs and advised the ARVN Ranger forces. Expedient, organizational-minded and experts in small unit tactics, US Special Force advisers were also highly capable in training and staff work. During over a decade of deployment, they single-handedly organized and trained various groups of Montagnards in the central highlands and contributed significantly to the defense and control of the border areas, a perilous and most difficult task.

As US forces began to redeploy from South Vietnam in 1969, MACV increased its emphasis on the quality of US officers assigned to training centers. Since there was no longer a requirement for replacements in US units, more combat-experienced personnel were diverted to advisory duties, many of them having served several combat tours. Being familiar with the war, and having lived in various combat situations, they were thoroughly conversant with problems faced by tactical units. Their assignment to ARVN schools and training centers tremendously benefited not only ARVN students but also our instructors.

When arriving in country for the first tour of duty, every US training adviser had a difficult time familiarizing himself with the new environment, local culture and manners and the ARVN unit to which he was attached. It took him at least a month, frequently longer, to make himself feel at home in the new environment and job and to be productive. An adviser's usefulness, therefore, was short-lived, given his normal one-year tour. His personal experience could not be completely transferred to his successor. It was as if everything had to start anew every year as far as his counterpart was concerned. Obviously, the annual turnover of US advisers brought about many inconveniences for ARVN units. For one thing, Vietnamese commanders were never sure how they would approach a new adviser and whether the new relationship would be as good as the old one.

Some ARVN school commandants recommended that US training advisers should be assigned for longer tours with their schools. After all, they argued, there was no problem of insecurity or hardship since almost all service schools and training centers were located in the Saigon area, in cities or secure areas. By comparison with their colleagues in tactical units, US training advisers often had a much more comfortable life and a less demanding job. In terms of self-interest, naturally these arguments were valid and it appeared that the longer an adviser stayed with a school or a training center, the better his services would be. However, these arguments failed to take into account the strain imposed on these US officers and enlisted men living in prolonged separation from their families. If only this problem could have been resolved in some convenient way, the prolonged tour would have been easier for most US advisers. And as far as the RVNAF were concerned, it would have been a most welcome event.

Should a US training adviser try to be intimate with his Vietnamese counterpart or keep him at a certain distance? Some argued that too much intimacy might lead to disrespect or disdain which adversely affected a good working relationship. It was true that all excesses were harmful. But to the extent that I knew of this problem, there was never too much intimacy between US officers and ARVN counterparts. It was equally true that if an adviser was too reserved he was not only artificial but it also created undue difficulties for both sides, not to mention a tendency to suspect and misunderstand each other. Both extremes had to be avoided if a good working relationship was the objective to be attained. To Vietnamese officers of all grades in general, neither excessive intimacy nor too much distance was acceptable. What was important to them was sincerity, compassion and mutual respect. To them, a respectable adviser was someone who would not go beyond his advisory area, kept to his duties and never interfere with command responsibilities. A sincere adviser was someone who never put on an affected personality, abstained from showering his counterparts with superlative words of praise and always behaved true to his feelings and nature. A good, understanding adviser always tried to think as if he were in his counterpart's shoes, measured his own opinions and got things done by induction and persuasion, never by threats of leverage. Professional competence and experience alone would not necessarily make a well-heeded adviser, but tact and compassion helped him accomplish his difficult mission. Vietnamese in general were sentimental and sensitive. Rudeness, vulgarity, abrasive words were apt to hurt and alienate them. During the incipient period of US advisory effort when language was still an important barrier and the problem of culture largely ignored by both sides, most Vietnamese could not understand these American jokes and certain gestures and words were considered insolent. But these cultural misunderstandings gradually diminished as we learned the English language and familiarized ourselves with American culture through offshore courses and as US training advisers learned more about Vietnamese culture.

Important as it was, language was not an absolute requirement for an adviser's success. This was increasingly true during the later years of the US advisory effort in Vietnam. The ability to speak Vietnamese was certainly valuable if a high degree of proficiency was attained. Even a smattering knowledge of conversational Vietnamese helped break the ice faster than anything else. But this was not a must as far as an adviser's usefulness was concerned. He could always communicate through the intermediary of a good interpreter and his effectiveness was in no way affected by his inability to speak Vietnamese. Most Vietnamese, in fact, thought that it was better for them to learn English since this helped widen their horizons of knowledge. So US training advisers complied by giving English lessons and gradually, with the establishment of the RVNAF Languages School and the mushrooming of private English courses, many Vietnamese servicemen became in time proficient with the language. By the time US combat forces arrived in Vietnam, language was no longer a major problem. There were few US advisers who could speak Vietnamese as a native but those who did, mostly district advisers, really enjoyed great popularity among the local officials and population.

The contributions of training advisers to the enlightment and improvement of the RVNAF were indeed monumental achievements. Their tenacious efforts spanned two long decades of war and hardship. If there was a proper epitaph dedicated to the US training adviser of the Vietnam war, this epitaph ought to be: "The First to Arrive and the Last to Depart."

CHAPTER VIII

Observations and Conclusions

The Paris Agreement of January 1973 ended eighteen years of American military advisory effort in South Vietnam. Looking back on the evolution of the system and the achievements of the effort, no one can escape the feeling that this was indeed the most ambitious program the US Army and its sister services had ever undertaken for the benefit of an allied military force. That this effort had been a success, there was no single doubt. By the time the last US advisers departed, the RVNAF had become a formidable instrument of peace enforcement with its 13 well-equipped, well-trained army divisions, a strong and modern air force, and an efficient logistical support system. Under better leadership and with continued American support, this modern military force could well have been an invincible opponent against any invasion.

In terms of system and mission evolution, the US advisory effort appeared to have developed in four distinct phases or periods which all reflected the changing US policies toward Vietnam. From 1955 to 1960, this effort was modest but far-reaching in consequence. This was a period of reorganization and retraining during which the nascent Vietnamese Army was molded into what could be called the mirror-image of the US Army, structurally and doctrinally. While there appeared to be a strong strategic sense in the creation of a division-based army with ancillary combat and service support units, this conventionally trained and organized military force was ill-prepared for the type of counter-insurgency warfare it was called upon to fight in the late 1950's. If the lessons of the First Indochina War had been of any use, it would have been much better to develop at the same time the kind of territorial forces that were to play such an important role during the latter stages of the war. But support for these forces was late in coming and not until 1961 was there any conscious effort to expand and train the Civil Guard and People's Militia (later to become Regional and Popular Forces).

The period from 1961 to 1965 was devoted to developing counterinsurgency capabilities on the one hand and to providing combat support assistance to the regular forces on the other. The role of the US Special Forces was most significant at this juncture in the training of the CIDGs and strike forces. Despite the usefulness of these organizations, they were an irritation to the GVN which did not find its image enhanced by the presence of US-paid and supported auxiliaries. Some RVN leaders even suspected American motives behind the program, and when the Rhade rebellion broke out in 1964, they were convinced that it had been condoned by some Americans. US Special Forces also provided training and advisers for the ARVN Ranger forces whose creation met with initial opposition from the Military Assistance Advisory Group which apparently suspected a political motive behind it. American concern over counterinsurgency further led to the assignment of US advisers to work with Vietnamese province chiefs and assist them in the training and employment of territorial forces. But this effort was at first viewed by the Diem government as a move to control GVN activities in exchange for extended support. Therefore, the expansion of the US advisory effort to the district level in 1964, albeit occasioned by circumstantial needs, would have met with GVN opposition had Mr. Diem survived as President. In the area of combat support, US Army aviation units, although not operating in an advisory capacity, did familiarize ARVN troops and commanders with heliborne tactics and gave them the additional mobility required by counterinsurgency warfare.

The next period, 1965-1969, saw the role of US advisers almost completely overshadowed by the presence of US combat units and their active participation in the ground war. Despite a gradual force structure increase, the RVNAF were relegated to the role of pacification support in view of their limited capabilities. During this period, the advisory effort seemed to be reduced to maintaining liaison and obtaining US logistical and tactical support for the benefit of ARVN units. The generosity with which this support was dispensed could be attributed to the US advisers' eagerness to oblige and to be useful. Its adverse effect was felt only much later when the RVNAF had to rely on their own means. Training continued but was impeded and sometimes suspended altogether by operational requirements. But it was during this period that the US advisory effort expanded considerably in another direction: pacification support. It was this expansion that made available direct advisory benefits to the growing territorial forces for the first time and the gradual upgrading of these forces began. This training advisory effort alone, to include all the MATs and MALTs, absorbed a sizeable portion of total US advisory strength in the field, but it was an effort well expended.

The advent of Vietnamization brought back to US advisers their proper role and to the advisory effort, a new sense of dedication. Improved selection of US field advisers coupled with various programs to enhance the RVNAF tactical and logistical capabilities quickly yielded remarkable returns. The RVNAF, on their way to full growth, welcomed the effort but were overwhelmed by the speed with which the programs accelerated. It appeared as if the US was more concerned about getting out than willing to take the time for the entire process of Vietnamization to produce solid, lasting results; although it was true that by the time the last US adviser departed, the RVNAF had been left with substantial amounts of assets and had grown into a military giant. The trouble was that the flood of equipment in the few months before the cease-fire engulfed the RVNAF logistical and operational system which still lacked the technicians needed to store, control or maintain the more sophisticated materiel. Disaster was averted, however, by the provision of the large contractor-operated technical assistance system under the USDAO.

In general, except for the first few years, almost all US advisers seemed to have been well prepared for their role which they usually performed with dedication and effectiveness. Depending on the level and specialized area of interest, there were certain dissimilarities in approach and techniques but the objectives to be achieved remained essentially the same. In this regard, it was difficult to tell the difference from one adviser to another for they were all dedicated to a similar cause. However, it appeared that the higher the echelon, the less emphasis was placed on advising. In fact, only at the division and lower levels did US advisers truly act as advisers in the sense that they directly assisted in day-to-day operations and completely devoted their time and energy to advisory duties.

At the top level, the relationship between the JGS and MACV was both advisory and cooperation. The successive MACV commanders and staff division chiefs and members were professional diplomats, tactful and respectful of the authority and professional competence of their counterparts. Advice was usually provided during informal meetings and discussions. Combined planning activities were always conducted by combined committees under combined chairmanship. The relationship, therefore, resembled a partnership between co-workers in which neither side assumed the predominant role. It was as if in the eyes of MACV commanders, the JGS needed little advice as a control body for the entire RVNAF. But it was true that during the period of US active participation, MACV became a theater command and was more concerned about the conduct of the war and the control and support of US forces. Therefore, only a small fraction of MACV staff members were actually involved in advisory duties. Despite this and because of their extended tours, MACV commanders and staff division chiefs always had a deep insight into RVNAF problems, their strengths and weaknesses, and were thoroughly familiar with every major ARVN unit.

In its advisory relations with the JGS, MACV seemed to be bound by certain security regulations and restrained by US policies. As a result, the JGS was not always fully informed even though the information was desired for planning purposes. Also the JGS was never allowed to participate in or even comment on certain planning and programming actions of which it was the primary beneficiary and executor. The Military Assistance Program recommended funding was a case in point. Other JGS-initiated recommendations deemed vital to the improvement of the RVNAF, such as requests for the M-16 rifle, M-48 tank, 175-mm gun, etc., were satisfied only when such requirements had become all too evident. But these shortcomings apparently resulted from the dictates of US policies and procedures.

At the field level and in combat units, the usefulness of tactical advisers was not acutely felt during the period prior to the US participation in the war since their role was mostly confined to training assistance, and end-use and maintenance inspection. During the formative years of the RVNAF, the presence of tactical advisers was sometimes a source of irritation for a few ARVN commanders who felt that their own combat experience was far superior to the advice they could expect from a young American officer. As of 1965, however, stepped up combat activities and the increased reliance on US combat support assets such as airlift, helilift, tactical air and artillery support made the US advisers indispensable in ARVN combat units. At the battalion and regimental level, in addition to serving as intermediaries in obtaining US combat support, tactical advisers compensated for the basic weakness of ARVN units in operational planning not only by assisting and advising but sometimes by actually doing the work. In a few extreme cases, US advisers were also compelled to make decisions for their counterparts. Although not generalized, this tendency to overtake and patronize seemed to edge ARVN commanders toward a passive role, chiefly when modern warfare required so much skill in the employment of US-controlled combat support assets. At the division and corps levels, US advisers were also extremely useful in assisting ARVN staffs in developing plans and studies, a field in which ARVN officers were usually not strong. While the division senior adviser was able to devote his full time and effort to his advisory duties, the corps senior adviser was not, for the simple reason that he also commanded US troops. As a result, the corps staff benefited most from the work of the advisory group attached to the corps. Not being exposed to a counterpart US staff in action, ARVN staff officers naturally could not learn the fine points of American planning and coordination in combat situations.

In general, in ARVN combat units, US advisers stayed for only six months. The fact that an ARVN battalion commander had to accommodate several different advisers during this time of command did not help build the kind of working relationship conducive to steady progress and improvement.

If the tactical advisory effort were to be more effective, then it appeared that not every ARVN battalion needed an advisory team for the mere sake of it. This effort should have been selectively made and perhaps would have been more beneficial if confined to higher levels of command where the need for US advisers was more strongly indicated in order to help build a solid command, control and planning system for the entire RVNAF.

With regard to training, the task of US advisers was particularly difficult during the early years. In a certain sense, training the Vietnamese Army during that time was not unlike preaching a new gospel, but US advisers acquitted themselves admirably. The early effort of sending Vietnamese cadres to US service schools and making them instructors proved to be a sound policy since it alleviated the training burden placed on a limited number of US training advisers. At ARVN schools and training centers, in addition to providing training support, US advisers closely monitored individual and unit training results, the utilization of graduates, and carefully evaluated practical performances as compared to text book teachings. This evaluative contribution was most useful for ARVN service schools to update their training programs. Training manuals and materials made available through the advisory system were up-to-date and valuable for the training of a conventional military force to fight a conventional warfare. They should have been complemented by comprehensive literature on unconventional warfare and tactics.

The most tangible contribution of the US advisory effort to the RVNAF training base was the expansion and modernization of service schools and training centers. Some of the facilities were so modern that they ranked among the best in Southeast Asia. The RVNAF were particularly proud of the Dalat National Military Academy and the high caliber of its graduates.

In the area of intelligence, the US-RVNAF relationship took the unusual form of both advising and co-working. This relationship made both the adviser and the advisee feel close together since it implied an exchange which benefited both. Due to the close working relationship and better understanding of each other's strengths and weaknesses, the adviser was able to offer more practical advice and the advisee was also able to contribute something useful in return. ARVN intelligence officers did learn a great deal from US advisers, particularly in the highly sophisticated areas of signal and technical intelligence. They also benefitted from American experience in human intelligence which was a particularly difficult task of collection in Vietnam. In return, US intelligence officers gained deeper insight in their knowledge of the Vietnamese Communists through association with their ARVN counterparts.

US intelligence advisers performed their role extremely well in all areas of endeavor and at all levels, except for the sector and subsector where they had to handle problems not usually related to intelligence. A major constraint of the intelligence advisory effort was the one-year tour of duty. Although it applied equally to all branches of service, the one-year tour was most disadvantageous for intelligence since a new adviser usually required a longer time to familiarize himself with the intricate Vietnamese intelligence organization and the equally complex and extremely fluid enemy situation. The US intelligence adviser was, therefore, really useful only after his third month in the country. In general, the growth and maturity of ARVN intelligence was largely attributable to US advisers.

In the area of logistics, the importance and value of US advisers seemed to grow in proportion with the increase in US military aid and the ever enlarging stock of modern equipment. In daily contacts and working sessions, US logistical and technical advisers all proved to have a solid professional background, and were dedicated to their duties. They utilized every procedure and technique for providing advice, from written memoranda to joint visits, private meetings, review conferences and joint staff studies. During the period of US active participation, US advisers were the essential intermediaries between ARVN and US logistical units. They helped provide the additional support ARVN logistical units required to fulfill their mission. Over the years, ARVN logisticians were able to learn many modern operational concepts from US advisers, such as functional organization, automated materiel management, cost programming, etc. Under the sponsorship and tutelage of US advisers, they also worked out significant plans and programs for the improvement and modernization of the ARVN logistic system, such as Path Finders I and II, the Depot Upgrade Program, etc. All in all, US logistical and technical advisers succeeded remarkably in their missions. They had helped the RVNAF build a modern, functional, cost-effective logistical system and were instrumental in improving every aspect of its operations.

A significant aspect of the US advisory effort in the Vietnam war was pacification support. This support was more demanding because it involved many non-military areas as well. The role of the pacification adviser was, therefore, a dual military-civilian one requiring numerous skills and endurance. In view of its impact on the population, this role was also more difficult and more delicate than that assumed by purely military advisers. Although advisers began operating at the district level in 1964, the pacification support effort really made significant headway only as of 1967 with the advent of CORDS which gave it more cohesive direction and provided more systematic advisory assistance to the RF and PF, the mainstay of territorial security. The spectacular achievements obtained during the following years were largely attributable to US advisers, military and civilian, who helped push the program to success. Their contributions were monumental and affected every aspect of the program, from planning to execution, monitoring and evaluation. Without their efforts and the sizable American financial and materiel support, the pacification program would have progressed much more slowly.

There was no doubt that US pacification advisers performed their role with dedication and resourcefulness. But it seemed that in the context of an ideological conflict in which a solid popular base was the key to ultimate success, US advisers could have contributed much more had they been in closer contact with the population, and known more about their true aspirations and problems. It was no secret that the most successful and popular advisers were those who came back for a second or third tour and spoke the native language well. For a task as demanding and as people-oriented as pacification, those who were involved should have been carefully prepared for it and should have learned to speak the

language and to live among rural natives as well. In no other areas
were language and cultural adaptation so vital as in pacification because the sensitivity of the local population toward Americans stemmed
primarily from differences in way of life and most particularly, the
wide gap between American and Vietnamese modes of living.

Despite the constraints imposed by linguistic and cultural differences and a relative short tour of duty, most US advisers were successful in the performance of their role regardless of the level of assignment
and the area of specialty. This success was chiefly due to preparation
and the fact that every adviser was most conscious of his delicate and
difficult mission. In the eyes of the Vietnamese servicemen, there were
three things about US advisers and the advisory effort that were most
important: the adviser's personality, his procedures and techniques,
and his professional competence.

The issue of professional competence raised another often-asked
question about the suitability of US Army professionalism to the kind
of war fought in Vietnam. Predicated on technological and material
superiority, perhaps it was not suited for the ideological aspect of
the conflict. Perhaps because of this, no US adviser was ever assigned
to assist in RVNAF political warfare activities. But the Vietnam conflict, despite its ideological overtones, was still very much of a
military war which was fought with increasingly modern armaments by
both sides. During the later stages, it was primarily a showdown of
sheer military might. This was where and when US military assets and
professional know-how mattered and even became decisive. Of particular
importance for the RVNAF to fight this war was the technological advance
gained from the US Army in signal and technical intelligence, long and
short range communications, heliborne tactics, and logistic support
operations. If US Army professionalism seemed ill-fitted to the early
stage of the war, it proved to be indispensable as soon as warfare
escalated to the division level.

When US advisers first came into direct contact with the Vietnamese
armed forces eighteen years earlier, their problems were much less complicated. Then they were primarily concerned about the language barrier

and how to get along with their counterparts on a personal basis. In time, they learned to cope with both problems but only after going through a painful period of trials and errors.

The ability to communicate in Vietnamese or French was never a must for an adviser except in some specialized areas. In the early days, some US advisers spoke French and could communicate fairly well with Vietnamese officers of the older generation if the conversation did not involve military or technical terminology. But then only a few US advisers and not all Vietnamese officers could speak French, which was also banned as the official language in late 1955. The trend then was clearly indicated: it was either English or Vietnamese. It so happened that in view of the strong anti-colonialist feelings of that time, most high school students opted for English which had officially replaced French as the primary mandatory foreign language in their curriculum; and in time, the majority of these students became military officers. The same determination to learn English caught on with the military, who saw in it the immediate advantage of attending US service schools. And so, without formal planning and even unconsciously, the trend toward learning English picked up momentum on a national scale.

Learning Vietnamese proved to be difficult for the few US advisers who endeavored to master the language. Although syntactically simple, Vietnamese as a tonal language proved phonetically hard for Westerners. Even those who methodically took lessons for many months could only produce toneless, hence unintelligible, utterances. Then there was the problem of regional accents and vocabulary which differed to the point of incomprehensibility even among the natives. Experience indicated that very few Americans ever achieved a useful degree of fluency and even if fluency was attained, the colloquial vocabulary they used was hardly sufficient for professional communication. It was also true that Vietnamese had not yet developed a comprehensive and consistent technical terminology in such advanced areas as electronics, mechanical engineering, aerodynamics, etc. So the efforts of learning Vietnamese as an instrument of professional communication, even through the process of intensive training, was largely defeated not only by phonetic difficulties, but also by the limitations of the language itself.

Besides, since the Vietnamese were eager to learn English which somehow was easier for them to master linguistically and since all technical manuals were in English, there was added inhibition for US advisers to pursue language learning. To most Vietnamese, the value and usefulness of an adviser did not require his ability to communicate in Vietnamese. He could always communicate effectively through interpreters. Besides, more and more Vietnamese became proficient in English and language, in time, ceased to be a barrier altogether. In the areas of human intelligence and pacification, however, the ability to understand and communicate in Vietnamese was paramount to the effectiveness of US advisers. Thorough knowledge about the Vietnamese Communists required direct exposure to their language and culture which could not be obtained through interpretation. In pacification work, even a smattering of colloquial Vietnamese could earn a US adviser instant rapport with the local population. And if he knew the language well enough to communicate directly with them, then he could be assured of certain success. This was particularly true with the case of district level advisers.

How to get along with a Vietnamese counterpart and have him receptive required the whole art of human relations and depended on how well the US adviser knew the Vietnamese character and temperament. Too much intimacy or the total lack of it was unadvisable. Both were extremes to be avoided. But too much intimacy was definitely better than a total lack of it. What really mattered in the eyes of Vietnamese was a correct attitude, sincerity and mutual respect. A warm personal friendship would not necessarily lead to disrespect or disregard if it was based on mutual affection, mutual compatibility and mutual respect; it need not involve too much intimacy which, culturally, was repulsive to most Vietnamese, nor did it detract the partners from the pursuit of their business if both did not seek it as an end in itself.

The inability of some Americans to adjust to local living conditions naturally led to the recreation of American environments. This was a cultural trait that distinguished Americans from the French who mixed more easily with the Vietnamese. It seemed that no American could survive without his PX, his compound and his daily bath. In time,

American compounds and PXs became monumental institutions of American culture in Vietnam. To the underprivileged Vietnamese, these constituted a whole world apart, a world so distant that Vietnamese seldom really felt close to Americans in a cultural sense. Exposure to American material opulence induced envy and greed that led to the practice of illicit business. This, added to the insecure psychology of wartime, the miseries of economic life and the largesse of American aid, contributed to corruption. "American money corrupts" the Vietnamese press used to say. Although there was some slanting insinuation in it, the fact should be admitted that the presence of Americans and their conspicuous display of materialistic wealth created the conditions for, and not infrequently invited, corruption. There were never any written procedures on how to obtain goods through the adviser but the good-natured and dedicated adviser was usually eager to assist his counterpart if asked.

The American propensity for living well was a cultural trait that Vietnamese officers freely admitted as a difference they could do nothing about, nor did they feel annoyed by it. In a determinist sense, they were resigned to their economic condition and never expected that Americans should live otherwise. But exposure to an unattainable good life somehow instilled, on their part, a certain complex of inferiority and sometimes bitterness, which accounted for the distance they always tried to keep from American advisers in order not to be hurt. And this was not good for the pursuit of a common goal. An ARVN officer, if criticized for not keeping pace with American drive, was usually heard retorting, "If I lived that kind of life, I could do the same." To give a proper advisory example, not every adviser was required to live a spartan Vietnamese way of life since this was not only unnatural but also conveyed some hypocritical undertone. But it certainly helped reduce the cultural gap if the American way of life could be kept as inconspicuous and low-keyed as the environment permitted.

There was no doubt that US Army advisers did an excellent job and the US advisory effort in South Vietnam indeed helped the RVNAF attain remarkable achievements in terms of combat effectiveness and technical and managerial skills. But there was one thing that this effort seemed never able to achieve: the inculcation of motivation and effective leadership. This was, after all, neither the fault of US advisers nor a shortcoming of the advisory effort, but a basic weakness of our political regime. The US adviser, as an individual, did all he could to fulfill his mission, and he did it well.

The majority of US Army advisers came out of their tour of duty with a better, more sober, understanding of the problems the RVNAF had to face in the war. More importantly, they invariably came away with profound compassion and a heart felt affection for their counterparts with whom they had shared the hazards and spartan conditions of combat. Many such relationships had developed into lasting personal friendships. This was perhaps the least publicized human aspect of the US advisory effort that had brought two entirely different nations together for some period of their histories.

APPENDIX A

	State of Vietnam
	Ministry of National Defense
	General Staff
MEMORANDUM	The Chief of Staff
	Telephone: Aubepine 10
	No. 1891/TTM/MG
	APO 4002, 10 April 1955

PRINCIPLES AUTHORIZING TRIM ADVISERS WITH UNITS AND FORMATIONS OF THE VIETNAMESE NATIONAL ARMED FORCES.

I/- GENERAL

The Vietnamese, French and American Governments, in a common agreement, have decided to create "A Liaison Mission" (TRIM) to train and instruct the Vietnamese Armed Forces.

Composed of American and French Officers assigned according to their particular abilities, TRIM will be personally directed by the Chief MAAG (US Military Assistance Advisory Group) under the authority of the Commander in Chief.

This organization includes a Staff and subordinate Advisory Teams placed at the principal echelons of the Vietnamese Armed Forces.

II/- TRIM GENERAL ADVISORY MISSION

The TRIM advisers' mission is to assist and advise, on strictly technical aspects, the Vietnamese military authorities to whom they are assigned, to rapidly and effectively rebuild the Vietnamese Armed Forces on a new basis.

III/- TRIM ADVISERS' AUTHORITY

TRIM advisers are empowered to:

- Represent the Chief TRIM among the Vietnamese organizations to which they are assigned to the exclusion of all others.
- Advise, in the event of need, and assist, when requested by the Vietnamese officers to whom they are attached, in the preparation and execution of tasks which are their responsibilities.
- Visit the Vietnamese organizations of interest in the presence of their commanders or delegated representatives, upon request.

- Be kept informed of current regulations, orders and documents not strictly confidential or secret which are deemed absolutely indispensable for the execution and effectiveness of their mission.

- Submit written reports to the Chief TRIM on the organization status of the units they advise, particularly from an instructional point of view, their training, equipment, morale, combat effectiveness aptitude on the condition that the same copies be forwarded to the interested Vietnamese unit commanders. These reports will be identified by a special numbering marker (such as single or double underline).

IV/- TRIM ADVISERS' RESPONSIBILITIES

a. TRIM advisers have no command or supervisory authority over the Vietnamese Armed Forces organizations or activities.

b. On the other hand, the senior adviser of each team is responsible only to his TRIM superviser for the organization and use of his subordinates. In addition, he has the particular duty of having his personnel respect the regulations established by the Vietnamese Armed Forces concerning organizational security, for which the Vietnamese Military is responsible.

V/- VIETNAMESE ARMED FORCES OFFICERS' RESPONSIBILITIES TOWARD THEIR TRIM ADVISERS

a. Only Vietnamese Armed Forces officers will assume command authority, and are entirely responsible for the performance and results obtained in the Vietnamese organizations.

b. It is their responsibility to assure TRIM advisers of:

- Security
- Satisfaction in their operational requirements, billets, office space, vehicles, drivers, mess personnel, interpreters, signal and emergency medical services.

Specific instructions pertaining to this subject will be published by the General Staff, Vietnamese Armed Forces.

c. With regard to TRIM advisers, Vietnamese Armed Forces Officers are required to:

- Facilitate to the maximum of their ability, the performance of their tasks, particularly on the following points: the routing of documents essential to their mission, whether coming from higher, subordinate or lateral echelons, orders issued consequently, activity programs, visits to units, assistance at firing range, maneuver instruction sessions, etc.
- To invite necessary counsel, particularly in the areas of new and misunderstood techniques, instruction, training, logistics and organization.

- To examine with care the recommendations made by TRIM advisers, and using their own judgement, to make use of those that appear to be the most propitious to develop the effectiveness of the organizations under their command.

d. Relations between Vietnamese Armed Forces officers and TRIM advisers will naturally develop through daily contacts and official ceremonies, and particularly, through an inter-allied spirit, cooperative, courteous and appropriate for maintaining the Vietnamese Armed Forces Officer Corps' prestige.

GENERAL DISTRIBUTION

LE VAN TY
Brigadier General
Chief of Staff
Vietnamese Armed Forces

APPENDIX B

MEMORANDUM

Republic of Vietnam
Ministry of National Defense
General Staff
Bureau of
General Studies and Plans
Telephone: 30.857
No. 1442/TTM/TNDKH/KH/MK
APO 4002 dated April 24, 1958

SUBJECT: The Assistance of American Advisers

REFERENCE: Memo No. 1891/TMT/MG April 10, 1955

I. In their organization process the RVNAF need the continued assistance of American advisers. They are our truthful friends who wish to use their accumulated experience to guide and help reorganize our armed forces into an efficient anti-Communist force. Consequently, it is the duty of every unit commander to help them accomplish their mission.

II. This memorandum serves as a reminder to unit commanders of their duties and responsibilities towards American advisers assigned to their respective units.

Unit commanders should:

- Provide security for American advisory teams.
- Satisfy, with available means, their needs concerning lodging, transportation, driver, office, mess personnel, interpreter, mail, information and medical emergencies.
- Provide documents necessary for their advisory works.
- Provide information concerning the unit's projects, decisions from higher echelon authorities, and related orders issued to its own subordinate units.
- Confer with them on all problems concerning technical, organizational and training matters.
- Thoroughly study their advice and opinions and make efficient use of them.

Moreover, to demonstrate their understanding of responsibilities and duties unit commanders should show due consideration to MAAG high-ranking officers making visits to their units, and brief them on the activities and the actual status of their units.

    III. It is also requested that officers be civil and courteous in their daily contacts with American advisers in order to contribute to friendly Vietnamese-American relations.

                                                   Lt. General LE VAN TY
                                                   Chief, General Staff
                                                   RVNAF

Restricted Distribution
(officers only)

Glossary

ARVN	Army of the Republic of Vietnam
CAP	Combined Action Program
CAT	Combat Assistance Team
CATO	Combat Arms Training and Organization
C-E	Communications-Electronics
CIDG	Civilian Irregular Defense Group
CLC	Central Logistics Command
CORDS	Civil Operations and Rural Development Support
CTC	Central Training Command
CTZ	Corps Tactical Zone
DMZ	Demilitarized Zone
DSA	District Senior Adviser
GVN	Government of the Republic of Vietnam
JGS	Joint General Staff
JUSPAO	Joint United States Public Affairs Office
MAAG	Military Assistance Advisory Group
MACV	Military Assistance Command, Vietnam
MAP	Military Assistance Program
MAT	Mobile Advisory Team
MALT	Mobile Advisory Logistic Team
MDAP	Mutual Defense Assistance Program
MR	Military Region
MSS	Military Security Service
MTT	Mobile Training Team
NVA	North Vietnamese Army
PSA	Province Senior Adviser
PSDF	People's Self Defense Forces

RAC	Regional Assistance Command
RD	Rural (or Revolutionary) Development
RF-PF	Regional and Popular Forces
RVN	Republic of Vietnam
RVNAF	Republic of Vietnam Armed Forces
TERM	Temporary Equipment Recovery Mission
TRIM	Training Relations and Instruction Mission
USAAG	United States Army Advisory Group
USAID	United States Agency for International Development
USARV	United States Army, Vietnam
USDAO	United States Defense Attache Office
USOM	United States Operations Mission
VC	Viet Cong

www.ingramcontent.com/pod-product-compliance
Lightning Source LLC
Chambersburg PA
CBHW080540170426
43195CB00016B/2625